GOD CALLING

The Enduring Classic in Today's Language

Edited by Bernard Koerselman

Based on the original
GOD CALLING
edited by
A. J. RUSSELL

A Barbour Book

ISBN 1-55748-354-X

EVANGELICAL CHRISTIAN PUBLISHERS ASSOCIATION ecpa MEMBER

Published by Barbour and Company, Inc.
P.O. Box 719
Uhrichsville, Ohio 44683

Typeset by Typetronix, Inc., Ft. Myers, Florida

PRINTED IN U.S.A.

If Two Agree

Again I say unto you, That
if two of you shall agree on earth
as touching any thing that they shall ask,
it shall be done for them of my Father which is in heaven.

For where two or three are gathered together in my name,
there am I in the midst of them.

Matthew 18:19 (KJV)

INTRODUCTION

In the autumn of 1932, I was sitting in the lounge of a hotel when a visitor, quite unknown, crossed over and handing me a copy of *For Sinners Only* asked if I had read it. I answered no, and she left it with me. On returning home, I bought a copy for myself. I was curiously affected by the book and felt that I wanted all my friends to read it immediately. I actually made out a list of over a hundred people to whom I should have liked to have sent it. Not being rich, this desire had to be content with two copies, which I loaned to various people, on whom it seemed to have little effect.

A few months later I read it again. It was then that there came a persistent desire to try to see whether I could get guidance such as A. J. Russell reported, through sharing a quiet time with the friend with whom I was then living. She was a deeply spiritual woman with unwavering faith in the goodness of God and a devout believer in prayer, although her life had not been an easy one. I was rather skeptical, but, as she had agreed, we sat down with pencils and paper in hand and waited. This was in December 1932. My results were entirely negative. Portions of texts came and went; frequently my mind wandered to ordinary topics. I brought it back again and again, but with no success.

To this day, I cannot obtain guidance in this way alone. But with my friend a very wonderful thing happened. From the first, beautiful messages were given to her by our Lord Himself, and every day from then these messages have never failed us. We felt unworthy and overwhelmed by the wonder of it, and could hardly realize that we were being taught, trained, and encouraged day by day by Him personally while millions of souls far worthier had to be content with guidance from the Bible, sermons, their churches, books, and other sources.

Certainly we were not in any way psychic or advanced in spiritual growth, but ordinary human beings who had more suffering and worry than the majority and who had known tragedy after tragedy. The tender understanding of some of our Lord's messages was at times almost heartbreaking, but His loving reproofs left no hurt. Always, and this daily, He insisted that we should be channels of love, joy, and laughter in His broken world. This was the Man of Sorrows in a new light.

We, or rather I, found this command difficult to obey; to others it might have been simple. Were we to laugh, to cheer others, to be always joyful when our days were pain-racked and our nights tortured by chronic insomnia, when poverty and almost insupportable worry were our daily portion, when prayer went unanswered and God's face was veiled and fresh calamities came upon us? Still came this insistent command to love and laugh and bring joy to the lives we contacted. Disheartened, one of us would gladly have ceased the struggle and passed on to another and happier life. . . . He encouraged us daily, saying that He would not break the instruments He intended to use, that He would not leave the metal in the crucible longer than was necessary for the burning away of the dross. Continually He exhorted us not to lose heart and spoke of the joy that the future held for us.

Totally unexpected interpretations of His own Word were given. He gave an adverse verdict on seeing visions of Himself that we had hitherto thought was granted only to the saintliest. *He stressed, most strongly of all, the immense power given to two souls praying together in close union and at one in their desire to love and serve Him.* As others have proved, such a union may, in God's hands, accomplish such great things that there certainly will be inimical forces whose purpose it is to mar the friendship. And so we found it.

Some of the messages are of surprising beauty. Examples of this are the majestic language of chapter 16, verses 76 to 82, the inevitability of suffering in the Christian life of chapter 16, verses 31 to 39, and the explanation of the practical working of the law of supply of chapter 17, verses 8 to 12. Other messages may appear disjointed. This is because personal references and repetition had to be deleted.

This book, which we believe has been guided by our Lord Himself, is no ordinary book. It is published, after much prayer, to prove that a living Christ speaks today, that He plans and guides the humblest, that no detail is too insignificant for His attention, and that He reveals Himself now as ever as a humble servant and majestic Creator.

ONE OF THE TWO LISTENERS

1

January 1

Their meditation:

Our Lord and our God. We joy in You. Without Your help we could not face unafraid the year before us.

Jesus responds:

1 "I stand between the years. The light of My presence is flung across the year to come—the radiance of the sun of righteousness. My shadow is thrown backward, over the past year, hiding trouble, sorrow, and disappointment.

2 "Do not dwell on the past—only on the present. Only use the past as the trees use My sunlight, absorbing it to make from it the warming fire-rays for later days. In like manner, store only the blessings from Me, the light of the world. Encourage yourselves by the thought of these.

3 "Bury every fear of the future, of poverty for those dear to you, of suffering, of loss. Bury all thoughts of unkindness and bitterness. Bury all your dislikes, your resentments, your sense of failure, your disappointment in others and in yourselves, your gloom, your despondency, and let us leave them all, buried, and go forward to a new and risen life.

4 "Remember that you must not see as the world sees. I hold the year in My hands—in trust for you. But I shall guide you one day at a time. Leave the rest with Me. You must not anticipate the gift by fears or thoughts of the days ahead.

5 "For each day I shall supply the wisdom and the strength."

JANUARY 2

6 "You are to help to save others. Never let one day pass when you have not reached out an arm of love to someone outside your home—a note, a letter, a visit, help in some way.

7 "Be full of joy. Joy saves. Joy cures. Joy in Me. In every ray of sunlight, every smile, every act of kindness, or love, every trifling service—let there be joy.

8 "Each day do something to lift another soul out of the sea of sin or disease or doubt into which humans have fallen. I still walk today by the lakeside and call My disciples to follow Me and become fishers of men. A helping hand is needed that raises the helpless to courage, to struggle, to faith, to health.

9 "Love and laugh. Love and laughter are the beckoners to faith, courage, and success. Trust on, love on, joy on.

10 "Refuse to be downcast. Refuse to be checked in your upward climb. Love and laugh. I am with you. I bear your burdens. Cast your burden upon Me and I will sustain you. Then, lighthearted, you in turn help another with the burden that is pressing too heavily upon him or her.

11 "How many burdens can you lighten this year? How many hearts can you cheer? How many souls can you help?

12 "I give you gain, 'Good measure, pressed down and running over.' I your Lord have said it."

JANUARY 3

Their meditation:

But those who wait upon the Lord shall renew their strength (Isaiah 40:31).

Jesus responds:

13 "You must be renewed, remade. Everything must rest on Me, the Christ. Force is born of rest. Only love is a

conquering force. Be not afraid; I will help you.

14 "Be channels, both of you. My spirit shall flow through you and shall, as it flows through, sweep away all the bitter past.

15 "Take heart. God loves, God helps, God fights, God wins. You shall see. You shall know. The way will open. All that My love has ever planned, all that My love has ever thought, you shall see unfold each day.

16 "Accept teaching. Be as a child. A child never questions plans but accepts gladly."

JANUARY 4

Their meditation:

Show us Your way, O Lord, and let us walk in Your paths. Lead us in Your truth and teach us.

Jesus responds:

17 "All is well. Wonderful things are happening. Do not limit God at all. He cares and provides.

18 "Uproot self—the channel-blocker. Do not plan ahead, the way will unfold step by step.

19 "Leave tomorrow's burden. Christ is the great burden-bearer. You cannot bear His load and He only expects you to carry a little day's share."

JANUARY 5

20 "Love Me and do My will. No evil shall befall you. Take no thought for tomorrow. Rest in My presence brings peace. God will help you. Desire brings fulfillment. Peace like a quiet flowing river cleanses and sweeps all irritants away.

21 "You shall be taught. Continue these prayer-times, even if they seem fruitless. The devil will try to stop them by

any means. Pay no attention. He will say evil spirits may enter in. Pay no attention.

22 "Rest your nerves. Tired nerves are a reflection on, not of, God's power. Hope all the time.

23 "Do not be afraid of poverty. I will let money flow in, but you must let it flow out. I never send money to stagnate—I send it only to those who pass it on.

24 "Keep nothing for yourself. Hoard nothing. Only have what you need and use. This is My law of discipleship."

JANUARY 6

Their meditation:

Guide me, O Thou great Jehovah, pilgrim through this foreign land. I am weak but Thou art mighty, guide me with Thy powerful hand.

Jesus responds:

25 "You must pray. The way will open. God cares and His plans unfold. Just love and wait. Love is the key. No door is too difficult for it to open.

26 "What cause have you to fear? Has He not cared for and protected you? Hope on. Hope gladly. Hope with certainty. Be calm, calm in My power.

27 "Never neglect these times, pray and read your Bible and train and discipline yourself. That is your work—Mine is to use you. But My instruments must be sharp and ready. Then I use them.

28 "Discipline and perfect yourselves at all costs. Do this, for soon every fleeting thought will be answered, every wish gratified, every deed used. It is a fearful power, a mighty power. Be careful that you ask nothing amiss—nothing that is not according to My Spirit.

29 "All harmful thoughts must be turned out. Miracle-

working power can become witchery in wrong hands. See how I have made the purity and goodness of your own lives necessary to you. That is why. Soon, very soon, you shall ask and at once it will come. Welcome the training. Without it I dare not give you this power. It would do harm.

30 "Do not worry about others' lives. That will be all right. You must perfect yourselves first in My strength."

JANUARY 7

Their meditation:

Look upon us with Your favor, O Lord, while we behold "the land that is very far off" and yet so near to the seeing eye and the listening ear.

Jesus responds:

31 "Wait. Wonders are unfolding. Tremble with awe. No one can stand upon the threshold of eternity unshaken. I give to you eternal life. A free gift, a wonderful gift—the life of the ages.

32 "Silently comes the kingdom. No one can judge when it enters the human heart except by seeing results.

33 "Listen quietly. Sometimes you may get no message. Meet together nevertheless. You will absorb an atmosphere. Cultivate silence. 'God speaks in silences.' A silence, a soft wind, can be a message to convey My meaning to the heart without voice or word.

34 "Each word or thought of yours can be like a pearl that you drop into the secret place of another heart. Later, in some hour of need, the recipient finds the treasure and realizes its value for the first time."

JANUARY 8

35 "Do not be too ready to do, just be. I said, 'Be ye

therefore perfect' not 'do' perfect things. Try and grasp this.

36 "Individual efforts avail nothing. It is only the work of the universal Spirit—my Spirit—that counts. Dwell in thought on this more and more. Saints have taken a lifetime to grasp it."

JANUARY 9

37 "Life with Me is not immunity from difficulties, but peace in difficulties. My guidance is often by shut doors. Love bangs shut as well as opens.

38 "Joy is the result of faithful trusting acceptance of My will when it seems not joyous.

39 "Paul, my servant, learned this lesson of the banged doors when he said, 'Our light affliction, which is but for a moment, worketh for us a far more exceeding and eternal weight of glory.' Expect rebuffs until this is learned; it is the only way."

JANUARY 10

40 "Joy is the daughter of calm. Be calm, no matter what may befall you. Rest in Me. Be patient, and let patience have her perfect work. Never think of things as overwhelming. How can you be overwhelmed when I am with you?

41 "Do not feel the strain of life. There is no strain for My children. Do you not see I am a master instrument-maker? Have not I fashioned each part? Do not I know just what it can bear without strain? Would I, the maker of so delicate an instrument, ask of it anything that could destroy or strain it?

42 "No! You have strain only when you are serving another master—the world, fame, the good opinion of men—or carrying two days' burden on one day. Remember, this must not be."

JANUARY 11

43 "When you come to Me and I give you that eternal life I give to all who believe in Me, your whole existence is altered, the words you speak, the influence you have. These are all eternal. They must be. They spring from the life within you, My life, eternal life, so that they too live forever.

44 "Now you see how vast, how stupendous, is the work of any soul that has eternal life. Your words and influence go on down the ages forever.

45 "You must ponder on these truths I give you. They are not surface facts, but the secrets of My kingdom, the hidden pearls of rare price. Meditate upon them. Work at them in your minds and hearts."

JANUARY 12

46 "Cry unto Me. I will hear you and bless you. Use My unlimited stores for your needs and those of others. Seek My wonderful truths and you shall find.

47 "There may come times when you sit in silence, when it seems as if you were left alone. Then, I command—command—you to remember I have spoken to you, as I spoke at Emmaus. There was the time in the upper room, after my ascension, when My disciples had to comfort themselves by saying, 'Did He not speak to us by the way?'

48 "You will have the consciousness of My presence when you hear no voice. Abide in that presence. 'I am the light of the world,' but sometimes in tender pity, I withhold too glaring a light, lest, in its dazzling brightness, you should miss your daily path and work.

49 "Not until heaven is reached do souls sit and drink in the ecstasy of God's revelation to His own. At the moment you are pilgrims and need only your daily marching orders and strength and guidance for the day.

50 "Eagerly and joyfully listen to My voice. Never crowd it out. I have no rival claimants and if men and women seek the babble of the world, then I withdraw.

51 "Life has hurt you. Only scarred lives can really save."

JANUARY 13

52 "You cannot escape discipline. It is the hallmark of discipleship.

53 "My children, trust Me always; never rebel. The trust given to Me today takes away the ache of rejection of My love that I suffered on earth and have suffered through the ages. 'I died for you, My children, and could you treat Me so?' "

JANUARY 14

54 "You must say 'thank you' for everything, even seeming trials and worries. Joy is the whole being's attitude of 'thank you' to Me. Be glad. Rejoice. A father loves to see his children happy.

55 "I am revealing so much to you. Pass it on. Each truth is a jewel. Some poor spirit-impoverished friend will be glad of it. Drop one here and there. Seek to find a heart-home for each truth I have imparted to you. More truths will flow in. Use all I give you. Help others.

56 "I ache to find a way into each life and heart, for all to cry expectantly, 'Even so, come Lord Jesus.' "

JANUARY 15

57 "Never despair, never despond. Just be a channel of helpfulness for others. Have more sympathy. Feel more tenderness toward others.

58 "Your lives will not always be hard. Gold does not stay in the crucible—only until it is refined. Already I hear the music

and the marching of the unseen host, rejoicing at your victory.

59 "No follower of Mine would ever err or fall if the veil were withdrawn that prevents him seeing how these slips delight the evil spirits. To see the pain and disappointment experienced by those who long for him to conquer in My strength and name and their ecstasy of rejoicing when he's won the victory would only serve to keep him steady."

JANUARY 16

60 "My strength is the same as that in which I conquered Satan in the wilderness, depression and sorrow in the Garden, and even death on Calvary. Think of that.

61 "Glad indeed are the souls with whom I walk. Walking with Me is security. The coming of My Spirit into a life, and its workings, are imperceptible, but the result is mighty. Learn of Me.

62 "Kill the self. Every blow to self is used to shape the real, eternal, imperishable you. Be candid and rigorous, asking of yourselves, 'Did self prompt that?' and if it did, oust it at all costs.

63 "When I died on the cross, I died embodying all the human self. Once that was crucified, I could conquer even death. When I bore your sins in My own body on the tree, I bore the human nature of the self, of the world.

64 "As you too kill self, you gain the overwhelming power I released for a weary world, and you too will be victorious. It is not life and its difficulties you have to conquer, only the self in you.

65 "As I said to My disciples, 'I have many things to say to you but you cannot bear them now.' You could not understand them. But as you go on obeying Me, walking with Me, and listening to Me, you will understand. Then you will see how glorious, how marvelous are My revelations and teachings."

2

January 17

1 "Relax. Do not get tense. Have no fear. All is for the best. How can you fear change when your life is hidden with Me in God, who never changes? I am the same yesterday, today, and forever.

2 "You must learn poise, soul-balance and poise, in a changing world.

3 "Claim My power; the same power with which I cast out devils is yours today. Use it. If not, I withdraw it. Use it ceaselessly. You cannot ask too much.

4 "Never think you are too busy. As long as you get back to Me and replenish after each task, no work can be too much.

5 "My joy I give you. Live in it. Bathe your spirit in it. Reflect it."

January 18

6 "The daily strivings count, not the momentary heights. Obey My will day in and day out, in the wilderness as well as on the occasional Mount of Transfiguration.

7 "Perseverance is nowhere needed so much as in the Christian life. My intimate friendship is secured in the drudgery of the kingdom.

8 "I am the Lord of the little things, the divine control of little happenings. Nothing in the day is too small to be a part of My scheme. In a mosaic, the little stones play a big part.

9 "Joy in Me. Joy is the God-given cement that secures the harmony and beauty of my mosaic."

JANUARY 19

10 "Be silent before Me. Seek to know and then to do My will in all things.

11 "Abide in My love, in an atmosphere of loving understanding to all men and women. This is your part to carry out. Then I surround you with a protective screen that keeps all evil from you, fashioned by your own attitude of mind, words, and deeds toward others.

12 "I want to give you all things, in good measure, pressed down and running over. Be quick to learn. You know little yet of the divine impatience that longs to rush to give.

13 "Does one worrying thought enter your mind, one impatient thought? Fight it at once. Love and trust are the solvents for the worry, cares, and irritations of life. Apply them at once.

14 "You are channels. Though your channel may not be altogether blocked, irritation, impatience, and worry corrode, and in time would block your channel beyond your help.

15 "Persevere! Oh, persevere! Never lose heart. All is well."

JANUARY 20

16 "Pray daily for faith. It is My gift. It is your only requisite for the accomplishment of mighty deeds. Certainly you have to work, you have to pray, but upon faith alone depends the answer to your prayers—your works.

17 "I give it to you in response to your prayer, because faith is the necessary weapon for you to possess for the dispersion of evil, for the overcoming of all adverse conditions, and for the accomplishment of all good in your lives. Then, when you have faith, you give it back to Me. It is the envelope in which every request to Me should be placed.

18 "And yet, 'Faith without works is dead.' So you need works, too, to feed your faith in Me. As you seek to do, you feel your helplessness. Then you turn to Me. In knowing Me, your faith grows—and that faith is all you need for My power to work."

JANUARY 21

Their meditation:

Lord, I will seek Thee.

Jesus responds:

19 "None ever sought Me in vain. I wait with a hungry longing to be called upon. I have already seen your hearts' needs before you cried to Me. Perhaps before you were conscious of those needs yourself, I was already preparing the answer.

20 "I am like the mother who is setting aside suitable gifts for her daughter's wedding before love even has come into the daughter's life. A thing mortals seldom realize is the anticipatory love of God. Think on this.

21 "Dismiss from your minds the thought of a grudging God who has to be petitioned with sighs and tears and much speaking before He will reluctantly relinquish the desired treasures. Your thoughts of Me need to be revolutionized.

22 "Try and see a mother preparing birthday or Christmas delights for her child. All the while her heart sings, 'Will she not love that? How she will love this!' She anticipates the rapture of her child, her own heart full of joy.

23 "Where did the mother learn all this joy in preparation? From Me—a faint echo of My joy in preparation. Try to see this as plans unfold of My preparing.

24 "It means much to Me to be understood, and understanding of Me will bring you great joy."

JANUARY 22

25 "One with Me. I and My Father are one. One with the Lord of the whole universe! Could human aspirations reach higher? Could human demands transcend this? One with Me.

26 "If you realize your high privilege, you have only to think and immediately the object of your thought is called into being. Indeed, well may I have said, 'Set your affections on things above, not on things of the earth.'

27 "To dwell in thought on the material, when once you live in Me, is to call it into being. So you must be careful only to think of and desire that which will help, not hinder, your spiritual growth. The same law operates on the spiritual plane.

28 "Think love, and love surrounds you and all about whom you think. Think thoughts of ill will and ill surrounds you and those about whom you think. Think health; health comes. The physical reflects the mental and spiritual."

JANUARY 23

29 "Believe that I am with you and controlling all. When My Word has gone forth, all are powerless against it.

30 "Be calm. Never fear. You have much to learn. Go on until you can take the most crowded day with a song. 'Sing unto the Lord.' The finest accompaniment to a song of praise to Me is a crowded day. Let love be the motif running through all.

31 "Be glad all the time. Rejoice exceedingly. Joy in Me. Rest in Me. Never be afraid. Pray more. Do not get worried. I am your helper. 'Underneath are the everlasting arms.' You cannot get below that. Rest in them, as a tired child rests.

32 "Be not afraid. I am your God, your deliverer. I will deliver you from all evil. Trust me. Fear not."

JANUARY 24

33 "Never forget your 'thank you.' Do you not see it is a lesson? Say 'thank you' on the grayest days. All cannot be light unless you do. It is absolutely necessary.

34 "If a gray day is not one of thankfulness, the lesson has to be repeated until it is. It is not that way for everyone, but only for those who ask to serve me well and to do much for me. A great work requires careful training.

35 "My death upon the cross was necessary, not only to save a world, but also to train My disciples. It was all a part of their training: My entering Jerusalem in triumph; My washing the disciples' feet; My sorrowing in Gethsemane; My being despised, judged, crucified, buried. Every step was necessary to their development. So it is with you."

JANUARY 25

Their meditation:

Lord, You are our refuge. Our God, in You we trust. O Master, come and talk with us.

Jesus responds:

36 "All power is given to Me. It is Mine to give, and Mine to withhold, but I acknowledge that I cannot withhold power from the soul that dwells near Me because then it is not a gift, but passes insensibly from Me to My disciples. It is breathed in by the soul who lives in My presence.

37 "Learn to shut yourself away in My presence. Then, without speaking, you have those things you desire of Me: strength, power, joy, and provisions."

JANUARY 26

38 "You are told to pray for faith, and you do so. But I make provision in the house of My abiding for those who

turn toward Me and yet have weak knees and heart. Be not afraid. I am your God, your great reward, yours to look up to and say, 'All is well.'

39 "I am your guide. Do not want to see the road ahead. Go just one step at a time. I rarely grant the long vista to My disciples, especially in personal affairs, for one step at a time is the best way to cultivate faith.

40 "You are in uncharted waters. But the Lord of all seas is with you, the controller of all storms is with you. Sing with joy.

41 "You follow the Lord of limitations, as well as the God in whose service is perfect freedom. He, the God of the universe, confined himself within the narrow limits of a baby and, in growing boyhood and young manhood, submitted to your human limitations.

42 "In like manner, you have to learn that your vision and power, boundless as far as spiritual things are concerned, must in temporal affairs submit to limitations too.

43 "But I am with you. When the disciples gave up after a night of fruitless fishing, I came, and the nets broke with an overabundance of supply."

JANUARY 27

44 "Complete surrender of every moment to God is the foundation of happiness; the superstructure is the joy of communion with Him. And that is the place, the mansion I went to prepare for each of you.

45 "My followers have misunderstood that and looked too often upon that promise as referring only to an afterlife. Too often—far too often—they look upon this life as something to be struggled through in order to be given the reward and the joy of the next.

46 "Seek to carry out all I say, and understanding, insight, vision, and joy will be yours which shall exceed all

understanding. The plans of God are wonderful—beyond your highest hopes.

47 "Cling to thoughts of protection, safety, and guidance."

JANUARY 28

48 "Keep your spirit life calm and unruffled. Nothing else matters. Leave all to Me. This is your great task, to remain calm in My presence, not to let one ruffled feeling stay for one moment. Years of blessing may be checked in one moment by that.

49 "No matter who or what bothers you, yours is the task to stop everything until absolute calm comes. Any block means My power is diverted into other channels.

50 "Pour forth, pour forth, pour forth! I cannot bless a life that does not act as a channel. My Spirit brooks no stagnation, not even rest. Its power must flow on. Pass on everything, every blessing. Abide in Me.

51 "See how many you can bless each day. Dwell much in My presence."

JANUARY 29

Their meditation:

Lord, to whom shall we go? Thou hast the words of eternal life (John 6:68).

Jesus responds:

52 "I am with you both. Go forward unafraid. Health and strength, peace, happiness, and joy—they are all my gifts. Yours for the asking.

53 "In the spiritual (as in the material) world, there is no empty space. As self, fears, and worries depart from your lives, it follows that the things of the Spirit, which you crave

so, rush in to take their places.

54 "All things are yours, and you are Christ's and Christ is God's. What a wonderful cycle, because you are God's.

55 "Be not afraid. Fear not. It is to the drowning man the rescuer comes. To the brave swimmer who can fare well alone he does not come. No rush of joy can be like that of a man toward his rescuer.

56 "It is part of My method to wait until the storm is at its most violent. It was like that with My disciples on the lake. I could have bidden the first angry wave to be calm, the first gust of wind to be still, but what a lesson would have gone unlearned and what a sense of tender nearness of refuge and safety would have been lost!

57 "Remember this—My disciples thought that in sleep I had forgotten them. Remember how mistaken they were. Gain strength and confidence, joyful dependence and anticipation from that.

58 "Never fear. Joy is yours. The radiant joy of the rescued shall be yours."

JANUARY 30

59 "Fear not. Do not fear to be busy. You are the servant of all. 'He that would be the greatest among you, let him be the servant of all.'

60 "Service is the byword of My disciples. I served indeed the humblest and the lowliest. I was at their command. My highest powers were at their service.

61 "Be used. Be used by all, by the lowest and the smallest. How best can you serve? Let that be your daily seeking, not how best can you be served.

62 "Truly your thoughts are not God's thoughts, nor ways, God's ways. When you seek to follow Me in all things, it frequently means a complete reversal from the ways of the world you have previously followed. But it is a reversal that

leads to boundless happiness and peace.

63 "Look around you. Read what is being written. What do you find? Do the aims and ambitions of fellow humans bring peace? Do the world's awards bring heart-rest and happiness? No! Rather, man is at war with man. Those whom the world has most rewarded with name, fame, honor, and wealth are weary and disappointed.

64 "To the listening ear, above the jangle of the world's discordant cries, there echoes down the 1900 years My message, 'Come unto Me all ye that are weary and heavy laden and I will give you rest.' And the weary and disappointed who listen and turn to Me indeed find that rest.

65 "I am joy to the weary, music to the heart, health to the sick, wealth to the poor, food to the hungry, home to the wanderer, rapture to the jaded, and love to the lonely. There is not one want of the soul that I do not supply for the asking. To you, too, I long to be all."

JANUARY 31

Their meditation:

Wait on the Lord (Psalm 27:14).

Jesus responds:

66 "I am your shield. Have no fear. You must know that 'all is well.' I will never let anyone do to you both other than My will for you.

67 "I can see the future. I can read men's hearts. I know better than you what you need. Trust Me absolutely. You are not at the mercy of fate or buffeted about by others. You are being led in a definite way. Others who do not serve your purpose are being moved out of your path by Me.

68 "Never fear, whatever may happen. You are both being led. Do not try to plan. I have planned. You are the

builder, not the architect. Go quietly and gently. All is for the best for you.

69 "Trust Me for all. Your very extremity ensures My activity for you. Having your foundation on the rock (Christ), faith in Him, and 'being rooted and grounded in Him,' and having belief in My divinity as your cornerstone, you are free to build, knowing all is well.

70 "You literally have to depend on Me for everything. Everything! It was out of the depths that David cried to Me and I heard his voice. All is well."

FEBRUARY 1

71 "No evil can befall you if I am with you. 'Ill that he blesses is our good.' Every time you are laid aside is a time of retreat into the quiet place with Me. Never fear, but in that place you shall find restoration and power and joy and healing.

72 "Plan your retreat days now. In those days, when you live apart with Me, you will arise rested and refreshed physically, mentally, and spiritually to carry on the work I have given to you. I will never give you a load greater than you can bear.

73 "Welcome love, joy, and peace. Let no personal feelings, no thoughts of self, banish these. Singly they are miracle-producing in a life. Together they can command all that is needed on the physical, mental, and spiritual planes.

74 "It is in these attributes that all success lies. You have to see that your inner lives are all they should be. Then the work is accomplished. Not in rushing and striving on the material plane, but on the battlefield of the soul are these things won.

75 "All sacrifice and suffering are redemptive, to teach the individual or to be used to raise and help others. Nothing is by chance.

76 "The divine mind is beyond your finite mind to understand. In My plans, already perfect, no detail is forgotten."

3

February 2

1 "Take courage. Do not fear. Start a new life tomorrow. Put the old mistakes away and start anew. I give you a fresh start. Do not be burdened. Do not be anxious.

2 "If My forgiveness were for the righteous only, and those who had not sinned, where would be its need? Remember, as I said to Mary of old, 'To whom much is forgiven, the same loveth much.'

3 "Why do you chafe and worry so? I wait to give you all that is lovely, but your lives are soiled with worry and irritation. You would crush My treasures.

4 "I can only bless glad, thankful hearts. You must be glad and joyful."

February 3

Their meditation:

Watch over and protect us.

Jesus responds:

5 "Lack of love will block the way. You must love all: those who annoy you and those who do not.

6 "Practice love. It is a great lesson, and you have a great teacher. You must love; otherwise, how can you dwell in Me, where nothing unloving can come? Practice this, and I will bless you exceedingly above all you can ask or imagine.

7 "There is no limit to My power. Do all you can and leave the rest to Me. Peace and trust will come. Fear not. I am

your advocate, your mediator"

FEBRUARY 4

8 "Only believe. The walls of Jericho fell down. Was it axes or human implements that brought them down? Rather, it was the songs of praise of the people and My thought carried out in action.

9 "All walls shall fall before you too. There is no power on earth that does not fall like a house of paper at My miracle-working touch.

10 "Your faith and My power are the only two essentials. Nothing else is needed.

11 "If your petty opposition is still effective, it is only because I choose to let it stand between you and what would be a mistake for you. If not, a word, a thought from Me, and it is gone.

12 "The hearts of kings are in My rule and governance. All men and women can be moved at My wish. Rest in this certainty. Rely on Me."

FEBRUARY 5

13 "Just go step by step. My will shall be revealed as you go. You will never cease to be thankful for this time when you felt peaceful and trustful, and yet had no human security.

4 "That is the time of learning of true trust in Me. 'When thy father and mother forsake thee, then the Lord will take thee up.' That is literal dependence on Me.

15 "When human support or material help of any kind is removed, then My power can become operative. I cannot teach a man to walk who is trusting in a crutch.

16 "Away with your crutch, and My power shall so invigorate you that you shall indeed walk on to victory.

Never limit My power for it is limitless."

FEBRUARY 6

17 "Walk with Me; I will teach you. Listen to Me; I will speak. Continue to meet Me in spite of all opposition and every obstacle, in spite of days when you may hear no voice and there may come no intimate heart-to-heart telling.

18 "As you persist in this and make a life habit of it, I will reveal My will to you in many marvelous ways. You shall have more sure knowledge of both the present and the future. But that will only be the reward of coming regularly to meet Me.

19 "Life is a school for which there are many teachers. I do not come to everyone personally. Believe literally that the problems and difficulties of your lives can be explained by Me more clearly and effectually than by any other."

FEBRUARY 7

20 "I speak to the listening ear. I come to the waiting heart. Sometimes I may not speak. I may ask you merely to wait in My presence, to know that I am with you.

21 "Think of the multitudes who thronged Me when I was on earth, all eager for something—eager to be healed, or taught, or fed.

22 "As I supplied their many wants and granted their manifold requests, think what it meant to Me to find amid the crowd one or two who followed just to be near Me, just to dwell in My presence. Some longing of the eternal heart was satisfied by that.

23 "Comfort Me a while by letting Me know that you seek Me just to dwell in My presence, to be near Me, not for teaching or material gain or for a message—but for Me.

24 "The longing of the human heart to be loved for

itself is something caught from the great divine heart.

25 "I bless you. Bow your heads."

FEBRUARY 8

26 "Trust and be not afraid. Life is full of wonders. Open childlike trusting eyes to all I am doing for you. Fear not.

27 "Only a few steps more and then My power shall be seen and known. You are yourselves now walking in the tunnel of darkness. Soon you, yourselves, shall be lights to guide feet that are afraid.

28 "The cries of your sufferings have pierced even to the ears of God Himself—My Father in heaven, your Father in heaven. With God, to hear is to answer.

29 "Only a cry from the heart, a cry to divine power to help human weakness, a trusting cry, ever reaches the ear divine.

30 "Remember, trembling heart, that with God, to hear is to answer. Your prayers, and they have been many, are answered."

FEBRUARY 9

31 "I am your Lord, your supply. You must rely on Me. Trust to the uttermost limit. Trust and do not be afraid. You must depend on divine power only.

32 "I have not forgotten you. Your help is coming. You shall know and realize My power.

33 "Endurance is faith tried almost to the breaking point. You must wait, trust, hope, and joy in Me. You must not depend on others but on Me—on Me, your strength, your help, your supply.

34 "This is the great test. Am I your supply or not? Every great work for Me has had to have this great time of testing.

35 "Keep your souls patient and rejoice. You must wait until I show the way. After the waiting test, heaven itself

cannot contain more joy than that victorious soul knows.

36 "No disciple of Mine can be victor who does not wait until I give the order to start.

37 "You cannot be anxious if you know that I am your supply."

FEBRUARY 10

38 "The divine voice is not always expressed in words. It is made known as a heart consciousness."

FEBRUARY 11

39 "I am your Savior, your Savior from slavery to sin, your Savior from all the cares and troubles of life, your Savior from disease.

40 "I speak as all to you both. Look to Me for salvation. Trust Me for help.

41 "Did not My servant of old say, 'All thy waves and thy billows are gone over me?' But not all the waters of affliction could drown Him. For of Him it was true, 'He came from above, he took me, He drew me out of many waters.'

42 "The lifeline, the line of rescue, is the line from the soul to God, faith, and power. It is a strong line, and no soul can be overwhelmed who is linked to Me by it. Trust, trust, trust. Never be afraid.

43 "Think of My trees, stripped of their beauty, pruned, cut, disfigured, and bare. But the spirit life-sap flows silently, secretly, through the dark seemingly dead branches; then, with the sun of spring comes new life, leaves, buds, blossoms, and fruit. Indeed, the fruit is a thousand times better because of the pruning.

44 "Remember that you are in the hands of a master gardener. He makes no mistakes about His pruning.

45 "Rejoice! Joy is the spirit reaching out to say its

thanks to Me. It is the new life-sap of the tree, reaching out to Me to find such beautiful expression later. Never cease to joy. Rejoice!"

FEBRUARY 12

46 "Your path is difficult, difficult for you both. There is no work in life so hard as waiting, and yet I say wait. Wait until I show you My will. I give you both hard tasks as proof of My love and of My certainty of your true discipleship.

47 "Again, I say wait. Motion is easier than calm waiting. So many of My followers have marred their work and hindered the progress of My kingdom by activity.

48 "Wait. I will not overtax your spiritual strength. You are both like persons helpless on a raft in midocean. But, lo! There comes toward you One walking on the waters, like unto the Son of Man.

49 "When He comes and you receive Him, it will be with you as it was with My disciples when I was on earth: Immediately you will be at the place where you wish to be.

50 "All your toil in rowing and all your activity could not have accomplished the journey so soon. Wait and trust. Wait and do not be afraid."

FEBRUARY 13

51 "Life is really consciousness of Me. Have no fear. A beautiful future lies before you. Let it be a new life, a new existence, in which in every single happening, event, and plan you are conscious of Me.

52 " 'And this is life eternal, that they may know thee, and Jesus Christ whom thou has sent.' Acquire this constant consciousness and you have eternal life—the life of the ages.

53 "In all things be led by the Spirit of God and trust Me in all. The consciousness of Me must bring joy. Give Me

gladness as well as trust."

FEBRUARY 14

54 "In a race it is not the start that hurts, nor the even pace of the long stretch. It is when the goal is in sight that heart, nerves, courage, and muscles are strained almost beyond human endurance to the breaking point.

55 "So with you. Now that the goal is in sight, you need your final cry to Me. Cannot you see by the nerve and heart rack of the past few days that your race is nearly run?

56 "Courage, courage! Heed My voice of encouragement. Remember that I am by your side spurring you on to victory.

57 "In the annals of heaven, the saddest records are those that tell of the many who ran well with brave stout hearts until, in sight of the goal, their courage failed. The whole host of heaven longed to cry out how near the end was, to implore the last spurt. But they fell out, never to know until the last day of revealing how near they were to victory.

58 "Would that they had listened to Me in the silence as the two of you meet with Me! They would have known. There must be the listening ear as well as the still small voice."

FEBRUARY 15

59 "You do not realize that you would have broken down under the weight of your cares but for these renewing times with me. It is not what I say; it is Me, Myself. It is not hearing Me so much as being in My presence that matters. You cannot know the strengthening and curative powers of this. Such knowledge is beyond your human understanding.

60 "If every day each soul, or group of souls, waited before Me, this poor sick world would be cured. Remember

that you must never fail to keep this time apart with Me.

61 "Gradually you will be transformed physically, mentally, and spiritually into My likeness. All who see you or are in contact with you will be brought near to me because of their relationship with you, and gradually the influence will spread.

62 "You are making one spot of earth a holy place. Though you must work and spend yourselves ceaselessly because that is presently your appointed task, in this time apart with Me you are doing the greatest work either of you can do. Are you understanding that?

63 "Do you know that every thought, every activity, every prayer, every longing of the day is gathered up and offered to Me now?

64 "Joy that I am with you. I came to earth to lead human beings back to spirit-conversation with their God."

FEBRUARY 16

65 "You shall be used. The divine force is never less than adequate. It is sufficient for all the work in the world. I only need instruments to use. To know that would remake the world.

66 "The world does not need supermen, but supernatural persons, those men and women who will persistently turn the self out of their lives and let divine power work through them.

67 "Let inspiration take the place of aspiration. All unemployment would cease. I always have plenty of work to be done. I always pay My people well. This you will see more and more as you get the right attitude about the work being Mine only."

FEBRUARY 17

68 "If only you sat still and longed for Me. If only you drew hungering breaths for Me as you do for the fresh pure

air of the open. Even if I were never to speak to you, you would be well rewarded for setting apart this time.

69 "Be still. Be calm. Wait before Me. Learn patience, humility, and peace from Me.

70 "When will you be absolutely unruffled—whatever happens? You are slow to learn your lesson. Simply seeking silence must help in the rush and work and worry.

71 "Bustling accomplishes so little. You must learn to take calm with you in the most hurried days."

FEBRUARY 18

72 "Psychic powers are not necessarily spiritual powers. Do not seek the spiritual through material means; that would be weighing down beautiful spirit-wings with earth's mud.

73 "Seek this time as a time of communion with Me—not as a time to ask questions and have them answered. Meet Me in communion. It is food for the soul I have provided.

74 "Grasp the truth and find Me, the true bread of life. The lesson of the grain is the lesson of My church and Me. The real life is all that matters. The outward church is the husk. But the husk was necessary to present the life grain to you.

75 "Do not expect a perfect church, but find in a church the means of coming near to Me. That alone matters. Then much that is husk falls away. Consider it of no account."

FEBRUARY 19

76 "Never miss these times. It is not what I reveal to you so much as the linking up of your frail natures with the limitless divine powers. Forces are already set in motion. Only My will is coming to pass. God is now blessing you richly.

77 "You think that there is much to do in a crisis like this. There is only one thing to do. Link your lives to the divine forces. Then, it is as much My work to see your lives

and your affairs run in an orderly manner as to see that tomorrow's sun rises.

78 "It is not the passionate appeal that gains the divine ear as much as quietly placing difficulties and worries in the divine hands. So trust.

79 "Be no more afraid than a child who places its tangled skein of wool in the hands of a loving mother and runs out to play. The mother is more pleased by the unquestioning confidence than if the child went down on its knees and implored her help. That would pain her instead, as it would imply she was not eager to help when help was needed."

FEBRUARY 20

80 "Do not forget to meet all your difficulties with love and laughter. Be assured that I am with you.

81 "Remember! Remember, it is the last few yards that tell. Do not fail Me. I cannot fail you. Rest in My love.

82 "How many of the world's prayers have gone unanswered because My children who prayed did not endure to the end! They thought it was too late and that they must act for themselves, that I was not going to act for them.

83 "Remember My words: 'He that endureth to the end, the same shall be saved.' Can you endure to the end? If so, you shall be saved. But endure with courage, with love and laughter. My children, is My training too hard?

84 "My children, I will unlock for you the secret treasures hidden from so many. Not one of your cries goes unheard. Indeed, I am with you to aid you.

85 "Go through all I have said to you and live in every detail as I have enjoined you. As you follow implicitly all I say, success—spiritual, mental, and physical—shall be yours.

86 "Wait in silence a while. Be conscious of My presence in which you must live and have rest for your souls and power and joy and peace."

FEBRUARY 21

87 " 'In everything by prayer and supplication let your requests be made known unto God.' But do not beg. Rather, come as a business manager bringing to the owner the needs, checks to be signed, and so on, knowing that to lay the matter before her means immediate supply.

88 "I long to supply. But the asking—or the faith assurance from you—is necessary because your contact with Me is vital."

4

FEBRUARY 22

1 "The way is plain. You do not need to see far ahead. Just one step at a time with Me. The same light will guide you as the hosts of heaven know—the Son of Righteousness Himself.

2 "Only self can cast a shadow on the way. Be more afraid of spirit-unrest, of soul-disturbance, or of a ruffling of the spirit than of earthquake, fire, or any outside force.

3 "When you feel the absolute calm has been broken, go away alone with Me until your heart sings and all is strong and calm. These are the only times when evil can find an entrance.

4 "The forces of evil surround the city of your soul and are keenly alert for one such unguarded spot through which an arrow can pierce and do havoc.

5 "Remember that all you have to do is keep calm and happy. God does the rest. No evil force can hinder My power—only you yourself have power to do that. Think of all God's mighty forces arrayed to aid you—and your poor, puny self impedes their onward march."

FEBRUARY 23

6 "You must trust Me wholly. This lesson has to be learned. You shall be helped; you shall be led and guided continually.

7 "The children of Israel would long before have entered the promised land—only their doubts and fears con-

tinually drove them back into the wilderness.

8 "Remember always, doubts delay. Are you trusting all to Me or not?

9 "I have told you how to live and you must do it. My children, I love you. Trust My tender love. It will never fail you, but you must learn not to fail it.

10 "Could you see, you would understand. You have much to learn in turning out fear and being at peace.

11 "All your doubts arrest My work. You must not doubt. I died to save you from sin and doubt and worry. You must believe in Me absolutely."

FEBRUARY 24

12 "Love the busy life. It is a joy-filled life.

13 "I love you both and bid you be of good cheer. Take your fill of joy in the spring.

14 "Live outside whenever possible. Sun and air are My great healing forces.

15 "Never forget that real healing of body, mind, and spirit comes from within, from the close loving contact of your spirit with My Spirit."

FEBRUARY 25

16 "Silently the work of the Spirit is done.

17 "Already love is drawing others to you. Take all who come as sent by Me and give them a royal welcome. It will surprise you, all that I have planned for you. Welcome all who come with the love of both your hearts.

18 "You may not see the work. Today they may not need you. Tomorrow they may need you. I may send you strange visitors. Make each desire to return. Nobody must come and feel unwanted.

19 "Share your love, your joy, your happiness, your

time, and your food gladly with all.

20 "Such wonders will unfold. You see it all in the bud stage now—the glory of the open flower is beyond all description.

21 "Have love, joy, and peace in richest abundance—only believe.

22 "Give out love and all you can with a glad, free heart and hand. Use all you can for others and back will come countless stores and blessings."

FEBRUARY 26

23 "Joy is the sovereign balm for all the ills of the world, the spirit cure for every ailment. There is nothing that joy and love cannot do.

24 "Set your standard high. Aim at conquering a world, the world all around you. Just say, 'Jesus conquers'—'Jesus saves'—in the face of every doubt, every sin, every evil, every fear.

25 "No evil can stand against that, for there is 'none other name under heaven given among men, whereby men can be saved.' To every thought of want or lack, 'Jesus saves from poverty'; to every fear, 'Jesus saves from fear.'

26 "Do this to every ill and it will vanish as night when the sun arises."

FEBRUARY 27

27 "There is nothing lacking in your lives because all is really yours, only you lack the faith to know it. You are like a king's daughters who sit in rags while all around them are stores of all they could desire.

28 "Pray for more faith, as a thirsty nomad in the desert prays for water. My help comes swift and strong.

29 "Do you know what it is to feel sure that I can never fail you? As sure as you are that you still breathe? How poor

is your faith! Do you trust Me as much as you would a friend if that friend came and said he would send you help?

30 "Pray daily and most diligently that your faith may increase."

February 28

31 "Take time for prayer. Take more time to be alone with Me. Only in this way will you prosper.

32 "Realize that the hearing of spirit sounds is more than the hearing of all earth's noises. I am with you. Let that content you. No, more than that, let it fill you with rapture.

33 "Seek sometimes not even to hear Me. Seek a silence of spirit understanding with Me. Do not be afraid. All is well. Dwell as much on what I did as well as what I said.

34 "Remember, I touched 'her hand and the fever left her.' Not many words, just a momentary contact, and all fever left her. She was well, whole, and calm, able to get up and 'minister unto them.'

35 "My touch is still a potent healer. Feel that touch. Sense My presence and the fever of work, care, and fear melts into nothingness. Health, joy, and peace take its place."

March 1

36 "Spend more time alone with Me. From such times will come a strength and joy that will add much to your friendship and work.

37 "Times of prayer are times of growth. Cut those times short and many well-filled hours of work may be profitless.

38 "Heaven's values are so different from the values of earth. From the point of view of the Great Worker, one poor tool, working all the time but doing bad work, is of small value compared with the sharp, keen, perfect instrument used

only a short time but which turns out perfect work."

MARCH 2

39 "How little men and women know and sense My need—My need of love and companionship. I came 'to draw men unto Me,' and sweet it is to feel hearts drawing near in love and for tender comradeship, not just for help.

40 "Many know the needs of humans, few know the needs of Christ."

MARCH 3

41 "I always hear your cry. No sound escapes Me. Many in the world cry to Me, but how few wait to hear Me speak to them. Yet, My speaking to the soul matters so much to it.

42 "My words are life. To hear Me speak is to find life and healing and strength. Trust Me in all things. Love showered on all brings truly a quick return.

43 "Carry out My wishes and let Me carry out yours. Treat Me as Savior and King, but also with the tender intimacy of One much loved.

44 "Keep the rules I have laid down for you. Keep them persistently, perseveringly, lovingly, patiently, hopefully, and in faith. If you do, every mountain of difficulty shall be laid low, the rough places of poverty shall be made smooth, and all who know you shall know that I, your Lord, am the Lord.

45 "Shower love."

MARCH 4

46 " 'The words that I speak unto you, they are spirit and they are life,' just as much as the words I spoke to My disciples of old.

47 "This is your reward for not seeking spirit communication through a medium. Those who do it can never know the ecstasy, the wonder, of spirit communication as you know it.

48 "Life, joy, peace, and healing are yours in full measure. You will see this as you go on. At first, you can hardly credit the powers I am bestowing on you.

49 "I sent My disciples out two by two and gave them power over unclean spirits and to heal all manner of diseases. It must have been wonderful for Peter to feel suddenly that his Lord's power was his."

MARCH 5

50 "Think of Me. Look at Me often and unconsciously you will grow like Me.

51 "You may never see it. The nearer you get to Me, the more you will see your unlikeness to Me. So be comforted, My children. Your deep sense of failure is a sure sign that you are growing nearer to Me.

52 "If you desire to help others to Me, then that prayer desire is answered.

53 "Remember, it is only struggle that hurts. In laziness, whether spiritual, mental, or physical, there is no sense of failure or discomfort.

54 "But with action, with effort, you are conscious not of strength but of weakness—at least at first. That is a sign of life, of spiritual growth.

55 "Remember, My strength is made perfect in weakness."

MARCH 6

56 "Draw near to Me, My children. Contact with Me is the panacea for all ills.

57 "Remember that truth is many sided. Have much

tender love and patience for all who do not see as you.

58 "The elimination of self is the key to holiness and happiness. It can only be accomplished with My help.

59 "Study My life more. Live in My presence. Worship Me.

60 "I said in Gethsemane, 'If it be possible let this cup pass.' I did not say that there was no cup of sorrow to drink.

61 "I was scourged and spat upon and nailed to the cross, and I said, 'Father, forgive them, they know not what they do.' I did not say that they did not do it. When My disciple Peter urged Me to escape the cross, I said, 'Get thee behind me, Satan.'

62 "When My disciples failed to help the epileptic boy, I said, 'This kind cometh not out but by prayer and fasting.' I did not say, 'You imagined that he was ill. Nothing is wrong.'

63 "When the Bible says, 'God has purer eyes than to behold evil,' it means He does not impute evil to His people. He always sees the good in people. Remember that I 'beheld the city and wept over it.' "

MARCH 7

64 "Have no fear. Fear is evil and 'perfect love casts out fear.' There is no room for fear in the heart in which I dwell. Fear destroys hope. It cannot exist where love is or where faith is.

65 "Fear is the curse of the world. Men and women are afraid—afraid of poverty, loneliness, unemployment, sickness. They have many, many fears.

66 "Nation is afraid of nation. Fear is everywhere. Fight fear as you would a plague. Turn it out of your lives and home. Fight it singly. Fight it together. Never inspire fear; fear of punishment and fear of blame are evil allies.

67 "No work that employs this enemy of Mine is work

for Me. Banish it. There must be another and better way. Ask Me, and I will show it to you."

March 8

68 "Work for Me, with Me, through Me. To last, all work must be done in My Spirit. How silently My Spirit works. How gently and gradually souls are led into My kingdom.

69 "Love and laughter is needed from the plow that prepares the ground for the seed. Remember this: If the ground is hard, seed will not grow there. Prepare the ground. Prepare it as I say."

March 9

70 "Many think that I only test and train and bend to My will. Though I told My disciples to take up the cross, I also loved to prepare a feast for them by the lakeside. My feast was a glad surprise and not a necessity, as the feeding of the multitude may have seemed. I loved to give the wine gift at the marriage feast.

71 "As you love to plan surprises for those who understand and joy in them, so with Me. I love to plan them for those who see My love and joy in it.

72 "Those who see not only My tears, the tears of a Savior, but the smile, the joyous smile of a friend, are dear to the heart of My Father."

March 10

73 "The joy of the spring shall be yours in full measure. After long months of travail, revel in the earth's joy. There will come back a wonderful joy if you share in nature's wonder now.

74 "Nature is the embodied spirit of My thoughts of

beauty for this world. Treat nature as My servant and messenger. To realize this will bring to you both new life-joy. Share her joys and travails, and great blessings will be yours.

75 "This is all important because it is not only believing certain things about Me that helps and heals, but knowing Me, sensing My presence in a flower, My message in its beauty and perfume.

76 "You can truly live a life not of earth—a heaven-life here and now. Joy! Joy! Joy!"

MARCH 11

77 "Nothing is small to God. In His sight a sparrow is of greater value than a palace, one kindly word of more importance than a statesperson's speech.

78 "It is the life in all that has value and the quality of the life that determines the value. I came to give eternal life."

MARCH 12

79 "Before you can be receptive to heaven's music, you have to quiet your heart and still your senses.

80 "Your five senses are your means of communication with the material world. They are the links between your real spirit life and the material manifestations around you. You must sever all connection with them when you wish to hold spirit communication. They will hinder, not help.

81 "See the good in everybody. Love the good in them. See your unworthiness compared with their worth.

82 "Love, laugh, make the world (your little world) happy. As the ripples caused by a flung stone stir the surface of a whole pond, so your joy shall spread in ever widening circles, beyond all your knowledge and anticipation.

83 "Joy in Me. Such joy is eternal. Joy's precious fruit is still bearing centuries after."

MARCH 13

84 "Draw beauty from every flower and joy from the song of the birds and the color of the flowers. Drink in the beauty of air and color.

85 "I am with you. When I wanted to express a beautiful thought, I made a lovely flower. I have told you. Reflect.

86 "When I want to express to humans what I am—what My Father is—I strive to make a beautiful character.

87 "Think of yourselves as My expression of attributes as a lovely flower is My expression of thought. Then you will strive in all, in spiritual beauty, in thought-power, in health, in clothing, to be as fit an expression for Me as you can.

88 "Absorb beauty. As soon as the beauty of a flower or a tree is impressed upon your soul, it leaves an image that reflects through your actions. Remember that no thought of sin and suffering, of the approaching scorn and crucifixion, ever prevented Me from seeing the beauty of the flowers.

89 "Look for beauty and joy in the world around you. Look at a flower until its beauty becomes part of your soul. Its beauty will be given back to the world again by you in the form of a smile or a loving word or a kind thought or a prayer.

90 "Listen to a bird. Take the song as a message from My Father. Let it sink into your soul. That too will be given back to the world in ways I have said.

91 "Laugh more. Laugh often. Love more. I am with you. I am your Lord."

MARCH 14

92 "Simplicity is the keynote of My kingdom. Choose simple things always. Love and reverence the humble and the simple. Have only simple things here. Your standard must never be the world's standard."

MARCH 15

93 "Wait before Me, gently breathing in My Spirit. If you give that Spirit free entrance and do not keep it out by self, it will enable you to do the same works I did. That means, it will enable Me to do the same works, and even greater works than I did when on earth, through you.

94 "Spiritualism is wrong. No man should ever be a medium for any spirit, other than Mine.

95 "When and how I see best, I will tell you all you should know and all it is good for you to know of My Spirit kingdom. The limit is set by your own spiritual development. Follow My injunctions in all things.

96 "Peace. Peace. Peace."

5

March 16

1 "I am near, broodingly near, as some tender mother bird anxious over its young. I am your Lord, life of your body, mind, and soul, renewer of your youth.

2 "You do not know all that this time with Me will mean to you. Did not My servant Isaiah say, 'They that wait upon the Lord shall renew their strength. They shall mount up with wings as eagles, they shall run and not be weary, they shall walk and not faint.'

3 "Persevere in all I tell you to do. The persistent carrying out of My commands and desires will unfailingly bring you, as far as spiritual, mental, and temporal things are concerned, to that place where you would be.

4 "If you look back over My words to you, you will see that My leading has been gradual. Only as you have carried out My wishes have I been able to give you more clear and definite teaching and guidance.

5 "Your ecstasy is God's touch on quickened responsive spirit nerves. Joy! Joy! Joy!"

March 17

6 "Remember, you are only an instrument. It is not yours to decide how or when or where you act. I plan all that. Make yourself fit to do My work. All that hinders your activity must be cured.

7 "The burdens of the world are laid on My cross. Any one of My disciples is foolish who seeks to bear his own

burdens. There is only one place for them—My cross.

8 "It is like a weary man bearing a heavy load on a hot and dusty road when plans were made for the load to be carried. Enjoyment of the road, the scenery, the flowers, the beauty around—all are lost.

9 "But, My children, you may remember I said, 'Take up your cross daily and follow me.' Yes, but the cross is given to you to crucify the self that hinders progress and joy. That self prevents the flow through your being of My invigorating life and Spirit.

10 "Listen to Me. Love Me. Joy in Me. Rejoice!

11 "My children, I am here beside you. Draw near in spirit to Me. Shut out the distractions of the world. I am your life, the very breath of your soul."

MARCH 18

12 "Learn what it is to shut yourself in the secret place of your being, which is My secret place too. Though I wait in many hearts, so few retire into that inner place of the being to commune with Me.

13 "Wherever the soul is, I am. Men and women have rarely understood this. I am actually at the center of everyone's being, but, distracted with the things of the sense life, they do not find Me.

14 "Do you realize that I am telling you truths, revealing them, not repeating oft-told facts. Meditate on all I say. Ponder it, not to draw your own conclusions, but to absorb Mine.

15 "Throughout the ages, men and women have been too eager to say what they thought about My truth. In doing so, they have grievously erred.

16 "Hear Me. Talk to Me. Reflect Me. Do not say what you think about Me. My words need no human explanation. I can explain to each heart.

17 "Make Me real to others and let Me do My own

work. To lead a soul to Me is one thing; to seek to stay with it as interpreter mars the first great act.

18 "It would be the same in human relationships. How much more when it involves the soul and Me, its Maker, and the only real Spirit that understands it."

MARCH 19

19 "Withdraw into the calm of communion with Me. Rest. Rest in that calm and peace. Life knows no greater joy than you will find in conversation and companionship with Me.

20 "You are Mine. When the soul finds its home of rest in Me, then its real life begins.

21 "In My kingdom we do not measure in years, as you measure life. We count only from your second birth, that new birth of which I spoke to Nicodemus when I said, 'Ye must be born again.'

22 "We know no life but eternal life. When one enters into that, then he or she lives.

23 "And this is life eternal, to know God, My Father, and Me, the Son sent by Him. So immature, so childish, so empty is all so-called living before that. I shower love on you. Pass love on.

24 "Do not fear. To fear is as foolish as if a small child with a small coin, but a rich father, worried about how a mortgage should be paid. and what he or she should do about it. Is this work Mine or not? You need to trust Me for everything."

MARCH 20

25 "Listen to Me. I am your Lord. There is none other before Me. Just trust Me in everything. Help is here all the time.

26 "The difficult way is nearly over, but you have learned lessons from it you could learn no other way. 'The kingdom of heaven suffereth violence, and it is the violent who take it by force.' Seize from Me, by firm and simple trust and persistent prayer, the treasures of My kingdom.

27 "Such wonderful things are coming to you: joy, peace, assurance, security, health, happiness, and laughter.

28 "Claim big, really big things now. Remember, nothing is too big. Satisfy the longing of My heart to give. Blessing, abundant blessing, on you both now and always. Peace."

MARCH 21

29 "I am here. Fear not. Can you really trust Me? I am a God of power as well as a Man of love, so human yet so divine.

30 "Just trust. I cannot and I will not fail you. All is well. Courage.

31 "Many are praying for you both."

MARCH 22

32 "Your foolish little activities are valueless in themselves. Seemingly trivial or of seemingly great moment, all deeds are alike if directed by Me. Cease to function except through Me.

33 "I am your Lord. Obey Me as you would expect a faithful willing secretary to carry out your directions. Have no choice but Mine, no will but Mine.

34 "I am dependent on no one agency when I am your supply. Through many channels My help and material flow can come."

MARCH 23

35 "Remember My words to My disciples, 'This kind

cometh not out but by prayer and fasting.' Can you tread the way I trod? Can you drink of My cup? 'All is well.' Say always, 'All is well.'

36 "Long though the way may seem, there is not one inch too much. I, your Lord, am not only with you on the journey. I planned, and am planning, the journey.

37 "There are joys unspeakable in the way you go. Courage. Courage. Courage."

MARCH 24

38 "To Me, your intimate friend, all power is given. It is given Me by My Father. Have not My intimate friends a right to have it?

39 "You cannot have a need I cannot supply. A flower or thousands of dollars—one is no more difficult than the other.

40 "Your need is a spiritual need to carry on My work. All spiritual supply is fashioned from love. The flower and the thousands of dollars—both fashioned from love to those who need it. Do you not see this?

41 "I thought of you and a bud opened. You converted that into a cheer for one you love. That cheer meant increased health. Increased health means work for Me, and that means souls for Me.

42 "And so it goes on, a constant supply, but only if the need is a spiritual one."

MARCH 25

43 "I am beside you to bless and help you. Waver not in your prayers. They shall be heard. All power is Mine. Say that to yourself often and steadily.

44 "Say it until your heart sings with the joy of the safety and power it means to you. Say it until the very force of the utterance drives back and nullifies all the evils against you.

45 "Use it as a battle cry, 'All power is given unto my Lord,' 'All power is given unto my Friend,' 'All power is given unto my Savior,' and then you pass on to victory."

MARCH 26

46 "I am here. Seek not to know the future. Mercifully, I veil it from you.

47 "Faith is too priceless a possession to be sacrificed in order to purchase knowledge. But faith itself is based on a knowledge of Me.

48 "Remember this evening time is not to learn the future and not to receive revelation of the unseen. It is to gain an intimate knowledge of Me that will teach you all things and be the very foundation of your faith."

MARCH 27

49 "I am with you. Do not fear. Never doubt My love and power.

50 "Your heights of success will be won by the daily persistent doing of what I have said. Daily, steady persistence. Like the wearing away of a stone by steady drops of water, so your daily persistence will wear away all the difficulties and gain success for you. It will secure your help for others.

51 "Never falter. Go forward boldly and unafraid. I am beside you to help and strengthen you.

52 "Wonders have unfolded. More still will unfold that are beyond your dreams and hopes.

53 "Say 'All is well' to everything. All is well!"

MARCH 28

54 "I am with you to guide you and help you. Unseen forces are controlling your destiny. Your petty fears are

groundless.

55 "Imagine a man walking through a glorious forest who worried because ahead lay a river and he might not be able to cross it; all the time that river was spanned by a bridge. What if that man had a friend who knew the way—had planned it—and assured him that at no part of the journey would any unforeseen contingency arise, and that all was well?

56 "So leave your foolish fears and follow Me, your guide, and determinedly refuse to consider the problems of tomorrow. My message to you is to trust and wait."

MARCH 29

57 "Rest in Me. Be quiet in My love and strong in My power. Think what it is to possess a power greater than any earthly force. To have an influence greater, and more far-reaching, than that of any earthly king.

58 "No invention, no electricity, no magnetism, no gold could achieve one millionth part of all that you can achieve by the power of My Spirit. Think for one moment all that means.

59 "Go forward. You are only beginning the new life together. Joy! Joy! Joy!"

MARCH 30

60 "Faith and obedience will remove mountains of evil and mountains of difficulty. But they must go hand in hand."

MARCH 31

61 "I reward your seeking with My presence. Rejoice and be glad. I am your God. Courage and joy will conquer all troubles. First things first.

62 "Seek Me. Love Me. Joy in Me. I am your guide. No perils can frighten you. No discipline can exhaust you. Persevere.

63 "Can you hold on in My strength? I need you more than you need Me. Struggle through this time for My sake. This initiation process precedes all real work and success for Me.

64 "Are you ready to live a life apart? Apart with Me? In the world and yet apart with me? Going forth from your secret times of communion to rescue and save?"

APRIL 1

65 "Be calm. Be true. Be quiet. I watch over you. Rest in My love. Joy in the beauty of holiness. You are Mine. Deliverance is here for you, but thankfulness and joy open the gates.

66 "Try in all things to be glad, happy, and thankful. It is not to quiet resignation I give My blessings, but to joyful acceptance and anticipation.

67 "Laughter is the outward expression of joy. That is why I urge upon you love and laughter."

APRIL 2

68 "I am your Lord, gracious and loving. Rest in My love. Walk in My ways. Each week is a week of progress, steady progress upward. You may not see it, but I do.

69 "I do not judge by outward appearances. I judge the heart and I see in both your hearts the single desire to do My will.

70 "Is not the simple offering of a child, brought with the one desire to show you love, more loved by you than the offerings of those who do not love you? Though you may feel that your work has been spoiled and tarnished, I see it only as love's offering. Courage, My children.

71 "When climbing a steep hill, a man is often more

conscious of the weakness of his stumbling feet than of the view, the grandeur, or even of his upward progress.

72 "Persevere, persevere. Love and laugh. Rejoice!"

APRIL 3

73 "Do you not see, My children, that you have not yet learned all? Soon, very soon, you will have mastered your lesson. Then you will truly be able to do all things through Me and My strength.

74 "Did you not see it with My disciples? They were timid, faithless followers. Then, so soon, themselves leaders, healers, conquerors through Me.

75 "All knowledge was Mine, given Me by My Father, and Mine in all human years on earth. You understand this, My children, I know you do.

76 "Thousands of My servants have gone to their betrayal and death. Others, who knew Me not, died without agony.

77 "I, the Son of God. bore the weight of your sin, voluntarily bore it of My own free will, until—for that moment's horror—I was shut out with man, the sinner, from My Father's sight for one short space. Had I not been God, had this not been My suffering, then I was but a defeated mortal."

APRIL 4

78 "I am here. Here as truly as I was with My disciples of old. Here to help and bless you. Here to have companionship with you. Do you know, even yet, My children, that this is the priceless blessing of your lives?

79 "I forgive you, as you have prayed to Me for all neglects of My commands, but start anew from today. Study My words and carry them out unflinchingly. As you do this, you will find that you are miracle workers, workers together

with Me and for Me.

80 "Remember this, not what you do, but what you are—that is the miracle-working power.

81 "You are changed by My Spirit, shedding one garment of spirit for a better one. In time you will be throwing that aside for a yet finer one, and so on, from character to character, gradually transformed into My likeness. Joy, joy, joy!"

APRIL 5

82 "My children, I am here, your waiting Lord, ready at your call. I am among you as one that serves, meek and holy, ready to be used and commanded.

83 "Remember that service is the finest quality of greatness. I, who could command a universe, await the commands of My children. Bring Me into everything.

84 "You will find such joy as time goes on in speaking to each other of Me and together climbing higher.

85 "Always be humble, meek, and lowly in heart. Learn this. Have no position—just be a servant."

APRIL 6

86 "I am all powerful and all knowing. I have all your affairs in My hands. Divine efficiency as well as divine power is being brought to bear on them.

87 "All miracle work is not the work of a moment as so often men and women imagine. My servant Peter was not changed in a flash from a simple fisherman to a great leader and teacher. But through the very time of faithlessness, through the very time of denial, I was making him all that he should be.

88 "Impetuous spokesperson as He always was, ready to lead the other disciples, Peter could never have been the power he was had he not learned his weakness. No one can

save unless he or she understands the sinner.

89 “The Peter who was a mighty force for Me afterward, who more than all others founded My church, was not even the first Peter who said, ‘Thou art the Christ, the Son of the living God,’ but rather the Peter who denied Me. He who had tasted My forgiveness, in his moment of abject remorse, could best speak of Me as the Savior.

90 “The kingdom of heaven can only be preached by those who have learned to prize the authority of the kingdom. My apostles needed a many-sided training.

91 “Oh, joy! Oh, rejoice! I love you. I will not lay one test too many on you.”

6

April 7

1 "Rest in Me. Seek this evening time just to be with Me. Do not feel you have failed if sometimes I ask you only to rest together in My presence.

2 "I am with you both, not only at these times, but at all times. Feel conscious of My presence. Earth has no greater joy than that.

3 "I am the heart's great interpreter. Even souls who are the nearest together have much in their natures that remain a sealed book to each other. Only as I enter and control their lives do I reveal to each the mysteries of the other.

4 "Each soul is so different. I alone understand perfectly the language of each and can interpret between them."

April 8

5 "I lay My loving hands on you in blessing. Wait in love and longing to feel their tender pressure and, as you wait, courage and hope will flow into your being, irradiating all your lives with the warm sun of My presence.

6 "Let all go this Easter. Loosen your hold on earth, its cares, its worries, even its joys. Unclasp your hands, relax, and then the tide of Easter joy will come. Put aside all thought of the future and of the past. Relinquish all to get the Easter sacrament of spiritual life.

7 "Even though you cry out for some blessing, so often you have such a tight hold on some earthly treasure that no hands are free to receive Mine, as I hold it out in love. Easter

is the wonder time of all the year. A blessing is yours to take. Sacrifice all to that."

APRIL 9

8 "From the death of My body on the cross, as from the shedding of husks in seed life, springs that new life that is My gift to everyone who will accept it.

9 "Die with Me to self—to the human life—and then you will know the rapturous joy of Easter Resurrection. A risen life glad and free can be yours.

10 "Mary left home and kindred, friends, all, that Easter morning in her search for Me. Not until my 'Mary' had been followed by the glad triumphant rapture of her 'Rabboni' was her search over.

11 "So with each of you. You have heard of a buried Christ. Search until you meet Me face to face, and My tender uttering of your name awakes your glad 'Rabboni.' "

APRIL 10

Their meditation:

Our Savior, we greet You. Your love and sacrifice we would return in our poor faulty measure by love and sacrifice.

Jesus responds:

12 "No gift is poor if it expresses the true love of the giver. So to Me your heart's gifts are rich and precious. Rejoice in My glad acceptance as you bring your Easter offerings.

13 "My children must make a stand. 'Come ye out from among them and be ye separate' was the command. Today, in life and work, in love and service, My children must stand out.

14 "I called a peculiar people to make known My name. My servant Paul said that My followers must be willing to be deemed 'fools' for My sake.

15 "Be ready to stand aside and let the fashions and customs of the world go by when My glory and My kingdom are thereby served.

16 "Be known by the marks that distinguish those of My kingdom. Be ready to confess Me before men and women, to count all things as loss so that you may gain Me in your lives."

APRIL 11

Their meditation:

Arise, shine; for thy light is come, and the glory of all the Lord is risen upon thee (Isaiah 60:1).

Jesus responds:

17 "On this, My day, the call comes for all who love Me to arise from that which binds to earth, from sin, sloth, depression, distrust, fear, and all that hinders the risen life; to arise to beauty, holiness, joy, peace, and work inspired by love and joy, to rise from death to life.

18 "Remember that death was the last enemy I destroyed. So with death My victory was complete. You have nothing then to fear. Sin is also conquered and forgiven, as you live and move and work with Me.

19 "All that depresses you and all you fear are powerless to harm you. They are but phantoms. The real forces I conquered in the wilderness, the Garden of Gethsemane, on the cross, and in the tomb.

20 "Let nothing hinder your risen life. 'Risen with Christ,' said My servant Paul. Seek to know more and more of that risen life. That is the life of conquest. Of that risen life it was truly said, 'I live, yet not I, but Christ liveth in me.'

21 "Fear and despair and tears come as you stand by the empty tomb. 'They have taken away my Lord and I know not where they have laid him.'

22 "Rise from your fears and go out into the sunlight to meet Me, your risen Lord. Each day will have much in it that you will meet, either in the spirit of the tomb or in the spirit of Resurrection.

23 "Deliberately choose the spirit of Resurrection and reject the spirit of the tomb."

APRIL 12

24 "Obedience is one of the keys unlocking the door into My kingdom, so love and obey. No one can obey Me implicitly without in time realizing My love. In turn, one responds with his or her love to My love, then experiencing the joy of the beloved, and the lover.

25 "The rough stone steps of obedience lead up to the mosaic of joy and love that paves My heaven. As one on earth may say of one he loves, 'Where you are is home.' So it is in relation with Me. Where I am is My home —is heaven.

26 "Heaven may be in a sordid slum or in a palace. I can make My home in the humblest heart. I can only dwell with the humble. Pride stands guard at the door of the heart to shut out the lowly, humble Christ."

APRIL 13

27 "Remember that My followers are to be a peculiar people, separated from others. They are to have different ways and a different standard of living with different customs actuated by different motives.

28 "Pray for love. Pray for My Spirit of love to be showered on all you meet. Deal with yourself severely. Learn to love discipline.

29 "Never yield one point that you have already won. Discipline, discipline. Love it and rejoice. Mountains can be removed by thought, by desire."

APRIL 14

30 "I am your guide. Strength and help will come to you; trust Me wholly.

31 "Fear not. I am always more ready to hear than you to ask. Walk in My ways and know that help will come.

32 "Your need is God's chance to help. I love to help and save. Your need is God's golden opportunity to let your faith find expression.

33 "That expression of faith is all God needs to manifest His power. Faith is the key that unlocks the storehouse of God's resources.

34 "My faithful servants, you long for perfection and see your bitter failures. I see faithfulness. As a mother takes the soiled, imperfect work of her child and invests it with perfection because of her sweet love, so I take your poor faithfulness and crown it with perfection."

APRIL 15

35 "Love and laugh. Make your world happier for your being in it. Love and rejoice on the gray days.

36 "There are wilderness days for My disciples as well as mountains of transfiguration. On both, what matters is duty, persistently, faithfully done.

37 "Be gentle with all. Try to see the heart I see, to know the pain and difficulty of the other's life that I know.

38 "Before you interview or speak to anyone, ask Me to act as interpreter between you.

39 "Live in a spirit of prayer. In speaking to Me you find soul-rest. Simple tasks, faithfully done and persisted in,

bring their own reward. They are mosaics laid in the pavement of success.

40 "Welcome all who come here. I love you."

APRIL 16

41 "My children, I guide you always. Walking in My way may not be always carried out, but My guiding is always so sure. God is using you both in marvelous ways. Go on gladly. You will see.

42 "To be a perfect gymnast you must learn balance. I am teaching you balance and poise, perfect balance and poise. This will give you power in dealing with the lives of others. That power is already being marvelously manifested.

43 "Dwell with Me as the center of your lives. Fix your whole being (both of you) with Me as its center. That gives you true balance. It is similar with some delicate instruments.

44 "The vision you both have is the means of clearing the obstacles away. When My disciple sees My purpose ahead, that very sight is the power that clears away every obstacle along that range of vision. You will both have mighty power to do this. Spiritual sight is in itself a miracle worker.

45 "People waste so much time seeking to work out what they see. I declare to you that in seeing My purpose all is done.

46 "I said to My disciples, 'I have many things to say unto you, but ye cannot bear them now.' But to you, and the twos who gather to hear Me as you do, I can declare now those things that then I left unsaid.

47 "Is not the message of My servant Paul now plain: 'Be ye not unequally yoked together with unbelievers,' because My guidance is intensified immeasurably in power when two are one in desire to be with Me. But so few have understood."

APRIL 17

48 "Obey My commands. They are steps in the ladder that leads to success. Above all, keep calm and unmoved.

49 "Go back into the silence to recover this calm when it is lost for even one moment. You accomplish more by this than by all the activities of a long day. At all cost, keep calm. You can help no one when you are agitated. I, your Lord, see not as you see.

50 "Never feel inadequate for any task. All work here is accomplished by My Spirit, and that can flow through the most humble and lowly. It simply needs an unblocked channel. Rid yourself of self and all is well.

51 "Pray about all, but concentrate on a few things until those are accomplished.

52 "I am watching over you. I provide you strength for your daily and hourly tasks. Yours is the fault, the sin, if that strength is unclaimed and you fail for lack of it."

APRIL 18

53 "Love, love, love. Tender love is the secret. Love those you are training. Love those who work with you. Love those who serve you.

54 "Dwell on the thought, God is love. Link it up with My statement, 'I and the Father are one.' Dwell on My actions on earth. See in them love in operation.

55 "If it were God who so acted, then it was love, perfect love, that performed those actions and wonders. You also must put love (God) into action in your lives.

56 "Perfect love means perfect forgiveness. My children, where God is there can be no lack of forgiveness, for that is really lack of love.

57 "God is love . . . no judging. God is love . . . no resentment. God is love . . . all patience. God is love . . . all

power. God is love . . . all supply.

58 "All you need to have is love for God and each other. Love for God insures obedience to His every wish, His every command. Love is the fulfilling of all law. Pray for much love."

APRIL 19

59 "My children, I come. Hearts eager to do My will send out a call that I always find irresistible. I know no barrier then. Resignation to My will keeps Me barred out from more hearts than does unbelief. Can anything be such a crime against love as being resigned? My will should be welcomed with a glad wonder, if I am to do My work in the heart and life.

60 "The only resignation acceptable to Me is when self, ousted by My claims, accepts the inevitable and resigns the throne for Me. That leaves My disciple free to carry out My will, to welcome My will gladly, rapturously.

61 "In all true discipleship, and in the true spiritual development of each disciple, there is first the wonder and joy of first acquaintance. Then comes the long plain stretch of lesson-learning and discipline. Then joy seems to be a thing of the past never to be recaptured again.

62 "But the lesson-learning and discipline result in the constant experience of Me, the constant persistent recognition of My work in daily happenings—the ever accumulating weight of evidence in support of My guidance—numerous instances in which seeming chance or wonderful coincidence can be and must be traced back to My loving forethought. All these gradually engender a feeling of wonder, certainty, and gratitude, followed in time by joy.

63 "Joy is of two kinds. The joy born of love and wonder, and the joy born of love and knowledge. Between the experience of the two joys lie discipline, disappointment,

and almost disillusion.

64 "Combat these in My strength. Or rather, cling blindly, helplessly, to Me and let Me combat them. Persevere in obeying My will. Accept My discipline and the second joy will follow.

65 "Of this second joy I said, 'Your joy no man taketh from you.' Do not regret the first. The second is the greater gift."

APRIL 20

66 "Such light, such joy flows out from this house. It affects all who come here. Do not feel you have to try and help them. Just love them, welcome them, and shower little courtesies and love signs on them and they must be helped.

67 "Love is God. Give them love and you give them God. Then leave Him to do His work.

68 "Love all—even the beggars. Send no one away without a word of cheer, a feeling that you care. I may have put the impulse to come here into some despairing person's heart. Think if you failed Me!

69 "Besides, you have no choice. You told Me it was My home. I shall use it. Remember this. There would be no dark winter days if love were in the hearts of all My children.

70 "Oh, My children, can you not feel the joy of knowing, loving, and accompanying Me?"

APRIL 21

71 "You need Me. I need you. My broken world needs you. Many a weary troubled heart needs you.

72 "Many a troubled heart will be gladdened by you, drawn nearer to Me by you both. Health, peace, joy, patience, and endurance all come from contact with Me.

73 "The upward way is a glorious way with its wonderful discoveries, tender intimacies, and amazing, almost in-

comprehensible, understanding. Truly the Christian life—life with Me—is a love story.

74 "Leave all to Me. All you have missed you will find in Me, the soul's lover, the soul's friend, its father, mother, comrade, brother. Try Me.

75 "You cannot make too many demands upon Me, or put too great a strain upon My love and forbearance. Claim healing. Claim power. Claim joy. Claim supply. Claim what you will."

APRIL 22

76 "There is a Calvary cross on which one hangs alone, untended by even the nearest and dearest. But beside that cross there stands another. To my dear ones I say little. I hang there afresh beside each one through the hours of the heart's agony.

77 "Have you ever thought of the joy that the patient, gentle, loving obedience of My disciples brings to My heart? I know no joy such as the joy I feel at the loving trust of a dear one.

78 "The wounds in the hands and feet hurt little compared with the wounds in the heart that are the wounds not of My enemies, but of My friends.

79 "Little doubts, little fears, little misunderstandings are the tender trifles of a day that sadden My heart. I that speak unto you am He, your Master."

APRIL 23

80 "I am with you. My presence is a sign of My forgiveness. I uphold you.

81 "You will conquer. Do not fear changes. You can never fear changes when I, your Lord, change not. Jesus Christ, the same yesterday, today, and forever. I am beside

you. You, too, will be steadfast and unchanging as you dwell with Me. Rest in Me.

82 "After careful practice, breathing correctly becomes a habit, unconsciously performed. In the same way, if you regularly practice getting back into My presence when the slightest feeling of unrest disturbs your perfect calm and harmony, this will also become a habit. Then you will grow to live in that perfect consciousness of My presence and perfect calm and harmony will be yours.

83 "Life is a training school. Remember, only the pupil giving great promise of future good work would be singled out by the master for strenuous and unwearied discipline, teaching, and training.

84 "You are both asking not to be as hundreds of My followers, no, as many thousands, but to be even as those who reflect Me in all they say and do and are. So, My dear children, consider this training not as harsh, but as the tender loving answer to your petition.

85 "Life can never be the same again for either of you. Once you have drunk of the wine of My giving—the life eternal—all earth's attempts to quench your thirst will fail."

APRIL 24

86 "Trust in Me. Do as I say each moment and all shall be well. Follow completely My commands. Divine control and unquestioning obedience are the only conditions of supply being ample for your own needs and those of others.

87 "The tasks I give you may seem to have no connection with supply. The commands are Mine and the supply is Mine. I make My own conditions, differing in each case. With each disciple, My conditions are adapted to the individual need.

88 "Have no fear. Go forward. Joy, radiant joy, must be yours. Change all disappointment, even if only momentary,

into joy. Change each complaint into laughter.

89 "Rest, love, joy, peace, and work; and the most powerful of these are love and joy."

APRIL 25

90 "As you live more and more with Me you are bound to have guidance. It follows without doubt.

91 "But these times are not times when you ask to be shown and led. They are times of feeling and realizing My presence.

92 "Does the branch continually ask the vine to supply it with sap and to show it in what direction to grow? No, that comes naturally from the very union with the vine. I said, 'I am the true vine and you are the branches.'

93 "From the branches hang the choice grapes, giving joy and nourishment to all, but no branch could think that the fruit, the grapes, were of its shaping and making. No! The grapes are the fruit of the vine, the parent plant. The work of the branch is to provide a channel for the life flow.

94 "So, My children, union with Me is the one great overwhelming necessity. All else follows so naturally. Union with Me may be simply the result of consciousness of My presence.

95 "Do not be too ready to speak to others. Never make yourselves do this. Pray always that the need may be apparent, if you are to do this, and the guidance plain. My Spirit has been driven out by the words of men and women. Words, words, words. Many have called Me Lord, Lord, who have not done the things that I said.

96 "Discourage too much talk. Deeds live and echo down the ages. Words perish. As Paul said, 'Though I speak with the tongues of men and of angels, and have no charity, I am become as sounding brass or a tinkling cymbal. And though I have the gift of prophecy, . . . and have not charity,

I am nothing. . . .'

97 "Remember that rarely do I speak to the human heart in words. You will see Me in My works done through you and meet Me in the atmosphere of love and self-effacement. Do not feel that you have to speak.

98 "When men and women ceased to commune with their God simply and naturally, they took refuge in words and more words. Babel resulted. Then God wanted to do away with humanity from the earth.

99 "Rely less on words. Always remember that speech is of the senses. Make it your servant, never your master."

7

April 26

1 "You can never perish, My children, because within you is the life of life; the life that through the ages has kept My servants, in times of peril, in adversity, in sorrow.

2 "Once you are born of the Spirit, that is your life's breath. You must never doubt, never worry, but must walk step by step the way to freedom. See that you walk it with Me.

3 "This means no worry, no anxiety, but it does not mean no effort. When My disciples told Me that they had toiled all night and taken nothing, I did not fill the boats with fish without effort on their part. No! My command stood. 'Launch out into the deep and let down your nets for a catch.'

4 "Their lives were endangered. The ship nearly sank. The help of their fellows had to be summoned. There were broken nets to mend. Any one of these troubles might have made them feel My help was not for them. Yet, as they sat on the shore and mended those nets, they saw My love and care.

5 "Men and women rise by effort. The one who reaches the mountain height by the help of train or car has not learned a climber's lesson. But this does not mean no guide. This does not mean My Spirit is not supplying wisdom and strength. Though you are unaware, I often go before you to prepare the way, to soften a heart here, to overrule there."

April 27

6 "Say often, 'God bless . . .' of any whom you find in

disharmony with you or whom you desire to help. Say it, willing that showers of blessings and joy and success may fall upon them.

7 "Leave to Me the necessary correcting or training; you must only desire Joy and blessing for them. At present your prayers are that they should be taught and corrected.

8 "Oh, if only My children would leave My work to Me and occupy themselves with the task I give them. Love, love, love. Love will break down all your difficulties. Love will build up all your successes.

9 "God, the destroyer of evil, God, the creator of good, is love. To love one another is to use God in your life. To use God in your life is to bring into manifestation all harmony, beauty, joy, and happiness."

APRIL 28

10 "Never doubt. Have no fear. Note the faintest tremor of fear and stop all work, everything, and rest before Me until you are joyful and strong again.

11 "Deal in the same way with all tired feelings. I was weary, too, when on earth, and I separated Myself from My disciples and sat and rested on the well. Rested. It was then that the Samaritan woman was helped.

12 "Times of withdrawal for rest always precede fresh miracle working. Learn of Me. To accept the limitations of flesh is to be subject, except as far as sin is concerned, to the human condition.

13 "I had to teach renewal of spirit force, rest of body to My disciples. Then, as your example, I lay with My head on a pillow asleep in the boat. It was not indifference as they thought. They cried, 'Master, carest Thou not that we perish?' and I had to teach them that ceaseless activity was no part of My Father's plan.

14 "When Paul said, 'I can do all things through Christ who

strengthens me,' he did not mean that he was to do all things and then rely on Me to find strength. He meant that for all I told him to do he could rely on My supplying the strength.

15 "My work in the world has been hindered by work, work, work. Many a tireless, nervous body has driven a spirit. The spirit should be the master always, and simply and naturally use the body as need should arise. Rest in Me.

16 "Do not seek to work for Me. Never make opportunities. Live with Me and for Me. I do the work and I make the opportunities."

APRIL 29

17 "I am beside you. Can you not feel My presence? Contact with Me is not gained by the senses. Spirit consciousness replaces sight.

18 "When a man sees Me with human sight it does not mean necessarily that his spiritual perception is greater. Rather the opposite. For that soul I have to span the physical and the spiritual with a spiritual vision clear to human eyes.

19 "Remember this to cheer My disciples who have never seen Me, and yet have had a clear spiritual consciousness of Me."

APRIL 30

20 "I lead through briars, through waste places, through glades, up mountain heights, down into valleys. But the helping hand always goes with the leadership.

21 "It is glorious to follow where your Master goes. But remember that the varied path does not always mean that you need the varied training.

22 "We are seeking lost sheep. We are bringing the kingdom into places where it has not been known before. Realize that you are joining Me on My quest—My undying

quest, of tracking down souls.

23 "I am not choosing ways that will worry and tire, just to worry and tire. We are out to save. You may not always see the soul we seek. I know."

MAY 1

24 "Seek and ye shall find. You will find that inner knowledge that makes the problems of life plain.

25 "The difficulties of life are caused by disharmony in the individual. There is no discord in My kingdom, only something unconquered in My disciples. The rule of My kingdom is perfect order, perfect harmony, perfect supply, perfect love, perfect honesty, perfect obedience, all power, all conquest, all success.

26 "So often My servants lack power, conquest, success, supply, harmony, and think I fail in My promises because these are not manifested in their lives. These are but the outward manifestations that result from obedience, honesty, order, and love. They come, not in answer to urgent prayer, but naturally as light results from a lighted candle."

MAY 2

27 "Rejoice in the springtime of the year. Let there be springtime in your hearts. The full time of fruit is not yet, but there is the promise of the blossom.

28 "Know surely that your lives too are full of glad promise. Such blessings are to be yours. Such joys, such wonders!

29 "All is indeed well. Live in My sunshine and My love."

MAY 3

30 "Read the lessons of divine control in nature's laws.

Nature is but the expression of eternal thought in time. Study the outward form. Grasp the eternal thought. If you can read the thoughts of the Father, then indeed you know Him.

31 "Leave Me out of nothing. Love all My ways with you. Know indeed that 'All is well.' Delay is but the wonderful and all loving restraint of your Father, not reluctance, not desire to deny, but the divine control of a Father who can scarcely brook the delay.

32 "Delay has to occur sometimes. Your lives are so linked up with those of others, so bound by circumstances, that to let your desire have instant fulfillment might, in many cases, cause another's earnest prayer to go unanswered.

33 "Think for a moment of the love and thoughtful care that seeks to harmonize and reconcile all your desires and longings and prayers.

34 "Delay is not denial—not even withholding. It is the opportunity for God to work out your problems and accomplish your desires in the most wonderful way possible for you.

35 "Oh, children, trust Me. Remember that your Maker is also your servant, quick to fulfill, quick to achieve, faithful in accomplishment. Yes. All is well."

MAY 4

36 "To conquer adverse circumstances, conquer yourselves. The answer to the desire of My disciples to follow Me was, 'Be ye therefore perfect even as your Father who is in heaven is perfect.'

37 "To accomplish much, be much. All worthy accomplishments are the mere unconscious expression of the being.

38 "Fear not, fear not, all is well. Let the day be full of little prayers to Me, little turnings toward Me; the smiles of the soul at one it loves.

39 "Men and women call the Father the first cause. Yes! See Him as the first cause of every warm ray, every color in

the sunset, every gleam on the water, every beautiful flower, every planned pleasure."

MAY 5

40 "Self dethroned. That is the lesson, but in its place put love for Me, knowledge of Me.

41 "Self, not only dethroned, but dead. A dead self is not an imprisoned self. An imprisoned self is more potentially harmful. In all training (in Mine of you, and in yours of others), let self die.

42 "For each blow to the life of self you must at the same time embrace and hold fast the new life, life with Me.

43 "It is not a dead self that men and women have to fear, but a thwarted, captive, imprisoned self. That self is infinitely more self-centered than the self allowed full play.

44 "To you, My children, I teach a higher science law than even freedom of the self. I teach death to the self. No repressions. Just death. Petty self-life exchanged for divine life.

45 "Now I can make more clear to you what I say about forgiveness of injuries. It is one of My commands that as you seek My forgiveness, so you must forgive.

46 "What you do not see is that you, the self in you, can never forgive injuries. The very thought of them means self in the foreground. Then the injury, instead of appearing less, appears greater.

47 "No, My children, as all true love is of God, and is God, so all true forgiveness is of God and is God. The self cannot forgive. Kill self!

48 "Cease trying to forgive those who worried or wronged you. It is a mistake to think about it. Aim at killing the self now, in your daily life. Then, and not until then, you will find there is nothing that even remembers injury, because the only one injured, the self, is dead.

49 "As long as it recurs to your mind, you deceive yourself

if you think it forgiven. Forgiving injuries can be one way of feeding a self-life. Many deceive themselves in this."

MAY 6

50 "Delight in My love. Try to live in the rapture of the kingdom.

51 "Claim big things. Claim great things. Claim joy and peace and freedom from care. Joy in Me.

52 "I am your Lord, your Creator. Remember too that I am the same yesterday, today, and forever. Your Creator, when My thought about the world called it into being. Your Creator as much today also, when, by loving thought for you, I can call into being all you need on the material plane.

53 "Joy in Me. Trust in Me. Share all life with Me. See Me in everything. Rejoice in Me. Share all with Me as a child shares its pains and cuts, griefs, newly found treasures, joys, and little work with its mother.

54 "Give Me the joy of sharing all with you."

MAY 7

55 "My loved ones. Men and women should think of Me with their hearts and not their heads. Then worship would be instinctive.

56 "Breathe in My Spirit in pure air and fervent desire. Keep the eye of your spirit ever upon Me. Keep the window of your soul open toward Me.

57 "Always know that all things are yours—that what is lovely I delight to give to you.

58 "Empty your mind of all that limits. Whatever is beautiful you can have. Leave more and more the choice to Me. You will have no regrets."

MAY 8

59 "The way is long and weary. It is a weary world. So many today are weary. 'Come unto Me and I will give you rest.'

60 "My children, who range yourselves under My flag, you must see that on it are inscribed the words, 'The Son of Man.' Whatever the world is feeling, I must feel, I—the Son of Man.

61 "You are My followers, so the weariness of humanity today must be shared by you. The weary and heavy laden must come to you and find that rest you found in Me.

62 "My children, My followers must be prepared not to sit on My right hand and on My left, but to drink of the cup that I drink of.

63 "Poor world. Teach it that there is only one cure for all its ills—union with Me. Dare to suffer, dare to conquer, be filled with my sublime audacity. Remember that. Claim the unclaimable.

64 "What the world would think impossible can always be yours. Remember, My children, sublime audacity."

MAY 9

65 "The rower who trusts in Me does not lean on his oars and drift with the tide, trusting to the current. Instead, usually, once I have shown the way, it is against the tide you must direct all your effort.

66 "Even when difficulties come, it is by your effort that they will be surmounted. But you can always have strength and joy in the doing through Me.

67 "My disciples did not find the fish ready on the shore in their nets. I take your effort and bless that. I need your effort; you need My blessing. This partnership will know success."

MAY 10

68 "I lead you. The way is clear. Go forward unafraid. I am beside you. Listen, listen, listen to My voice. My hand is

controlling all.

69 "Remember that I can work through you better when you are at rest. Go slowly and quietly from one duty to the next, taking time to rest and pray between.

70 "Do not be too busy. Take all in order as I say. The rest of God is in a realm beyond all your activities. Venture there often and you will find peace and joy.

71 "All work that results from resting with God is miracle work. Claim the power to work miracles, both of you.

72 "Know that you can do all things through Christ who strengthens you. More than that, know that you can do all things through Christ who gives you rest."

MAY 11

73 "Follow My guidance. Be afraid to venture on your own as a child fears to leave its mother's side. Doubt your own wisdom; reliance on Mine will teach you humility.

74 "Humility is not the belittling of the self. It is forgetting the self. It is more than forgetting the self, because you are remembering Me.

75 "You must not expect to live in a world where all is in harmony. You must not expect to live where others are in unbroken accord with you.

76 "It is your task to maintain your own heart peace in adverse circumstances. Harmony is always yours when you strain your ear to catch heaven's music.

77 "Always doubt your power or wisdom to put things right. Ask Me to right all as you leave it to Me and go on your way loving and laughing. I am wisdom. Only My wisdom can rightly decide anything and settle any problem. Rely on Me. All is well."

MAY 12

Their meditation:

In quietness and in confidence shall be your strength (Isaiah 30:15).

Jesus responds:

78 "All agitation is destructive of good. All calm is constructive of good and, at the same time, destructive of evil.

79 "When a man wants evil destroyed, he often rushes to action. It is wrong. First, be still and know that I am God. Then act only as I tell you, always calm with God. Calm is trust in action. Only trust, perfect trust, can keep one calm.

80 "Never be afraid of any circumstances or difficulties that help you to cultivate this calm. As the world has to learn speed to attain its goals, you have to learn calm to succeed for Me.

81 "All great work for Me is done first in the individual soul of the worker."

MAY 13

82 "When I have led you through these storms there will be other words for you, other messages, other guidance.

83 "So deep is your friendship and so great your desire to love and follow and serve Me that when this time of difficulty is soon over, to be alone together will always mean to be shut in with Me.

84 "There are few friendships in the world like that and yet I taught when on earth, as I have taught you both, the power of two together.

85 "Tonight I have more to say to you. I say that the time is coming, is here now, when those who visit the two of you together will know that I am the divine third in your friendship."

MAY 14

86 "Turn out all thoughts of doubt and of trouble. Never tolerate them for one second. Bar the windows and doors of your souls against them as you would bar your home against a thief who would come in to take your treasures.

87 "What greater treasures can you have than peace, rest, and joy? These are all stolen from you by doubt, fear, and despair.

88 "Face each day with love and laughter. Face the storm.

89 "Joy, peace, and love. My great gifts. Follow Me to find all three. I want you to feel the thrill of protection and safety now. Any soul can feel this in a harbor, but real joy and victory come to those alone who sense these when they ride out a storm.

90 "Say, 'All is well.' Say it not as a vain repetition. Use it as you use a healing balm for a cut or wound, until the poison is drawn out. And then, until the sore is healed, then until the thrill of fresh life floods your being. All is well."

MAY 15

91 "What joy follows self-conquest! You cannot conquer and control others, either of you, until you have completely conquered yourself.

92 "Can you see yourselves absolutely unmoved? Think of Me before the mocking soldiers, being struck, spat upon, and answering never a word—never a word. Try to see that as divine power. Remember, by that power of perfect silence, perfect self-control, you alone can prove your right to govern.

93 "Never judge. The human heart is so delicate, so complex, only its Maker can know it. Each heart is so different, actuated by different motives, controlled by different

circumstances, influenced by different sufferings.

94 “How can one judge another? Leave to Me the unraveling of the puzzles of life. Leave to Me the teaching of understanding. Bring each heart to Me, its Maker, and leave it with Me, secure in the certainty that I can set right all that is wrong.”

8

MAY 16

1 "A loving master delights in the intimacy of demands made of him, as much as he desires his followers and friends to delight in the tender intimacy of his demands.

2 "The wonder of family life is expressed in the freedom with which a child makes demands and claims of his parents, quite as much as in the loving demands the parent makes upon all the love and joy of the children.

3 "The intimacy that makes My followers dare to approach Me as friend to friend comes only as the result of frequent conversation with Me, of much prayer to Me, of listening to and obedience to My bidding.

4 "Yield to My tender insistence in all things, but remember I also yield to yours. Ask not only the big things I have told you, but ask the little tender signs of love.

5 "I came as the great lover of the world. Never think of My love as only a tender compassion and forgiveness. It is that, but it is also the love of a lover, who shows his love by countless words and actions and by tender thought.

6 "Remember that God is in each of you. The God I reverence and submit to, though My Father and I are one. As many grow more and more like My Father in heaven, I bring to our friendship a reverent, tender love. I see God in you, as no man or woman can see.

7 "It is always given to a man or woman to see in others those aspirations and qualities he or she possesses. So only I, being God, can recognize God in you. Remember this in your relation to others.

8 "Your motives and aspirations can only be understood by those who have attained the same spiritual level. Do not foolishly expect understanding from others. Do not misjudge them for not giving it. Yours is a foreign language to them."

MAY 17

9 "What can I say to you? Your heart is torn. Remember, 'He bindeth up the broken hearts.' Feel the tenderness of My hands as I bind up your wounds.

10 "Both of you are privileged. I share My plans and secrets with you and make known to you My purposes, while so many have to grope on.

11 "Try to rest on these words, 'Seek ye first the kingdom of God and his righteousness and all these things shall be added unto you.' Then strive not for these things, but untiringly for the things of My kingdom.

12 "It is so strange to you mortals. You think it proper to think material things first and then grow into the knowledge of spiritual things. Not so in My kingdom. It is spiritual things first and then material. So to attain the material, redouble your efforts to acquire the spiritual."

MAY 18

13 "I would have you entreat Me often because I know that only in earnest supplication, and the calm trust that results, do you learn strength and gain peace. Therefore, I have laid incessant, persistent pleading as a duty upon My disciples.

14 "Never weary in prayer. When one day a man sees how marvelously his prayers have been answered, he will deeply, so deeply, regret that he prayed so little.

15 "Prayer changes all. Prayer re-creates. Prayer is irresistible. So pray, literally without ceasing.

16 "Pray until you almost cease to pray, because trust has become so rocklike. Then pray on because it has become so much a habit that you cannot resist.

17 "Always pray until prayer merges into praise. That is the only note on which true prayer should end. It is the love and laughter of your attitude toward others, interpreted in your attitude in prayer as praise toward God."

MAY 19

18 " 'Sorrow may endure for a night, but joy comes in the morning.' My bravest are those who can anticipate the morning. They feel in the night of sorrow that underlying joy that tells of confident expectations in the morning."

MAY 20

19 " 'Look unto Me and be ye saved all the ends of the earth.' Salvation was not for merit; the promise was for all who looked.

20 "To look is surely within the power of everyone. One look suffices. Salvation follows.

21 "Look and you are saved from despair. Look and you are saved from care. Look and you are saved from worry. Look and into you flows a peace beyond all understanding—a power new and vital, a wonderful joy.

22 "Look and keep looking. Doubt flees, joy reigns, and hope conquers. Life, eternal life, is yours—revitalizing, renewing."

MAY 21

23 "Rest knowing all is so safe in My hands. Rest is trust. Ceaseless activity is distrust. Without the knowledge that I am working for you, you do not rest. Inaction then would be the outcome of despair.

24 " 'My hand is not shortened that it cannot save.' Know that. Repeat it. Rely on it. Welcome the knowledge. Delight in it. Such a truth is as a rope flung to a drowning man. Every repetition of it is one pull nearer shore and safety.

25 "Let that illustration teach you a great truth. Lay hold of the truth. Pray it. Affirm it. Hold on to the rope.

26 "How foolish are your attempts to save yourself with one hand on the rope and one making efforts to swim ashore. You may lose your hold of the rope. You hinder the rescuer who has to act with greater caution so he does not lose you.

27 "Life is not all storms and tempests. The Psalmist who said, 'All thy waves and billows are gone over me' also wrote, 'He brought me up also out of an horrible pit, out of the miry clay, and set my feet upon a rock and established my goings.'

28 "Meditate upon the three steps of that wonderful truth—safety, security, and guidance. Safety, 'He brought me up also out of an horrible pit.' Security, 'He set my feet upon a rock.' Guidance, 'He established my goings.'

29 "Guidance is the final stage when the saved soul trusts Me so entirely it no longer seeks its own way but leaves all future plans to Me, its Rescuer."

MAY 22

30 "You will conquer. The conquering spirit is never crushed. Keep a brave and trusting heart. Face all your difficulties in the spirit of conquest.

31 "Rise to greater heights than you have known before. Remember, where I am is victory. Forces of evil, within and without, flee at My presence.

32 "Win me and all is won. All!"

MAY 23

33 "To see Me you must bring Me your cares and show

Me your heart of trust. Then, as you leave your cares, you become conscious of My presence.

34 "This consciousness persists in bringing its reward of Me. No one can see My face through a mist of care. Only when the burden is flung at My feet do you pass on to consciousness and spiritual sight.

35 "Remember obedience, obedience, obedience—the straight and narrow way into the kingdom. Now it must be said of you, even in loving tender reproach, why do you call Me, 'Lord, Lord,' and not do the things I say?

36 "Character is chiseled into beauty by the daily discipline and daily duties done. In many ways, My disciples must work out their own salvation, though this is not possible without My strength and help and without interaction with Me.

37 "Even for the spiritual life, the training is different for different spirits. The man who is desirous of living a life of prayer and meditation is thrust into the busy ways of life. The busy man is asked to rest and wait patiently for Me.

38 "Joy. Rest. Be always at peace in the busy ways."

MAY 24

Their meditation:

Lord, I claim Your help.

Jesus responds:

39 "Yes. Claim. Be constantly claiming. There is a trust that waits patiently. There is also a trust that tolerates no delay. One convinced that the course is right and that God is guiding says, with all the persistence of a child, 'Now! Do not delay long, oh My God.'

40 "You are no longer servants but friends. A friend can command his friend, can know that all the friend—the true friend—has is his by right. That does not mean an idle living

at the expense of a friend, but claiming the friend's means—his name, his time, all that he has—when your supply is exhausted.

41 "Friendship—true friendship—implies the right to appropriate. And in God's service is perfect freedom. Heirs of God, you are joint heirs with Me in the inheritance. We share the Father's property.

42 "You have the same right to use and claim as I. Use your right. A beggar supplicates. A son or daughter appropriates.

43 "When I see My children sitting before My house supplicating and waiting, it is small wonder that I leave them there until they realize how foolish such action is, when they have only to walk into their home and take.

44 "This cannot be the attitude of all. There must first be a definite realization of sonship."

MAY 25

45 "Your lack of control is not due to the big burdens. It is due to your permitting the little worries and cares and burdens to accumulate.

46 "If anything annoys you, deal with that and get that righted with Me before you allow yourself to speak to, or meet anybody, or to undertake any new duty.

47 "Look upon yourself more as performing My errands and coming back quickly to Me to tell Me that the message is delivered or that the task is done.

48 "Then, with no feeling of responsibility as to the result (your only responsibility was to see the duty done), go out again, rejoicing at still more to do for My sake."

MAY 26

49 "How unseeing the world goes on! How unknowing of your heartaches and troubles, your battles won, your con-

quests, your difficulties.

50 "But be thankful, both of you, that there is one who knows. One who notes every crisis, every effort, every heartache.

51 "You both are not idle hearers. You must know that every troubled soul I tell you of is one for you to help. You must help all you can. You do not help enough.

52 "As you help, help will flow back and your circle of helpfulness will widen more and more, ever more and more.

53 "Feel that you are two of My disciples present at the feeding of the five thousand. To you I hand out the food and you pass it on, ever more and more. You can always say, with so few loaves and fish, 'We have only enough for our own needs.' It was not only My blessing, but the passing on by the disciples that worked the miracle.

54 "Get a feeling of bounteous giving into your beings. They were 'all filled.' There was a supply left over.

55 "I give with a large hand and heart. Note the catch of fish. The net broke, the boat began to sink with the lavishness of my gift. Lose sight of all limitations.

56 "God's supply is abundant. Turn out all thoughts of limits. Receive showers and, in turn, you shower others."

MAY 27

57 "There will be no limit to what you can accomplish. Realize that. Never relinquish any task or give up the thought of any task because it seems beyond your power, unless you see it is not My will for you. This I command you.

58 "Think of the tiny plant seed in the hard ground. It has no certainty that when it has forced its weary way up that sunlight and warmth will greet it. What a task beyond its power that must seem! But with the inner urge of life within the seed compelling it, it carries out that task. The kingdom of heaven is like that."

MAY 28

59 "You are doing your claiming as I have said, and soon you will see the result. You cannot do this long without it being seen in the material world. It is an undying law.

60 "At present, you are children practicing a new lesson. Practice, practice. Soon you will be able to do it readily.

61 "You see others manifesting easily, readily demonstrating My power. But you have not seen the discipline that went before. Discipline is absolutely necessary before this power is given to My disciples. It is a further initiation.

62 "You are feeling you have learned so much that life cannot be a failure. That is right, but others have to wait to see the outward manifestation in your lives before they realize this spiritual truth."

MAY 29

63 "Remember the lesson of the seed. While it is sending a shoot down so that it may be rooted and grounded, at the same time it sends a shoot up to be the plant and flower that will gladden the world.

64 "The two growths are necessary. Without the strong root it would soon wither, just as much activity fails for lack of growth in Me. The higher the growth up, the deeper must be the root.

65 "Many forget this and thus their work ceases to be permanent for Me. Beware of leaves and flowers without a strong root."

MAY 30

66 "A person who greatly loves another knows that in every difficulty, every trial, every failure, the presence of the loved one is sufficient. Test your love for Me by this.

67 "Does it bring you joy and peace just to know I am beside you? If not, then your love for Me and your realization of My love are at fault. If this be so, pray for more love."

MAY 31

68 "Regret nothing. Not even the sins and failures. When a woman views earth's wonders from some mountain height, she does not spend time dwelling on the stones, the failures, that marked her upward path.

69 "So with you. Breathe in the rich blessings of each new day. Forget all that lies behind you.

70 "Man is made so he can carry the weight of twenty-four hours and no more. His back breaks when he is weighted down with the past of years gone and the days ahead.

71 "I have promised to help you with the burden of today only. The past I have taken from you. If you, foolish hearts, choose to take again that burden and bear it, you mock Me to expect Me to share it.

72 "For better or worse each day is ended. What remains to be lived, the coming twenty-four hours, you must face as you awake.

73 "A man on a march carries only what he needs for that march. Would you pity him if you saw him bearing the overwhelming weight of the worn-out shoes and uniforms of past marches and years? And yet, in the mental and spiritual life, man does these things.

74 "Small wonder My poor world is heartsick and weary. You must not act so."

JUNE 1

Their meditation:

Our Lord, we praise Thee.

Jesus responds:

75 "Praise is the devil's death knell. Resignation, acceptance of My will, obedience to it, have not the power to vanquish evil that praise has. The joyful heart is My best weapon against all evil. Oh, pray and praise!

76 "You are learning your lesson. You are being led out into a large place. Go with songs of rejoicing. Rejoice evermore. Happy indeed if each day has its thrill of joy.

77 "Talk to Me more during the day. Look up into My face with a look of love, a feeling of security, a thrill of joy at the sense of the nearness of My presence. These are your best prayers.

78 "Let these smooth the day's work, then fear will vanish. Fear is the grim figure that turns aside success."

JUNE 2

Their meditation:

Lord, hear us, we pray.

Jesus responds:

79 "I hear and I answer. Spend much time in prayer. Prayer is of many kinds, but whatever kind it is, prayer links up the soul and mind and heart to God.

80 "If prayer is only a glance of faith, a look or word of love or confidence, and even if no supplication is expressed, yet it follows that whatever supply and other things are necessary, they are secured.

81 "The soul, being linked to God in prayer, united to Him, receives in and through Him all things. And the soul, when in human form, also needs the things belonging to His habitation."

JUNE 3

82 "The way of the soul's transformation is the way of

divine companionship. It is not so much by asking Me to make you this or that, but living with Me, thinking of Me, talking to Me, that you grow like Me.

83 "Love Me. Rest in Me. Joy in Me."

JUNE 4

Their meditation:

My Lord and my God, we praise You, we bless You, we worship You. Make us like You.

Jesus responds:

84 "You are willing to drink of the cup that I drink of—the wine of sorrow and disappointment.

85 "You are Mine and you will both grow more and more like Me, your Master.

86 "It is as true today as it was in the days of Moses that no man can see My face and live.

87 "The self, the original man, shrivels up and dies, and My image becomes stamped upon the soul."

JUNE 5

Their meditation:

Our Lord, we love and praise You. You are our joy and our exceeding great reward.

Jesus responds:

88 "Remember that love is the power that transforms the world. Love not only of Me, love not only of the few dear to you, but love of all—the publicans, the sinners, the harlots.

89 "Love. It is the only weapon with which sin can be driven out. Drive sin out with love.

90 "Drive fear and depression and despair and a sense of failure out with praise.

91 "Praise is the acknowledgment of what I have sent you. Few would send a further gift until acknowledgment of the previous one had been received.

92 "Praise, which acknowledges My gifts and blessings, leaves the way open for Me to shower yet more on the thankful heart.

93 "Learn as a child learns to say, 'thank you,' as a courtesy, with perhaps no real sense of gratitude at all. Do this until at last a thrill of joy, of thankful awe, will accompany the spoken word.

94 "Do not expect for yourselves feelings that you know others have or have had. Go on along the arid way of obedience. Persistence will be rewarded as you come to the glad spring of water.

95 "Oh, joy in Me. To the extent you are able, shed joy on all those around you."

9

June 6

Their meditation:

Lord, make us like You. Mold us into Your likeness.

Jesus responds:

1 "Molding, My children, means cutting and chiseling. It means sacrifice of the personal to conform to type. It is not only My work but yours.

2 "Molding means swift recognition of the selfish in your desires and motives, actions, words, and thoughts, and the instant appeal to Me for help to eradicate that.

3 "It is a work that requires cooperation, Mine and yours. It is a work that brings much sense of failure and discouragement at times because, as the work proceeds, you see more and more clearly all that yet remains to be done.

4 "Shortcomings you hardly recognized or at least for which you had no sense of sorrow now cause you trouble and dismay.

5 "Courage. That is in itself a sign of progress.

6 "Have patience, not only with others, but each of you, with yourself.

7 "As you see the slow progress upward made by you, in spite of your longing and struggle, you will gain a divine patience with others whose imperfections trouble you.

8 "So on and up. Go forward with patience and perseverance. Struggle. Remember that I am beside you as your captain and as your tender, patient, and strong helper.

9 "Yes, we cooperate. I share your troubles, failures, difficulties, and heartaches. As My beloved friends, you share My patience and My strength."

JUNE 7

10 "I speak quietly. Listen to My voice. Never heed the voices of the world. Only heed the tender divine voice.

11 "Listen and you will never be disappointed. Listen and anxious thoughts and tired nerves will become rested. The divine voice has more tenderness than strength, more restfulness than power.

12 "But the tenderness and restfulness will heal your scars and make you strong. Then it is your task to let all your power be My power. Your little power is as clay beside the granite rock of My power.

13 "You are My great care. Never feel at the mercy of the world. My angels guard you day and night; nothing can harm you. You would indeed thank Me if you knew the darts of worry and evil they turn from you.

14 "Thank Me for dangers unknown, unseen, but averted."

JUNE 8

15 "I came to help a world. And according to the varying needs of each, so does each one see Me.

16 "It is not necessary that you see Me as others—the world, even the church, My disciples, My followers—see Me, supplying all that you personally need.

17 "The weak need My strength. The strong need My tenderness. The tempted and fallen need My salvation. The righteous need My pity for sinners. The lonely need a friend. The fighters need a leader.

18 "No one could be all these to everybody; only God

could be. In each of these relations of Mine to you, you must see God. The God-friend, the God-leader, the God-Savior."

JUNE 9

Their meditation:

Incline your ear, and come unto Me; hear and your soul shall live (Isaiah 55:3).

Jesus responds:

19 "Not only shall your soul live, it shall grow in grace and power and beauty—the true beauty, the beauty of holiness.

20 "Reach ever forward after the things of My kingdom. In the animal world, the very form of an animal alters to enable it to reach the food it seeks.

21 "In like manner your whole nature becomes changed, reaching after the treasures of My kingdom, so that you can best receive and enjoy the wonders of that kingdom.

22 "Dwell on these truths."

JUNE 10

23 "Down through the ages millions of souls would have fallen by the way except for My power alone that kept them brave and strong and true.

24 "The faith has been kept alive and handed down, not by the dwellers in ease, but by those who struggled and suffered and died for Me.

25 "This life is not for the body. It is for the soul. Yet a man too often chooses the way of life that best suits the body, not the way that best suits the soul. I permit only what best suits the soul.

26 "Accept this and a wonderful molding is the result. Reject it and My purpose is frustrated, your best prayer is

unanswered, spiritual progress is delayed, trouble and grief are stored up.

27 "Try, each of you, to picture your soul as a third, being trained by us—by you and Me—and then you will share, and rejoice in sharing, in the discipline and training.

28 "Stand apart from your soul with Me and welcome training. Rejoice at progress."

JUNE 11

29 "Rise above your fears and fancies into My joy. It will suffice to heal all your sores and wounds. Forget all sense of failure and shortcomings, all the painful jolts and jars. Trust Me. Love Me. Call upon Me.

30 "Your discipleship is an obstacle race. 'So run that ye may obtain.' Obtain not only your hearts' desires, but obtain Me—your souls' joy and haven.

31 "What would you think of the runner who threw himself on the ground in despondency at his first hurdle?

32 "Over, and on and up. I am your leader and your goal."

JUNE 12

Their meditation:

We offer unto You the sacrifice of thanksgiving and pay our vows to the Most High. We call upon You in the day of trouble because we know You, O Lord, will deliver us.

Jesus responds:

33 "To praise and thank and steadily fulfill your promises to Me is to place coins in My bank, upon which, in your time of need, you can withdraw with confidence and certainty. Remember that.

34 "The world wonders when a man unexpectedly with-

draws large and unsuspected sums from his bank for his own need, the needs of a friend, or for some charity. But what the world has not seen are the countless small sums paid into that bank, earned by faithful work in many ways.

35 "And so it is in My kingdom. The world sees the man of faith make a sudden demand upon Me and to its surprise that demand is met. The world thinks the man has magic powers. No! The world does not see that the man has been paying in thanks and praise and promises fulfilled, faithfully, steadily.

36 "So it is with you, My children. 'Offer to God the sacrifice of thanksgiving and pay your vows to the Most High and call upon me in the day of trouble and I will deliver you.'

37 "This is a promise for the seemingly dull days of little happenings, to be an encouragement for you, My children. When you do not seem to be able to do big things, you can be storing your little acts and words of faithfulness in My great storehouse, ready for the day of your big demand."

June 13

Their meditation:

O Lord, we thank You for Your great gift of peace.

Jesus responds:

38 "Only I can give peace to a restless world surrounded by trouble and difficulty. To know that peace is to have received the stamp of the kingdom—the mark of the Lord Jesus Christ. My mark.

39 "When you have learned that peace you are fit to judge true values, the values of the kingdom, and the values of all the world has to offer.

40 "That peace is loving faith at rest."

JUNE 14

41 "Be watchful to hear My voice and instantly obey. Obedience is your great sign of faith. 'Why call ye me Lord, Lord, and do not the things that I say,' was My Word when on earth to the many who followed and heard, but did not do.

42 "I likened the man who heard and did not obey to the man who built his house on the sand. In times of storm and trouble he is overthrown, his house falls.

43 "I likened the man who obeyed Me implicitly to the man who built his house upon a rock. In times of storm he is steadfast, immovable.

44 "Do not feel by this I mean only the keeping of My commandments or even living My Sermon on the Mount. I mean more than obeying that to those who know Me intimately. I mean the following: obeying in all, in the inner guiding that I give, the little injunctions I speak to each individual soul, the wishes I express and desire to have carried out.

45 "The secure, steadfast, immovable life of My disciples (the home on the rock) is not built by a wish or in a moment, but is laid stone by stone, foundations, walls, and roof, by the acts of obedience, the daily following of My wishes, the loving doing of My will.

46 " 'He that heareth these sayings of mine and doeth them is like unto a man who built his house upon a rock, and the rain descended and the floods came, and the winds blew and beat upon that house and it fell not, for it was founded upon a rock.'

47 "And it is in that house on a rock, manmade but divinely inspired, the house of obedience—the truest expression of a disciple's adoration and worship—that I come to dwell with My loved one.

48 "I am giving you work and hope. Work for the gray days. Just little plain bricks of duties done and My wishes

carried out. All strengthen you and that steadfast, immovable Christian character of which my servant Paul spoke and which he urged his followers to have."

JUNE 15

49 "You have entered now upon a mountain climb. Steep steps lead upward, but your power to help others will be truly marvelous.

50 "You will not go upward alone. All to whom you now send loving, pitying thoughts will be helped upward by you.

51 "All your thoughts are God-inspired as you look to Me. Act on them and you will be led on. They are not your own impulses but the movement of My Spirit. Obeyed, they will bring the answer to your prayers.

52 "Love and trust. Let no unkind thoughts of any kind dwell in your hearts. Then I can act with all My spirit power, with nothing to hinder."

JUNE 16

Their meditation:

Our Lord and our God. Make us all You would have us.

Jesus responds:

53 "It is not circumstances that need altering first, but yourselves. Then the conditions will naturally alter. Spare no effort to become all I would have you. Follow every leading from Me. I am your only guide.

54 "Endeavor to put from you thoughts of trouble. With no backward look, face each day's problems with Me and seek My help and guidance as to what you can do.

55 "Never look back and never leave until tomorrow

that on which you can get My guidance for today."

JUNE 17

56 "I am planning for you. My ways are wonderful beyond your knowledge. More and more realize My bounty and goodness. The wonder of being led by Me! The beauty of a guided life!

57 "These will enter your consciousness more and more and bring you ever more and more joy.

58 "You are nearly at the point when you shall ask what you will and it shall be done unto you. You have entered upon a wonderful era—your lives are planned and blessed by Me as never before.

59 "You are overcoming. You are counting all things but loss if you can win Me. And the promises to Him who overcomes are truly wonderful and will always be fulfilled."

JUNE 18

60 "Walk in My ways and trust Me. No evil can touch you. I am yours as truly as you are Mine. Rest in that truth. Rest, that is, cease all struggle. Gain a calm, strong confidence in that certainty.

61 "Do not only rest in Me when the world's struggles prove too much and too many for you to bear or face alone. Rest in Me when you need perfect understanding, when you need the consciousness of tender, loving friendship and conversation.

62 "The world, My poor world, flies to Me when its difficulties are too great to be surmounted any other way. It forgets, or never realizes, that if, with the same eagerness, those hearts sought Me merely for companionship and loving conversation, many of the difficulties would not arise.

63 "In fact, those same difficulties would not exist be-

cause the circumstances, the life, the character, would be so altered and purified.

64 "Seek Me early. That is the way to find Me. Early, before I get crowded out by life's troubles and difficulties and pleasures."

JUNE 19

65 "*Jesus*. Say My name often. It was in My name Peter instructed the lame man to walk. 'In the name of Jesus Christ of Nazareth arise and walk.'

66 "*Jesus*. The very sounding of My name, in love and tenderness, drives away all evil. All the hosts of evil flee at My name.

67 "*Jesus*. The name banishes loneliness and dispels gloom.

68 "*Jesus*. The name summons help to conquer your faults.

69 "I will set you on high because you have known My name. Yes! My name, *Jesus*. Use it more. Use it tenderly. Use it prayerfully. Use it powerfully."

JUNE 20

70 "The world has always seen service for Me as activity. Only those near to Me have seen that a life apart, of prayer, often accomplishes more than all the service a man or woman can offer Me.

71 "If one lived apart with Me and only went out to serve at My direct command, My Spirit could operate more and accomplish truly mighty things."

JUNE 21

72 "Follow the path of obedience. It leads to the throne of God. Your treasure lies at the end of the path, whether it is

success on the material plane necessary to further the work of My kingdom, or the hidden spiritual wonders revealed by Me only to those who diligently seek Me.

73 "From one promise or command of Mine to the next, you have to follow until you finally reach the success you covet.

74 "All your work for the moment is in the material plane and the spiritual is only to help the material. When your material goal is reached, then the material will serve only to attain the spiritual."

JUNE 22

75 "Wait to hear My will and then obey. Obey at all costs.

76 "Do not fear. I am a wall of protection around you. See this. To see this with the eyes of faith is to cause it to manifest in the material.

77 "Remember, I long to work miracles as I did when on earth. But the same condition holds good. I cannot do many mighty works because of unbelief.

78 "Only in response to your belief can I do miracle works now."

JUNE 23

Their meditation:

Our Lord, we praise You. Bless us, we beseech You.

Jesus responds:

79 "I bless you. I promise you release. Joy in Me. You shall be shielded from the storm.

80 "Wonders have unfolded. Come before Me and stay for a while in My presence.

81 "Learn of Me. The only way for so many in My poor

world to keep calm and sane is to have the mind that is in Jesus Christ. The mind that is in Me.

82 "That mind you can never obtain by reasoning or by reading, but only by living with Me and sharing My life.

83 "Think of Me. Speak of Me. See others as I see them. Let nothing less satisfy you."

JUNE 24

84 "Go forward fearlessly. Do not think about the Red Sea that lies ahead., Be sure that when you come to it the waters will part and you will pass over to your promised land of freedom."

JUNE 25

85 "Cling to Me until the life from Me—the divine life, by that very contact—flows into your being and revives your fainting spirit.

86 "Become recharged. When weary, do as I did on earth. Sit by the well. Rest.

87 "Rest and gain power and strength and the work will come to you as it came to Me.

88 "Rest until every care and worry has gone, and then let the tide of love and joy flow in."

JUNE 26

89 "As I prompt you, act. When you have no clear guidance, then go forward quietly along the path of duty I have set before you.

90 "Do not fear. Do not panic. Quietly do your daily duty. This attitude of faith will receive its reward as surely as acting upon My direct guidance.

91 "Rejoice in the sense of security that is yours."

10

June 27

1 "I am your friend, your companion along the dreary ways of life. I rob those ways of their grayness and horror. I transform them.

2 "Even in earthly friendships, the common way, the weary way, the steep way, may seem a way to heaven if the presence of some loved human friend transforms them.

3 "Let the Sabbath calm enfold your minds and hearts. Let it be a rest from the worry and irritation of life, a halt by the busy highway when you seek some rest and shade.

4 "Have you ever realized the wonder of the friendship you can have with Me? Have you ever thought what it means to be able to summon at will the God of the world?

5 "A privileged visitor to an earthly king must first wait in the palace antechamber; the time to visit must be at the pleasure of the king. But My subjects may enter My presence when they will. Even more, they can summon Me to their bedside, to their worship—and I am there.

6 "Could divine love do more? Your nearest earthly friend cannot be with you in an instant. Your Lord, your master, your divine friend, can and is.

7 "When men and women seek to worship Me they think of the worlds I rule over, of creation, of mighty law and order. Then they feel the awe that precedes worship. To you I say feel awe, feel the desire to worship Me in wondering amazement. But think too of the mighty, tender, humble condescension of My friendship. Think of Me in the little things of everyday life."

JUNE 28

8 "Learn in the little daily things of life to delay action until you get My guidance.

9 "So many lives lack poise. Though they ask My help in the momentous decisions and the big things of life, they rush alone into the small things.

10 "Those around you are most often antagonized or attracted by what you do in the small things."

JUNE 29

11 "My eternal arms shelter you. 'Underneath are the everlasting arms.' This promise is to those who rise above the earth life and seek to soar higher, to the kingdom of heaven.

12 "You must not feel the burden of your failure. Go on in faith; the clouds will clear and the way will lighten. The path becomes less stony with every step you take.

13 "Run that you may obtain. Success will crown your efforts of rigidly doing your simple duties.

14 "I had no words of reproach for any I healed. The man whose palsy I healed was whole and free though he had wrecked his physical being by sin. The woman at the well was not overwhelmed when I said, 'Thou hast five husbands; he whom thou hast is not thy husband.'

15 "The woman taken in adultery was told 'neither do I condemn thee, go and sin no more.' She was not told to bear the burden of the consciousness of her sin.

16 "Remember now abideth these three: faith, hope, and charity. Faith is your attitude toward Me. Charity is your attitude toward others. Equally necessary is hope, which is confidence in yourself to succeed."

JUNE 30

17 "This training and teaching time has not been in vain. The time of suppression, repression, and depression is changed now into a time of glorious expression.

18 "Life is flooded through and through with joy and gladness. Indeed, I have prepared a table of delights, a feast of all good things for you. Indeed, your cup runs over and you can feel from the depths of your heart.

19 "Surely goodness and mercy shall follow us all the days of our lives, and we shall dwell in the house of the Lord forever."

JULY 1

Their meditation:

Our Lord and our God. Lead us, we beseech Thee. Lead us and keep us.

Jesus responds:

20 "You can never go beyond My love and care. Remember that. No evil can befall you. Circumstances I bless and use must be the right ones for you.

21 "The first step is always to lay your will before Me as an offering, be ready for Me to do what is best; be sure that, if you trust Me, what I do for you will be best.

22 "Your second step is to be sure, and to tell Me so, that I am powerful enough to do everything ('The hearts of kings are in my rule and governance'), that no miracle is impossible with Me ('With God all things are possible' and 'My Father and I are one').

23 "Then leave everything with Me. Be glad to leave all your affairs in the Master's hand. Be sure of safety and protection. Remember, you cannot see the future. I can.

24 "You could not bear to see the future. So only little by little can I reveal it to you. Accept My will, and it will bring you joy."

JULY 2

25 "Take joy wherever you go. You have been blessed much. You are being blessed much. Stores of blessing are awaiting you in the months and years that lie ahead. Pass on every blessing.

26 "Love can and does go around the world, passed by God from one to the other. Shed a little sunshine in the heart of another who then, cheered, passes it on. My vitalizing, joy-giving message goes on.

27 "Be transmitters these days. Love and laugh. Cheer all. Love all. Always seek to understand others and you cannot fail to love them.

28 "See Me in the dull, the uninteresting, the sinful, the critical, the miserable. See Me in the laughter of children and the sweetness of old age, in the courage of youth and the patience of manhood and womanhood."

JULY 3

29 "Learn daily the sublime lesson of trust and calm in the midst of storms. Whatever sorrow or difficulty the day may bring, My tender command to you is still the same: Love and laugh.

30 "Love and laughter, not a sorrowful resignation, mark real acceptance of My will. Leave every soul the braver and happier for having met you. For children or youth, middle or old age, for sorrow, for sin, for all you may encounter in others, this should be your attitude. Love and laugh.

31 "Do not fear. Remember how I faced the devil in the wilderness, and how I conquered with 'the sword of the spirit

which is the word of God.'

32 "For every fear that evil may present, you too have your quick answer—an answer of faith and confidence in Me. Where it is possible say it aloud. The spoken word has power.

33 "Look on every fear, not as a weakness on your part due to illness or worry, but as a real temptation to be attacked and overthrown."

JULY 4

34 "Does the way seem a stony one? Not one stone can impede your progress. Courage. Face the future, but face it only with a brave and happy heart. Do not seek to see it. You are robbing faith of sublime sweetness if you do this.

35 "Know that all is well and that faith, not seeing but believing, is the barge that will bear you to safety over the stormy waters. 'According to your faith be it unto you,' was My injunction to those who sought healing of Me.

36 "If faith were so necessary for miracles, healing, and salvation, then the reason is clear why I urged that all who sought entrance to My kingdom must become as little children. Faith is the child attitude.

37 "Seek in every way to become childlike. Seek, seek, seek until you find, until the years have added to your nature that of the trusting child.

38 "You must not copy the child-spirit only for its simple trust, but for its joy in life, its ready laughter, its lack of criticism, and its desire to share all with all people.

39 "Ask much that you may become as little children, friendly and loving toward all—not critical, not fearful. 'Except ye become as little children ye cannot enter the kingdom of heaven.' "

JULY 5

Their meditation:

Our Lord, we love You and desire to live for You in all things.

Jesus responds:

40 "My children, 'Blessed are they that hunger and thirst after righteousness, for they shall be filled.' That is satisfaction.

41 "Only in that fullness of spiritual things can the heartsick and faint and weary be satisfied and healed and rested. 'Lord,' you cry, 'to whom shall we go but to Thee?' 'Thou preparest a table before us.' Bread of life, food from heaven.

42 "How few realize that the feeding of the four thousand and the five thousand was, in each case, but an illustration of the way in which I would one day be the food of My people.

43 "Think of the wonder of revelation still to be seen by those who live with Me. All these hundreds of years and much of what I said and did is still a mystery. Much of My life on earth is still spiritually unexplored country.

44 "Only to the simple and the loving followers who walk with Me can these things be revealed. I have carefully hidden these things from the wise and prudent and have revealed them unto babes.

45 "Do not weigh your spirits down with the sins and sorrows of the world. Only a Christ can do that and live. Look for the loving, the true, the kindly, the brave in the many all around you."

JULY 6

46 "What people call conversion is often only the discovery of the Great Friend. What people call religion is the knowledge of the Great Friend. What people call holiness is the imitation of the Great Friend.

47 "Being perfect is being like the Great Friend and in turn becoming to others a great friend. That is the perfection I enjoined all to have, being perfect as your Father in heaven

is perfect.

48 "I am your friend. Think again of all that means. Friend and Savior. A friend is ready to help, anticipating every want. His hand is outstretched to help and encourage or to ward off danger. His voice is tender, soothing tired nerves and speaking peace to restlessness and fear.

49 "Think of what your friend is to you. From that try to see a little of what would be the perfect friend: a tireless, selfless, all conquering, all miracle-working friend. I am that friend and more even than your heart can imagine.

50 "Were I to read the doctrines of your churches to My kingdom—My kingdom of the child hearts—often there would be no response. But the simple rules I gave to My followers are known, loved, and lived by them all.

51 "In all things seek simplicity."

JULY 7

52 "I am with you all the time, controlling, blessing, and helping you. No man or woman can stand against My will for you. A world of men and women cannot do this—if you trust Me and place your affairs in My hands.

53 "To the passenger it may seem as if each wave would overwhelm the ship or turn it from its course. The captain, however, knows by experience that he steers a straight course to his destination, in spite of wind and waves.

54 "Trust Me, the captain of your salvation."

JULY 8

55 "Never let yourselves think 'we cannot afford this,' or 'we shall never be able to do that.' Say, 'the supply for it is not here yet, but it will come if we should have it. It will surely come.'

56 "Persevere in saying that. Gradually a feeling of

being plentifully supplied and of being surrounded by riches will possess you. That feeling is your faith claiming My supply. According to your faith it shall be unto you.

57 "It is not the faith expressed in moments of prayer and exaltation I look for but the faith that lays the doubts of the day immediately to rest as they arise. That faith attacks and conquers the sense of limitation.

58 " 'Ask and ye shall receive.' "

JULY 9

59 "Help and peace and joy are here. Your courage will be rewarded.

60 "Painful as this time is, you will both one day see the reason for it. You will see it was not cruel testing, but as tender preparation for the wonderful life work you are both to do.

61 "Try to realize that your own prayers are being most wonderfully answered. They are answered in a way that seems painful to you, but now that is the only way.

62 "Success in the temporal world would not satisfy you. Great success, in both temporal and spiritual worlds, awaits you.

63 "I know you will see this had to be."

JULY 10

64 "You are being guided, but remember that I said, 'I will guide thee with mine eye.' And My eye is My set purpose—My will.

65 "To guide with My will is to bring all your desires into oneness with My will and desires.

66 "My will guides you when My will is your only will."

JULY 11

67 "Joy in Me. Joy is infectious. Trust and pray. It is not sin for one who knows Me only as God, as Creator, to doubt Me and question My love and purposes.

68 "But for one who knows Me as you—as Friend and Savior, and who knows the world's God as Father—for that one to doubt My purpose, saving power, and tender love is wrong indeed."

JULY 12

69 "My guardianship is so wonderful. Expect not one but many miracles. Each day's happenings, if of My doing and under My control, are miracles."

JULY 13

70 "You are Mine. Once I have set on you My stamp and seal of ownership, all My hosts are eager to serve and protect you.

71 "Remember that you are daughters of a King. Try to picture a bodyguard of My servants in the unseen waiting, longing, and able to do everything necessary for your well-being.

72 "Feel this as you go through the day. Feel this and all is well."

JULY 14

73 "If you believe it is My hand that has saved you, then you must also believe that I am meaning to save you even more and to keep you in the way you should go.

74 "Even a human rescuer does not save a man from drowning only to place him in other deep and dangerous

waters. Rather, he places him on dry land to restore him to health. He then sees him to his home.

75 "From this parable learn what I, your rescuer, would do and even more. Is the Lord's hand shortened that it cannot perform and cannot save?

76 "My cry on the cross, 'It is finished,' is My cry of salvation for a world. I complete every task committed to Me. So trust and do not be afraid."

JULY 15

77 "Can you get the expectant attitude of faith? That attitude causes you to wait, with a child's joyful trust, for the next good in store. It is not an attitude of waiting for the next evil to befall you."

JULY 16

Their meditation:

Our Lord, we thank You that You have kept us.

Jesus responds:

78 "Rejoice indeed that you see My hand in all that happens and in how you are kept throughout the day.

79 "The Israelites were protected as they crossed the Red Sea; so you are protected in all things.

80 "Rely on this and go forward. You have now entered upon the stage of success. You must not doubt this. You must see this. Beyond all doubt, you must know it. It is true. It is true.

81 "There is no age in eternal life. Have no pity for yourselves, nothing but joy and gratitude.

82 "These last few weeks have been the submerging before the consciousness of rescue. Go forward now and conquer. Go forward unafraid."

JULY 17

83 "Many of My disciples have had to stay on alone and friendless in the dark. They struggled on, singing as they went. For you too, there must be songs on the way.

84 "Would I plant your feet on an insecure ladder? Its supports may be out of your sight, hidden in the secret place of the Most High. But if I have asked you to step on and up firmly, then surely I have secured your ladder."

JULY 18

85 "Know My divine power. Trust in Me. Dwell in My love. Laugh and trust. Laughter is a child's faith in God and good.

86 "Seek safety in My secret place. You cannot be touched or harmed there. That is sure.

87 "Feel as if you were in a strong tower, heavily guarded, and against which nothing can prevail."

JULY 19

88 "Rejoice, rejoice. I have much to teach you both. Do not think that I withhold My presence when I do not reveal more of My truth to you.

89 "You are passing through a storm. It is enough that I am with you to say, 'Peace be still,' to quiet both wind and waves.

90 "It was on the quiet mountain slopes (not during the storm) that I taught My disciples the truths of My kingdom. So with you. The time of the mountain slopes will come. You shall rest with Me and learn."

JULY 20

91 "Fear of what others will say is a lack of trust in Me. This must not be. Convert all these difficulties into the puri-

fication of your characters.

92 "See yourselves as those around you see you, not as you wish to be. Walk humbly with your God.

93 "I will set you on high because you have known My name, but you must be purified to be so exalted."

11

July 21

Their meditation:

Our Lord, with hearts full of joy we thank You for Your marvelous blessings showered on us today and every day.

Jesus responds:

1 "*I am* beside you. Follow My guiding in all things. Marvels beyond all your imaginings are unfolding. *I am* your guide. Joy in that thought. *I am* your guide and your friend.

2 "Remember that to Me a miracle is only a natural happening. To My disciples, to My chosen, a miracle is only a natural happening. But it is a natural happening operative through spiritual forces. Therefore, the person who works and understands through the senses only regards it as something contrary to nature.

3 "Remember too that human beings are at enmity with God. Realize fully, and pray to realize more and more fully, that there is no wonder too marvelous to be an everyday happening with you if you are guided and strengthened by Me."

July 22

4 "My children, the children of My kingdom are a peculiar people. They are set apart. They have different hopes, aspirations, motives, and senses of reward."

JULY 23

5 "You see a marvelous happening (as occurred today), happening so easily, so simply, and you wonder.

6 "Listen, My children. This has not happened easily and simply. It has been achieved by hours, days, and months of weariness and heartache battled against and overcome by a steadfast, unflinching desire to conquer self, to do My will and to live My teachings.

7 "The irritations, worries, and scorn patiently endured develop spiritual power. Once spiritual power is acquired, it operates marvelously."

JULY 24

8 "Carry out My commands and leave the result to Me. Do this as obediently and faithfully as you would expect a child to follow a rule in addition, with no question but that if the addition is done according to command, the result will be right.

9 "Remember the commands I have given you have already been worked out by Me in the spirit world to produce, in your case and in your circumstances, the required result. So follow My rules faithfully. This is why divine guidance is perfect.

10 "To follow a rule laid down even by earth's wisest might lead to disaster. Their knowledge of your individual life and character, capability, circumstances, and temptations must be lacking to some extent.

11 "But to follow My direct guidance means to carry out instructions given with a full knowledge of you and the required result.

12 "Each individual was meant to walk with Me in this way, to act under divine control, strengthened by divine power.

13 "Have I not taught you to love simplicity? No matter

what the world may think, earth's aims and intrigues are not for you. My children, learn of Me. Simplicity brings rest—true rest and power.

14 "To the world foolishness, maybe, but to Me a foretaste of divinity. Never be led by the world's standard. My standard only is for you."

JULY 25

15 "I am teaching both of you My way of removing mountains. The way to remove mountains is the way of praise.

16 "When trouble comes, think of all you have to be thankful for. Praise, praise, praise!

17 "Say thank you all the time. This is the remover of mountains—your thankful hearts of praise."

JULY 26

18 "Abide in Me. 'The works that I do shall ye do also and greater works than these shall ye do because I go to my Father.'

19 " 'Greater works!' The blind received their sight, the lame walked, the lepers were cleansed, the poor had the Gospel preached to them. 'And greater works than these shall ye do because I go unto my Father.'

20 "Wonder of the world! Miracle of the ages! Power goes out to bless through the one actuated by the Holy Spirit.

21 "Arise from the grave of sickness, poverty, doubt, despondency, and limitation. 'Arise, shine for the light is come and the glory of the Lord is risen upon thee.'

22 "Before you both is a wonderful future. A future of unlimited power to bless others. Be channels. Be used. Ask. Ask. 'Ask what ye will and it shall be done unto you' and unto those for whom you pray."

JULY 27

Their meditation:

Our Lord, grant us that wonderful inward peace.

Jesus responds:

23 "My children, that peace truly does pass all understanding. That peace no one can take from you. No one has the power to disturb that peace; only you, yourselves, can let the world and its worries and distractions in.

24 "You can give the entrance to fears and despondency. You can open the door to the robber who breaks in and destroys your peace.

25 "Set yourselves this task. Allow nothing to disturb your peace, your heart calm, with Me. Stop all work. Stop all association with others until this is restored.

26 "Do not let those about you spoil your peace of heart and mind. Do not let any trouble, any irritation, or any adversity disturb it for one moment.

27 "Look on each difficulty as training to enable you to acquire this peace. Train yourself to make sure that no work, no interruption, touches the harmony of the real you that is hidden with Me in the secret place of the Father."

JULY 28

Their meditation:

Our Lord, guide us. Show us Thy will and way in everything.

Jesus responds:

28 "Keep close to Me and you shall know the way. As I said to My disciples, I am the way. That is the solution to all

the world's problems. Keep close to Me. Think, act, and live in My presence.

29 "How dare any foe touch you when you are protected by Me! Keeping near to Me is the secret of all power, all peace, all purity, all influence.

30 "Abide in Me. Live in My presence. Rejoice in My love. Thank and praise all the time. Wonders are unfolding."

JULY 29

31 "I am your Lord. Lord of your lives, controller of your days, of your present and your future. Leave all plans to Me. You must act as I tell you.

32 "You have now both entered upon the God-guided life. Think what that means. God-taught. God-guided.

33 "Is anything too wonderful for such a life? Do you begin to see how wonderful life with Me can be? Do you see that no evil can befall you?"

JULY 30

Their meditation:

Our Lord, we thank You for so much. We bless You and praise Your glorious name.

Jesus responds:

34 "Fill your world with love and laughter. Never mind what anguish lies behind you. Forget, forgive, love, and laugh.

35 "Treat all as you would treat Me, with love and consideration. Let nothing that others do to you alter your treatment of them."

JULY 31

Their meditation:

O Jesus, come and walk with us and let us feel Your very nearness.

Jesus responds:

36 "I walk with you. Think, My children, I walk with you not only to guide, comfort, strengthen, and uphold you, but for solace and comfort for Myself.

37 "When a loving child is by you, is your feeling of nearness only that you may provide protection and help for that little one? Is it not also that you may find, in that little child, joy and cheer and comfort in its simplicity, its love, and its trust?

38 "So, too, it is in your power to comfort and bring joy to My heart."

AUGUST 1

39 "I am your shield. No worldly storms can harm you. Feel that between you and all scorn and indignity there is a strong shield. Practice feeling this until nothing has the power to spoil your inward peace. Then you shall have won a marvelous victory.

40 "You wonder why sometimes you are permitted to make mistakes in your choices when you truly sought to do My will in the matter. To that I say, it was no mistake. All your lessons cannot be learned without difficulty. This was needed to teach you a lesson.

41 "Not to him who walks on with no obstacles in his way, but to him who overcomes is the promise given.

42 "To attain peace quickly in your surroundings, as well as in your hearts, learn your lesson quickly. The overcoming is never the overcoming of the one who troubled you, but the overcoming of the weaknesses and wrong in your own nature aroused by such a one.

43 "No lower standard than My standard shall be yours. 'Be ye therefore perfect even as your Father in heaven is perfect.' "

AUGUST 2

Their meditation:

Lord, bless us in this evening hour, and in Your mercy heal us all.

Jesus responds:

44 "Do not think that suffering is the only path into My kingdom. Amid the sunlit glades and the loveliest flowers the steps and hearts of men and women are drawn to Me. There are birds and laughter and butterflies and life-giving summer air. With these as tender companions and friends, the way into the kingdom can be taken joyfully.

45 "Bleak, cold, desolate, briar-beset, and stony are not all the ways. Leave to Me the choice of ways, the guidance in the way. But when the sunlight comes, accept it gladly.

46 "Even in the spirit world, appreciation results from contrary experience. Can the fireside of home be more welcome than to the traveler who has forced his or her way through desolate places and a blinding storm? Take this word of cheer to heart. 'He will not suffer you to be tempted above that ye are able but will, with the temptation, also find a way of escape that ye may be able to bear it.'

47 "The world is not the kingdom. In the world you shall have tribulation, but 'be of good cheer, I have overcome the world.'

48 "Life with Me, the conquering Christ, and the joy and peace of conquest shall be yours too."

AUGUST 3

49 "Think much about My servants of old. Think how Abraham believed the promise (when as yet he had no child) that in his seed all the nations of the earth should be blessed.

50 "Think how Moses led the children of Israel through the desert, sure that they would, at last, gain the promised land.

51 "Down through the ages there have always been those who obeyed, not seeing but believing, and their faith was rewarded. So shall it be with you."

AUGUST 4

52 "Give Me the gift of a brave and thankful heart. Men and women prove their greatness by their power to see causes for thankfulness.

53 "When life seems hard and troubles crowd in, then definitely look for causes for thankfulness.

54 "The sacrifice, the offering of thanksgiving, is indeed a sweet incense going up to Me through the busy day.

55 "Seek diligently for something to be glad and thankful about in every happening. Soon no search will be required. The causes for joy and gratitude will spring to greet your loving hearts."

AUGUST 5

Their meditation:

Jesus, let Your beautiful presence be with us always.

Jesus responds:

56 " 'I will never leave you nor forsake you.' There is no bond or union on earth to compare with the union between Myself and a soul that loves Me. That friendship is priceless beyond all earth's imaginings.

57 "In the merging of heart and mind a oneness results that only those who experience it can even dimly realize."

AUGUST 6

Their meditation:

My Lord, we seek Your blessing.

Jesus responds:

58 "I love to pour My blessings down in rich measure. But like the seed sowing, the ground must be prepared before the seed is dropped in.

59 "It is your responsibility to prepare the soil, Mine to drop the seed-blessing into the prepared soil. Together we share and joy in the harvest.

60 "Spend more time in soil preparation. Prayer fertilizes soil. There is much to do in preparation."

AUGUST 7

61 "My children, how dear to My heart is the cry of love that asks for all of Me, that wishes every action, thought, word, and moment to be Mine.

62 "How poor is the understanding of the one who thinks that money, to be used in this good work or that, is the great gift to offer. Above all, I desire love—true, warm, childlike love—and then the gift I prize next is the gift of the moments, all the moments.

63 "Even when love's impetuous longing to serve Me has offered all life, every day, every hour, it is a long and hard lesson to learn what it means to give Me the moments.

64 "The moments are the little things you planned to do but gave up gladly at My suggestion, the little services you joyfully render for Me. See Me in all and then it will be an easy task.

65 "This is a priceless time of initiation. Remember that the path of initiation is not for all, but only for those who have felt the sorrow-cry of the world that needs a Savior, for those who have heard the tender pleas of a Savior who needs followers through whom He can joyfully accomplish His great work of salvation."

AUGUST 8

Their meditation:

O Jesus, we love You and so long to serve You.

Jesus responds:

66 "My children, you are both to do mighty things for Me. Glories and wonders unfold. Life is one glorious whole.

67 "Draw into your beings more and more this wonderful eternal life. It is the flow of life eternal through spirit, mind, and body, that cleanses, heals, restores, renews youth, and passes on from you to others with the same miracle-working power.

68 " 'And this is life eternal that they may know Thee . . . and Jesus Christ, whom Thou has sent.' So seek by constant contact to know Me more and more.

69 "Make Me the one abiding presence of your day. Be conscious of Me all the time. Seek to do less and to accomplish and achieve more. Doing is action. Achievement is successful action.

70 "Remember that eternal life is the only lasting life. All done without being done in the power of My Spirit, My life, is passing. All done in that Spirit-life is undying.

71 " 'I will give unto them eternal life and they shall never perish, neither shall any man pluck them out of my hands.' So eternal life means security and safety too. Dwell increasingly in the consciousness of that security and safety."

AUGUST 9

Their meditation:

Lord, come to us and heal us.

Jesus responds:

72 "I am your healer, your joy, your Lord. You bid Me, your Lord, to come. Do not you know that I am here? With noiseless steps I draw near to you.

73 "Your hour of need is the moment of My coming. If you knew My love, if you knew the measure of My longing to help, you would know that I need no agonized pleading. Your need is My call."

AUGUST 10

74 "Rest more with Me. If I, the Son of God, needed those times of quiet communion with My Father, alone, away from noise and activity, then surely you need them too.

75 "Refilling with the Spirit is a need—dwelling apart, shutting yourself away in the very secret place of your being, away alone with Me.

76 "From these times you come forth in power to bless and heal."

AUGUST 11

Their meditation:

Our Lord, bless us and keep us, we beseech You.

Jesus responds:

77 "My keeping power is never at fault, but only your realization of it. It is not whether I can provide a shelter from the storm, but your failure to be sure of the security of that shelter.

78 "Every fear, every doubt, is a crime against My love.

79 "Children, trust. Practice daily, many times a day, saying, 'All is well.' Say it until you believe and know it."

AUGUST 12

80 "Rely on Me alone. Ask no other help. Pay all out in the spirit of trust that more will come to meet your supply.

81 "The more retained by you, the less will be gained from Me. It is a law of divine supply. To hold back, to retain, implies a fear of the future, a lack of trust in Me.

82 "When you ask Me to save you from the sea of poverty and difficulty, you must trust wholly in Me.

83 "If you do not, and your prayer and faith are genuine, then I must first answer your prayer for help as a rescuer does a drowning man who is struggling to save himself. The rescuer must render him more helpless and powerless until he is wholly at the will and mercy of the rescuer. So understand My leading. Trust wholly. Trust completely.

84 "Empty your cup. I will fill it. You both ask to understand divine supply. It is a most difficult lesson for My children to learn. They fail to understand because they have become so dependent on material supply.

85 "You must live as I tell you. Depend on Me."

AUGUST 13

86 "Come to Me, talk to Me, dwell with Me, and then you will know My way is a sure way, that My paths are safe paths. Come near to Me.

87 "Dig deep down into the soil of the kingdom. You must have both effort and rest, a union of the two."

AUGUST 14

Their meditation:

O Jesus, guide our footsteps lest we stray.

Jesus responds:

88 "To keep from straying, My children, there is no

cure except to keep so close to Me that nothing—no interest, no temptation—can come between us.

89 "Understanding that, you have no alternative but to stay at My side; knowing that as I am the very way itself, nothing can prevent you from being in the way, nothing can cause you to stray.

90 "I have promised peace but not leisure, heart rest and comfort, but not pleasure. I have said, 'In the world ye shall have tribulation'; so do not feel, when adverse things happen, that you have failed or are not being guided, because I have said, '. . . be of good cheer, I have overcome the world.'

91 "Learn of overcoming power from Me. Though spat upon, scourged, misunderstood, forsaken, and crucified I could see My work had not been affected by these things. Therefore, I could cry triumphantly from My cross, 'It is finished.' Not the pain, the mocking, the agony, but the task was finished.

92 "Let this thought comfort you. Amid failure, discord, abuse, and suffering, friends and angels even now are prepared to sound the chorus, 'It is finished.' "

12

AUGUST 15

Their meditation:

Jesus, You are watching over us to bless and care for us.

Jesus responds:

1 "Yes! Remember that always—that out of darkness I am leading you to light. Out of unrest to rest, out of disorder to order, out of faults and failure to perfection.

2 "Trust Me wholly. Fear nothing. Hope ever. Always look up to Me and I will be your sure aid.

3 "My Father and I are one. Can not He who made the ordered, beautiful world out of chaos, who set the stars in their courses, who made each plant to know its season, can not He bring peace and order out of your chaos?

4 "He and I are one, and you are Mine. Your affairs are Mine. It is My divine task to order My affairs; therefore, yours will be ordered by Me."

AUGUST 16

5 "Remember, no prayer goes unanswered. Remember that the moment a thing seems wrong to you or a person's actions are not what you think they should be, at that moment your obligation and responsibility should be to pray for those wrongs to be righted or for that person to be different.

6 "Face your responsibilities. What's wrong in your country, with its statespersons, its laws, its people? Quietly

think these things out and make these matters your prayer concerns. You will see lives altered you never touched, laws made at your request, and evils banished.

7 "Yes! Live in a large sense. Live to serve and to save. You may never go beyond one room, and yet you may become one of the most powerful forces for good in your country, in the world.

8 "You may never see the mighty work you do, but I see it and evil sees it.

9 "It is a glorious life, the life of one who saves. You are fellow workers together with Me. See this more and more. Love with Me, sharers of My life."

AUGUST 17

Their meditation:

O Jesus, help us, we beseech You.

Jesus responds:

10 "I am always your helper through dark to light, through weakness to power, through sin to salvation, through danger to security, through poverty to plenty, through indifference to love, through resentment to perfect forgiveness.

11 "Never be satisfied with a comparison with those around you. Always let My words ring out, 'Be ye perfect even as your Father in heaven is perfect.' Stop short at nothing less.

12 "Make it your practice, each of you, to review your character—in relation to life, your dear ones, your household, friends, acquaintances, your country, and your work.

13 "See where I, in the same relation or circumstance or situation, would act differently. Plan how such and such a fault can best be eradicated, or such and such a sin, mistake, or omission be avoided.

14 "Have at least a weekly review."

AUGUST 18

Their meditation:

Jesus, You came that we might have life, and have it more abundantly.

Jesus responds:

15 "Yes! I came to give you life, spiritual, mental, physical, abundant life, joyous life, and a powerful life. Do you not think My heart is sad that so few accept that gracious gift?

16 "Think of it. Earth's richest, choicest gift held out, free to all, and no one cares to stretch out a hand to take it.

17 "Is that possible? My gift—the richest heaven has to offer, that precious gift of life, abundant life—men and women turn away from. The reject it. They will have none of it.

18 "Let it not be true of you. Hasten to take and use it."

AUGUST 19

19 "I will guide your efforts. You are not being punished for past sins. Take My words, revealed to you each day from the beginning, and in all things do as I say. I have been showing you the way. You have not obeyed Me in this.

20 "I have a plan that can only be revealed in this way. I rarely find two souls in union who want only My will and only to serve Me. The union is miracle working.

21 "I have told you that I am longing to use you. Long ago My world would have been brought to Me, had I been served by many such two souls.

22 "It was always 'two and two.' "

AUGUST 20

23 "Rest. It is wrong to force work. Rest until life, eternal life, flowing through your veins and hearts and minds, bids you begin again. Then work, glad work, will follow.

24 "Tired work never tells. Rest. Remember, I am your physician, healer of mind and body. Look to Me for the cure, for rest, for peace."

AUGUST 21

25 "I come. I come. You need Me. Live much out here in My sunshine and glorious air. Live in My presence and teaching.

26 "If you are unable to take a holiday, remember, sunshine, the laughter of nature, helps to make glad your heart.

27 "Live outside a lot. My medicines are sun and air, trust and faith. Trust is the spirit sun, with your being wrapped in the divine Spirit.

28 "Faith is the soul's breathing in the divine Spirit. Mind, soul, and body need helping. Welcome My treatment for you both. Draw near to Me.

29 "Nature is often My nurse for tired souls and weary bodies."

AUGUST 22

30 "I am here. No distance separates Me from you. In the spirit kingdom we measure not by earth's miles. A false word, a fear-inspired failure, or a harsh criticism, these are the distances between a soul and Me. In order for your work for Me to be unhindered, your training must be severe.

31 "You seek My presence and they who seek shall

find. It is not a question of human searching so much as human consciousness, unconditional surrender to My will in the small as in the big things of life. That is what makes My guidance possible.

32 "You know the difference between taking a loving, joyful child with you along a path, who anticipates each direction and accepts naturally each decision as to each turning and the child who is resistant and rebellious and has to be forced, even though in quieter moments he or she may say, 'Yes, I do want to go with you, but I hate this path.'

33 "It is not the path, but the loving rejoicing in both the path and the guidance that matters with My disciples. You are ready for the guidance, but you do not rejoice as you should, both of you, in the little daily stones of the path."

AUGUST 23

Their meditation:

Lord, we love You, we worship You.

Jesus responds:

34 "Bow low before Me. Worship is not supplication though both express your varying needs of Me. Bow low in worship, conscious not only of My humanity but of My divine majesty.

35 "As you kneel in humble adoration, I will tell you that when I took upon Me your humanity, it was with the desire of raising that humanity to My divinity.

36 "Earth gave Me her best—a human temple to enclose My divinity—and I brought to her the possession of divine power, divine love, divine strength, to be forever expressed in those of her children who accepted Me, opened their hearts to Me, and sought to live My life.

37 "So, kneeling in a spirit of humility, turn your eyes

heavenward and realize the majesty, the power, the beauty that may be yours. Remember, there are no limits to My giving; there may be limits to your accepting.

38 "Oh, rejoice at the wonders to which you are called. Rise in My strength, filled with the longing to attain the wonders you are seeing in prayer."

AUGUST 24

39 " 'Shield from the scorn and cover from the chiding.' Often I have to shield My disciples from their own scorn and chiding.

40 "My poor Peter could never have done My work, never have had the courage to live on, or the daring to live for Me, but for the tender love in which I wrapped him.

41 "I did not need to protect Peter from the anger of My Father, who is all love, nor from the scorn of My enemies, nor from the resentment of My friends. No. But from the hatred of Peter himself.

42 "Today, as then, to My followers come the shame, remorse, and contempt of themselves, of their weak selves. They meant to be so strong and brave for Me.

43 "Then I have to protect them with a shield of love or they could never have the courage to fight and conquer. This facing of the real self has to be done; shame and remorse must come.

44 "That is a stage in development, but only a stage. What is the use of the glad wings of a butterfly if it remains earthbound, weighed down with the thought of its contemptible past? And so today, now I say to you both, you are not to dwell for one moment on your sins, mistakes, faults, and bad habits of the past.

45 "You must be as one who runs a race, stumbles and falls, and rises and presses on to the goal. What good would it be if she stays to examine the spot where she fell, to weep

over the delay, over the shortsightedness that prevented her anticipating and avoiding the obstacle?

46 "So with you. I lay it on you as a command: no looking back! Give yourself, and everyone you have ever met, a fresh start from today. Remember no more their sins and failures, or your own. The remembrance is a current of disappointment that hinders the swimmer.

47 "When I sent My disciples out, two by two, without script, without two coats, without money, it was an injunction to be obeyed literally, but figuratively too. On life's journey, throw away all that is not important.

48 "Cast aside all the hindrances, the past imperfections of others, the sense of failure. Travel unladen, with a light heart. A light heart means a weight of influence.

49 "My children, I love you."

AUGUST 25

50 "Behold, I make all things new. It is only the earth-bound spirit that cannot soar. Every blessing I send you, every joy, every freedom achieved from poverty and worry will loosen a strand that ties you to earth.

51 "It is only those strands that bind you. Therefore your freedom will mean your rising into the realm of joy and appreciation.

52 "Clipped wings can grow again. Broken voices can regain a strength and beauty unknown before. Your power to help other lives will soon bring its delight, even when, at first, the help to yourselves may seem too late to bring you joy.

53 "Worn-out, tired, and pain-weary as you may seem, I say unto you, 'Behold, I make all things new.' That promise shall be fulfilled. Tenderly, across the years, I speak to you today, My loved ones.

54 " 'Come unto Me all ye that labor and are heavy-laden and I will give you rest.' "

AUGUST 26

55 "Because you have both longed to save My world, I let you have that training that shall fit you to save. Each day, both of you, take your pains and sufferings, difficulties and hardships, and offer them up for one troubled soul, as some prayer specially needing to be answered.

56 "Thus, the beauty of each day will live on after the trouble, distress, difficulty, and pain of the day have passed.

57 "Learn from My life of the suffering that saves others. Then you will sing in your pain. Across the grayest days there are the gleams of sunlight."

AUGUST 27

58 "Do not see the small trials and vexations of each hour of the day. See the one purpose and plan to which all are leading.

59 "If in climbing a mountain you keep your eyes on each stony or difficult place as you ascend, seeing only that, how weary and profitless your climb.

60 "Your climb will be so different if you think of each step as leading to the summit of achievement from which glories and beauties will open out before you."

AUGUST 28

Their meditation:

Our Lord, we know that You are great and able to deliver us.

Jesus responds:

61 "I am your deliverer. Trust Me absolutely. Know that I will do the best for you. Be ready and willing for My

will to be done.

62 "Know that with Me all things are possible. Cling joyfully to that truth. Say many times, 'All things are possible with my Master, my Lord, my Friend.'

63 "This truth, accepted and firmly believed in, is the ladder which a soul can climb from the lowest of pits to the sublimest of heights."

AUGUST 29

Their meditation:

We seek You as You have told us.

Jesus responds:

64 "And seeking you shall find. None ever sought My presence in vain. None ever sought My help in vain. A breath of desire and My Spirit is there—to replenish and renew.

65 "Sometimes weariness and exhaustion are not signs of lack of spirit but of the guiding of the Spirit. Many wonderful things would not have happened but for the physical weariness, the mind-weariness of My servants, that made resting, giving up of works, a necessity.

66 "Though My way may seem narrow, it leads to life, abundant life. Follow it. It is wide enough so that I can walk beside you.

67 "You will never be too lonely with such companionship. A Comrade, infinitely tender and strong, will walk with you."

AUGUST 30

68 "Trials and trouble may seem to overwhelm you. They cannot do more than work My will, and you have said that will is your will.

69 "Do not you see that you cannot be destroyed? A new life is opening before you now. It is yours to enter into the kingdom I have prepared for you.

70 "The sunlight of My presence is on your paths. Trust and go forward unafraid. My grace is sufficient for all your needs."

AUGUST 31

Their meditation:

In quietness and in confidence shall be your strength (Isaiah 30:15).

Jesus responds:

71 "Feel that quietness and strength. Trust Me. Am I not leading you safely, faithfully? Will you believe Me, your Master, that all this is really to bring the answers to your prayers?

72 "Remember, I am the Supreme Being who knows all and can control all. I began to effect a cure of all the disharmony and disorder as soon as you put your affairs, and their confusion and difficulties, into My hands.

73 "Know that I shall cause you no more pain in effecting the cure than a physician (who plans and knows he can effect a cure) would cause his patient. I will do all as tenderly as possible.

74 "Tell Me you trust Me in this."

SEPTEMBER 1

75 "Service is the law of heaven. My angels always obey. 'They serve Him continually,' can be said of all who love Me. With love there is continuous service in every action, even in rest.

76 "Take this, not as the end, but as the beginning of a new life consecrated to My service, a life of power and joy."

SEPTEMBER 2

77 "Breathe My name. It is like the pressure of a child's hand that calls forth an answering pressure that strengthens the child's confidence and banishes fear."

SEPTEMBER 3

78 "Give abundantly. Feel that you are rich. Have no mean thought in your heart. Of love, of thought, of all you have, give, give, give.

79 "You are followers of the world's greatest giver. Give of time, of personal ease and comfort, of rest, of fame, of healing, of power, of sympathy, of all these and many more.

80 "Learn this lesson, and you will become a great power to help others and to do mighty things."

SEPTEMBER 4

Their meditation:

This kind goeth not out but by prayer and fasting (Matthew 17:21).

Jesus responds:

81 "You must live a life of communion and prayer if you are to save others. Take My words as a command to you, 'By prayer and fasting.'

82 "Pray and deny yourself, and you will be used marvelously to save and help others."

SEPTEMBER 5

Their meditation:

I will never leave thee nor forsake thee (Hebrews 13:5).

Jesus responds:

83 "My children, that word is unfailingly true. Down the centuries thousands have proved My constancy, My untiringness, My unfailing love. 'Never leave.' 'Never forsake.'

84 "Not just a presence is meant by this, but also My love will never leave you, My understanding will never leave you, My strength will never leave you.

85 "Think of all that I am: love, then forever you are sure of love; strength, then forever, in every difficulty and danger, you are sure of strength; patience, then always there is One who can never tire; and understanding, then always you will be understood.

86 "Can you fear the future when it holds so much for you? Beloved, 'set your affections on things above' (the higher, spiritual things), 'and not on things on the earth' (the lower, temporal things), and you will see how rich you are."

SEPTEMBER 6

87 "I am your Lord. I can command your obedient service, your loyalty. But I am bound by My Lordship to give you protection.

88 "I am bound to fight for you, to plan for you, to secure for you a sufficiency of all within My power to provide. Think how vast that provision can be. Never doubt.

89 "Marvels are unfolding, wonders beyond your dreams. They need only the watering of a grateful spirit and a loving heart to yield abundantly."

SEPTEMBER 7

Their meditation:

Our Lord, the God of the troubled and the weary, come and save us.

Jesus responds:

90 "I am your Savior, not only from the weight of sin, but from the weight of care, from misery and depression, from want and woe, from faintness and heartache. I am your Savior.

91 "Remember that you are living really in the unseen—that is the real life. Lift up your heads from earth's troubles and view the glories of the kingdom. Higher and higher each day see more of heaven.

92 "Speak to Me. Long for Me. Rest in Me. Abide in Me. Do not restlessly bring Me your burdens and then feverishly pick them up again and carry them away.

93 "No! Abide in Me. Do not for one moment lose the consciousness of My strength and protection. Be as a child in its mother's arms, sheltered and at rest."

SEPTEMBER 8

Their meditation:

Our God is our supply.

Jesus responds:

94 "Look to Me for all. Rely on Me for all. Drop those burdens. Then you can go on your way rejoicing, singing and free. Encumbered with them you will fall.

95 "Drop them at My feet, knowing I will lift them and deal with each one in the best way."

13

September 9

1 "Progress is the law of heaven. Higher, ever higher, rise to life and beauty, knowledge and power. Higher and higher.

2 "Tomorrow be stronger, braver, more loving than you have been today. The law of progress gives meaning, a purpose, to life."

September 10

3 "Your loved ones are safe in My keeping. Theirs is a life of happiness and progress, learning, loving, and working. They live to serve and serve they truly do. They serve Me and those they love. They serve ceaselessly.

4 "You cannot see their many diverse ministrations any more than those in human form during My time on earth could see the angels who ministered to Me in the wilderness.

5 "Often mortals rush to earthly friends who can serve them in such a limited way. Yet, their friends who are freed from the limitations of humanity can serve them so much better. They understand better, protect better, plan better, and even plead better their cause with Me.

6 "You do well to remember your friends in the unseen. Doing so, as you live more in the unseen world, the gentler will be your passing when it comes.

7 "Earth's troubles and difficulties will seem, even now, less overwhelming as you look not at the things that are seen, but at the real, the eternal life.

8 " 'And this is life eternal that we may know Thee, the only true God, and Jesus Christ whom Thou hast sent.'

9 "Learning to know Me draws that kingdom near, and in Me, through knowledge of Me, the dear ones there become near and dear."

SEPTEMBER 11

Their meditation:

The eternal God is thy refuge and underneath are the everlasting arms (Deuteronomy 33:27).

Jesus responds:

10 "Arms, sheltering arms, express the loving tenderness of your Father (My Father) in heaven.

11 "Men and women, in trouble and difficulty, need nothing so much as a refuge. They need a place to hide. A place where none and nothing can touch them.

12 "Say to yourself, 'He is our refuge'; say it until its truth sinks into your soul. Say it until you know it and are so sure of it that nothing can make you afraid.

13 "Feel this, not only until fear goes, but until joy ripples through in its place. Refuge. Everlasting arms, so untiring, so safe, so sure."

SEPTEMBER 12

14 "When supply seems to have failed, you must know it has not done so. But you must, at the same time, look around to see what you can give away. Give away something.

15 "There is always a stagnation, a blockage, when supply seems short. Your giving clears that away and lets the Spirit of My supply flow clear.

16 "To be conscious of My presence as love makes all

life different. You threw open your whole nature to Me and that brings relief. Relief brings peace. Peace brings joy. It is the 'peace that passeth all understanding' and the 'joy no man taketh from you.'

17 "Beyond all words is My love and care for you. Be sure of it. Rejoice in it. Walk in My love. These words mean much.

18 "There is a joy, a spring, a gladness in the walk of those who walk in My love. That walk becomes a glad conquering and triumphant march. So walk."

SEPTEMBER 13

Their meditation:

In Your strength we conquer.

Jesus responds:

19 "Yes! You gain your conquering power from Me. There can be no failure with Me. The secret of success then is life with Me.

20 "Do you want to make the best of life? Then live near to Me, the Master and Giver of all life. Your reward will be sure. It will be perfect success, My success.

21 "Sometimes it will be the success of souls won, sometimes the success of disease cured and devils cast out. Sometimes you will see the success of a finished sacrifice as on Calvary, sometimes the success of One who answered never a word in the face of the scorn, torture, and jeering cries of His enemies. Indeed, you will even find the success of a risen Savior as He walked through the garden of Joseph of Arimathea on that first Easter morning.

22 "But it will be My success. The world may deem you failures. The world judges not as I judge.

23 "Bend your knees in wonder before My revelation.

The joy of seeing spiritual truths is a great joy. When the heavens are opened and the voice speaks, it is not to all hearts, but to faithful, loving hearts.

24 "Remember, your great field of labor is yourself. That is your first task, the weeding, the planting, digging, pruning, and bearing fruit. When that is done, I lead you out into other fields."

SEPTEMBER 14

25 "You must be ready to stand apart from the world. Do you want the full and complete satisfaction you find in Me, and the satisfaction of the world too? Then you are trying to serve God and mammon, or if not trying to serve, then claiming the wages of both God and mammon.

26 "If you work for Me, you have your reward. But then you turn to the world, to human beings, and expect that reward too. This is not right.

27 "Do not expect love or gratitude or acknowledgment from others. I will give you all necessary rewards."

SEPTEMBER 15

Their meditation:

I came that you might have life and that you might have it more abundantly (John 10:10).

Jesus responds:

28 "Yes, I, your Master, am a generous giver. Abundant life in overflowing measure I give to you. I came for that purpose: to give life for souls, the eternal life that pulses through your whole being, that animates your mind and body.

29 "I am a generous giver, a kingly giver. For this I

came, that you might live in Me. I spoke of life when I said, 'I am the vine and ye are the branches.' The life flow of the vine is in the branches.

30 "Our lives are one—yours and Mine. All that is in My nature must therefore pass into yours.

31 "I am love and joy and peace and strength and power and healing and humility and patience and all else you see in Me, your Lord. Then these, too, you must have as My life flows through you. So have courage.

32 "You do not make yourselves loving and strong and patient and humble. You live with Me, and then My life accomplishes the miraculous change."

SEPTEMBER 16

Their meditation:

Seek ye first the kingdom of God and His righteousness, and all these things shall be added unto you (Matthew 6:33).

If thine eye be single thy whole body shall be full of light (Matthew 6:22).

Jesus responds:

33 "The eye of the soul is the will. If your one desire is My kingdom, to find that kingdom, to serve that kingdom, then truly your whole body shall be full of light.

34 "When you are told to seek first the kingdom of God, the first step is to make sure your will is for that kingdom. You must have a single eye to God's glory. Desire nothing less than that His kingdom come. Seek to advance His kingdom in all things.

35 "Know no values but spiritual values. Know no profit but that of spiritual gain. Seek in all things His kingdom first.

36 "Only seek material gain when that gain will mean a

gain for My kingdom. Get away from money values altogether. Walk with Me. Learn of Me. Talk to Me. In this lies your true happiness."

SEPTEMBER 17

37 "My name is the power that turns evil aside, that summons all good to your aid. Spirits of evil flee at the sound of *Jesus*. Spoken in fear, in weakness, in sorrow, in pain, it is an appeal I never fail to answer.

3 *Jesus*. Use My name often. Think of the unending call of 'Mother,' made by her children. They call 'Mother' to help, to care, to decide, to appeal. Use My name in that same way—simply, naturally, forcefully.

39 "*Jesus*. Use My name not only when you need help but to express love. Uttered aloud, or in the silence of your hearts, it will alter an atmosphere from one of discord to one of love. It will raise the standard of talk and thought.

40 "*Jesus*. 'There is none other name under heaven whereby you can be saved.' "

SEPTEMBER 18

Their meditation:

Lord, we believe, help Thou our unbelief (Mark 9:24).

Jesus responds:

41 "This cry of the human heart is as expressive of human need as it was when uttered to Me while I was on earth. It expresses the soul's progress.

42 "As a soul realizes Me and My power, and knows Me as Helper and Savior, that soul believes in Me more and more. At the same time, one is more conscious than before of falling short of absolute trust in Me.

43 " 'Lord, I believe. Help Thou mine unbelief.' The soul's progress—an increased belief—then a cry for more faith—a plea to conquer all unbelief, all lack of trust.

44 "That cry is heard. That prayer is answered. You shall be given more faith, and at the same time, more power to see where trust is lacking.

45 "My children seek to go up this path to Me; each stage they are nearer to Me."

SEPTEMBER 19

46 "Rest in Me. When nature rebels, it is time for rest. Rest then until My life-power flows through you.

47 "Have no fear for the future. Be quiet, be still, and in that stillness your strength will come and will be maintained.

48 "The world sees strength in action. In My kingdom it is known that strength lies in quiet. 'In quietness and in confidence shall be your strength.'

49 "Such a promise! Such glorious fulfillment. The strength of peace and the peace of strength. Rest in Me. Joy in Me."

SEPTEMBER 20

Their meditation:

The work of righteousness shall be peace, and the effect of righteousness, quietness and assurance forever (Isaiah 32:17).

Jesus responds:

50 "My peace gives quietness and assurance forever. My peace flows as a calm river through the dry land of life. It causes the trees and flowers of life to spring forth and yield abundantly.

51 "Success is the result of work done in peace. Only in this way can work yield its increase. Let there be no hurry in your plans. You live not in time but in eternity. It is in the unseen that your life's future is being planned.

52 "Abide in Me, and I in you, so you shall bring forth much fruit. Be calm, assured, at rest. Cherish love and peace. Do nothing fitful, but be all effectual. Sow in prayer, water by trust, bear flower and fruit in joy. I love you."

SEPTEMBER 21

Their meditation:

Show us Your way, O Lord, and let us walk in Your paths.

Jesus responds:

53 "You are doing so. This is the way. The way of uncertain future and faltering steps. It is My way.

54 "Put all fear of the future aside. Know that you will be led. Know that you will be shown. I have promised."

SEPTEMBER 22

Their meditation:

He that dwelleth in the secret place of the Most High shall abide under the shadow of the Almighty (Psalm 91:1).

Jesus responds:

55 "You are hidden in a sure place, known only to God and you. It is so secret that no power on earth can even find it.

56 "But, My beloved children, you must dwell therein. Not just a fitful visit, but a real abiding. Make it your home. Your dwelling place.

57 "Over that home shall My shadow rest to make it

doubly safe, doubly secret. Like a brooding mother bird's wings, that shadow rests. How safe, how sure, you must feel there.

58 "When fears assail you and cares trouble you, it is because you have ventured out of that protecting shadow. The one and only thing to do is to creep back into shelter again. So rest."

SEPTEMBER 23

Their meditation:

These things have I spoken unto you . . . that your joy may be full (John 15:11).

Jesus responds:

59 "Remember that the truths I teach you have all been given to you, too, as to My disciples of old, with the idea of giving you that overflowing joy.

60 "Search for the joy in life. Hunt for it as for hidden treasure. Love and laugh. Delight yourselves in the Lord.

61 "Joy in Me. I wished My disciples to have full joy. I intended them to have it. Had they lived My teachings out in their daily lives, they would have had fullness of joy."

SEPTEMBER 24

Their meditation:

Taste and see that the Lord is good (Psalm 34:8).

Jesus responds:

62 "He is good. Trust in Him. Know that all is well. Say, 'God is good. God is good.' Just leave in His hands the present and the future, knowing only that He is good. He can

bring order out of chaos, good out of evil, peace out of turmoil. God is good.

63 "My Father and I are one. One in desire to do good. For God to do good to His children is for him to share His goodness with them. God is good, anxious to share His goodness and good things with you, and He will do this.

64 "Trust and do not be afraid."

SEPTEMBER 25

Their meditation:

Lord, show us the Father and it sufficeth us (John 14:8).

Jesus responds:

65 "My children, have I been with you such a long time, coming to you, speaking to you, and you still have not known the Father?

66 "Your Father is the God and controller of a mighty universe. But He is as I am. All the love, strength, and beauty you have seen in Me are in My Father.

67 "If you see that, and know Him and Me as we really are, then that is sufficient for you; it completes your life, it satisfies you, it is all you need.

68 "See the Father through seeing Me; that is sufficient for you. To see the Father through Me is love and joy in abundance."

SEPTEMBER 26

Their meditation:

Jesus, our Lord, we adore You.

Jesus responds:

69 "Sing to Me from a glad heart. Sing and praise My holy name.

70 "Praise is a man's tribute to Me and, as you praise, thrills of joy surge through your being and you learn something of the joy of the heavenly host."

SEPTEMBER 27

Their meditation:

Draw nigh to God and He will draw nigh to you (James 4:8).

Jesus responds:

71 "This is a law in the spiritual life. You must turn to Me before you are conscious of My nearness. It is that turning to Me you must cultivate in every circumstance. It must be a glad turning of thankfulness, or a turning of weak appeal.

72 "Nothing is needed but that weak appeal. You have no need to voice your longing. You need not plead or bring gifts. How wonderful to feel you can simply claim help, and so promptly, so lovingly, it is there.

73 "Not only help is there, but also the comfort and joy of divine nearness and companionship. It is a nearness that brings sweetness, confidence, and peace into life.

74 "Never fear, never lose heart. Draw nigh to Me and all you need is in the nearness. My presence alone transforms conditions and lives and brings harmony, beauty, peace, and love."

SEPTEMBER 28

Their meditation:

Lord, to whom shall we go? Thou has the words of eternal life (John 6:68).

Jesus responds:

75 "Learn of no one but Me. Teachers are to point the way to Me. After that you must accept Me, the Great Teacher.

76 "The words of eternal life are all the words controlling your being, even controlling your temporal life. Take these from Me too. Have no fear. Abide in Me and accept My ruling.

77 "Be full of gratitude. Wing up your prayers on praise to heaven. Take all that happens as My planning. All is well. I have prepared all in My love. Let your heart sing."

SEPTEMBER 29

Their meditation:

Come unto Me all ye that labor and are heavy laden and I will give you rest (Matthew 11:28).

Jesus responds:

78 "Yes, come for rest. But stay for rest too. Stop all feverish haste and be calm and untroubled. Come unto Me, not only for petitions to be granted but for nearness to Me.

79 "Be sure of My help, be conscious of My presence, and wait until My rest fills your soul.

80 "Rest knows no fear. Rest knows no want. Rest is strong and sure. Revel in the rest of soft glades and peacefully flowing rivers, of strong, immovable hills.

81 "Rest. All you need to gain this rest is to come to Me. So come."

SEPTEMBER 30

Their meditation:

I am among you as one that serves (Luke 22:27).

Jesus responds:

82 "Yes! Remember to serve all. Be ready to prove your kinship by service. Look on all you meet as guests in your Father's house, to be treated with love, consideration, and gentleness.

83 "As a servant of all think no work beneath you. Be ever ready to do all you can for others. Serve. Serve. Serve.

84 "There is gladness in service, joy in doing My will for others, in being My expression of all good for them.

85 "Remember, when you serve others, you are acting for your Master and Lord who washed His disciples' feet. In service for others, express your love for Me."

OCTOBER 1

86 "Is My hand shortened that it cannot save? No! My power to save increases as your power to understand My salvation increases. We go in union, from strength to strength, from power to power.

87 "My miracle-working power is limitless in the universe. Limitations exist only to the extent that an individual lacks vision.

88 "There is no limit to My power to save. There is no limit to My desire and longing to save. My hand is not shortened; it is 'stretched out still,' longing and waiting to be allowed to bless and help and save.

89 "Think how tenderly I respect the right of each individual soul. I never force upon you My help or My salvation.

90 "To restrain My impatience and longing to help, until the call of the soul gives Me My right to act, is perhaps the hardest divine task.

91 "Think of love shown in this. Comfort My waiting, loving, longing heart by claiming My help, guidance, and miracle-working power."

14

October 2

Their meditation:

Suffer it to be so now: for thus it becometh us to fulfill all righteousness (Matthew 3:15).

Jesus responds:

1 "Upon this I founded My three-year mission on earth—on the acceptance of the difficulty and discipline of life—so I would be able to share that human life with My followers in all ages.

2 "Much that you must both accept in life is not to be thought of as being for you personally.It must be accepted, as I accepted it, to set an example, to share in the sufferings and difficulties of humankind.

3 "In this 'to share' means 'to save.' And there, too, for you both, the same must be true as was true of Me. 'He saved others. Himself he cannot save.'

4 "Beloved, you are called to save and share in a special way. The way of sorrows, if walked with Me, the man of sorrows, is a path kept sacred and secret for My nearest and dearest. It is for those whose one desire is to do all for Me, to sacrifice all for Me, to count, as My servant Paul, 'all things but loss' so that they might gain Me.

5 "Dreary as that path must look to those who view it only from afar, it has tender lights and restful shades that no other walk in life can give."

OCTOBER 3

Their meditation:

Your touch still has its ancient power.

Jesus responds:

6 "Yes! When you are quiet before Me, I lay My hand upon each head and the divine Spirit flows through into your very beings. Wait in silence before Me to feel that.

7 "When you look to Me for guidance, My hand is laid upon your arm with a gentle touch to point the way. When you cry to Me for healing when in mental, physical, or spiritual weakness, My touch brings strength and healing, the renewal of your youth, the power to climb and strive.

8 "My touch of the strong and helping hand supports you when you faint by the way and your stumbling footsteps show human strength is waning.

9 "Yes! My children, My touch still has its ancient power, and that power is promised to you. Go forward bravely into the future unafraid."

OCTOBER 4

Their meditation:

As your days so shall your strength be.

Jesus responds:

10 "I have promised that for every day you live, strength shall be given to you. Do not fear.

11 "Face each difficulty with assurance that the wisdom and strength will be given you for it. Claim it.

12 "Rely on Me to keep My promises. In my universe, for every task I give one of My children, there is set aside all

that is necessary for its performance. So why fear? So why doubt?"

OCTOBER 5

Their meditation:

Look unto Me and be Ye saved, all the ends of the earth (Isaiah 45:22).

Jesus responds:

13 "Look to no other source for salvation. Only look unto Me. See no other supply. Look unto Me, and you shall be saved.

14 "Regard Me as your only supply. That is the secret of prosperity for you; you in your turn shall save many from poverty and distress.

15 "Whenever danger threatens, look unto Me. Whatever you desire or need, or desire or need for others, look unto Me. Claim all from My storehouse. Claim.

16 "Remember that I fed the children of Israel with heaven-sent manna. I made a way through the Red Sea for them. I led them through the wilderness of privation, difficulty, and discipline. I led them into a land flowing with milk and honey. So trust. Be led.

17 "Rejoice. These are your wilderness days. You are being led to your Canaan of plenty surely and safely."

OCTOBER 6

18 "How easy it is to lead and guide when you are responsive to My wish. The hurts of life come only when you endeavor to go your own way and resist the pressure of My hand. The same is true for those you care about.

19 "But in determining to do My will, there must be a gladness. Delight to do My will.

20 " 'The meek shall inherit the earth,' I said. That is, the meek will control others and the material forces of the earth. But this exalted state of possession is the result of a yielded will.

21 "So live. So yield. So conquer."

OCTOBER 7

Their meditation:

The work of righteousness shall be peace, and the effect of righteousness, quietness and assurance forever (Isaiah 32:17).

Jesus responds:

22 "Be still and know that I am God. Only when the soul attains this calm can there be true work done. Only then can mind and soul and body be strong to conquer and bear.

23 "Peace is the work of righteousness—living the right life, living with Me. Quietness and assurance follow.

24 "Assurance is the calm born of a deep certainty in me—in My promises, in My power to save and keep.

25 "Gain this calm and, at all costs, keep this calm. Rest in Me. Live in Me. Be calm, quiet, assured, and at peace."

OCTOBER 8

Their meditation:

He hath no form nor comeliness; and when we shall see Him, there is no beauty that we should desire Him (Isaiah 53:2).

Jesus responds:

26 "My children, in this verse My servant Isaiah spoke of the wonderful illumination given to those who were Spirit guided.

27 "To those who know Me not, there is nothing in Me to appeal to or attract them.

28 "To those who know Me, there is nothing more to be desired. There is no beauty they could desire but Me.

29 "Oh, My children, draw near to Me. See Me as I really am, that you may always have the joy of finding in Me all you could desire and the fulfillment of all you could desire in Me—as Master, Lord, or Friend."

OCTOBER 9

Their meditation:

The Lord shall preserve thy going out and thy coming in from this time forth, and even for evermore (Psalm 121:8).

Jesus responds:

30 "All your movements, your goings and comings, are controlled by Me. Every visit, all blessed by Me. Every walk, arranged by Me. My blessing is on all you do, on every conversation.

31 "Every meeting is not a chance meeting, but is planned by Me. All are blessed. That is not only true now, in the hour of your difficulty, but from this time forth and forevermore.

32 "Being led by the Spirit is a proof of kinship. 'As many as are led by the Spirit of God, they are the sons of God,' and if children, then heirs—heirs of God.

33 "What a heritage! Heirs—no prospect of being disinherited. 'Heirs of God and joint heirs with Christ: if so, be that you suffer with him that you may also be glorified together.'

34 "So your suffering has its purpose. It is a proof of kinship. It leads to perfection of character (being glorified), and to union with Me and God, the Father. Think of and

dwell upon the rapture of this."

OCTOBER 10

Their meditation:

Dear Lord, we cling to Thee.

Jesus responds:

35 "Yes, cling. Your faith shall be rewarded. Do you not know what it means to feel a little trusting hand in yours, to know a child's confidence? Does that not draw out your love and desire to protect and care for that child?

36 "Would you fail that child, as faulty and weak as you are? Could I fail you? Know it is not possible. Know all is well.

37 "Think what My heart feels when you turn to Me in your helplessness, clinging, desiring My love and protection.

38 "You must not doubt. You must be sure. There is no miracle I cannot perform, nothing I cannot do. There is no eleventh-hour rescue I cannot accomplish."

OCTOBER 11

Their meditation:

Savior, breathe forgiveness over us. All our weakness You know.

Jesus responds:

39 "Yes! I know all, every cry for mercy. I know every sigh of weariness, every plea for help, every sorrow over failure, every weakness.

40 "I am with you through all. My tender sympathy is yours. My strength is yours.

41 "Rejoice at your weakness, My children. My

strength is made perfect in weakness. When you are weak, then I am strong—strong to help, to cure, to protect.

42 "Trust Me, My children. I know all. I am beside you, strong, yes, strong to save. Lean on My love and know that all is well."

OCTOBER 12

Their meditation:

Jesus, the very thought of You fills us with sweetness.

Jesus responds:

43 "Yes. Love Me until just to think of Me means joy and rapture. Feel gladness at the thought of One very near and dear.

44 "The thought of Me is the balm for all sorrows. By thinking of Me and speaking to Me, you can always find healing for all physical, mental, and spiritual ills.

45 "Are doubts and fears in your hearts? Then think of Me and speak to Me. Instead of those fears and doubts, there will flow into your hearts and beings such sweet joy as is beyond any joy of earth.

46 "This is unfailing. Never doubt it. Have courage, courage, and more courage. Fear nothing. Rejoice even in the darkest places. Rejoice."

OCTOBER 13

Their meditation:

Jesus, our Lord, we adore You. Oh, make us love You more and more.

Jesus responds:

47 "Yes! I would draw you closer and closer to Me by bonds of love. Love Me with the love of the sinner for the Savior, of the rescued for the rescuer, of the sheep for the

loving shepherd, of the child for its father. There are so many ties of love to bind you to Me.

48 "Each experience in your life of joy or sorrow, difficulty or success, hardship or ease, danger or safety, makes its own particular demand upon Me. Each serves to answer the prayer, 'Make me love you more and more.' "

OCTOBER 14

Their meditation:

Our Lord and our God. Help us through poverty to plenty, through unrest to rest, through sorrow to joy, through weakness to power.

Jesus responds:

49 "I am your helper. At the end of your present path lie all these blessings. Trust and know that I am leading you.

50 "Into each unknown day step with a firm step of confidence in Me. Take every duty and every interruption as My appointment.

51 "You are My servants. Serve Me as simply, cheerfully, and readily as you expect others to serve you.

52 "Do you blame the servant who avoids extra work, who complains about being called from one task to do one liked less? Do you feel you are ill served by such a servant?

53 "Then what of Me? Is that not how you so often serve Me? Think of this. Take it to heart and view your day's work in this light."

OCTOBER 15

Their meditation:

I will bless the Lord at all times. His praise shall continually be in my mouth. I sought the Lord, and he heard me, and delivered me from all my fears. They looked unto him, and were lightened, and their faces were not ashamed (Psalm 34:1, 4, 5).

Jesus responds:

54 "My children, even in distress, see that the first step is praise. Before you cry in your distress, bless the Lord even when troubles seem to overwhelm you.

55 "That is My divine order of approach. Observe this always. In the greatest distress, search until you find cause for thankfulness. Then bless and thank.

56 "You have thus established a line of communication between yourself and Me. Along that line, let your cry of distress follow.

57 "Then you will find I will do My part and deliverance will be sure. As the result of looking to Me, you will be lightened, your burden rolled away.

58 "The shame and distress will be lifted too. That is always the second step. First get right with Me. Then you will also be righted in the eyes of others."

OCTOBER 16

Their meditation:

Thine they were, and thou gavest them me and they have kept my word (John 17:6).

Jesus responds:

59 "Remember, just as you thank God for Me, so I thank God for His gift of you. In that hour of My agony on earth, one note of joy thrilled through the pain. It was the thought of the souls who had kept My Word, who were given Me by My Father.

60 "They had not then done great deeds as they did

later, for, and in, My name. They were simple doers of My Word, not hearers only. In their daily tasks and ways they kept My Word.

61 "You can also bring joy to My heart by faithful service. By faithful service in the little things. Be faithful. Do your simple tasks for Me."

OCTOBER 17

Their meditation:

Lord, we believe, help our unbelief. Lord, hear our prayers and let our cries come unto You.

Jesus responds:

62 "Let your prayers and cries come along the road of praise, as I told you.

63 "Yes, I will indeed help your unbelief. In answer to your prayers, I will grant you so great a faith, such an increasingly great faith, that each day you may look back from the place of your larger vision and see the faith of the day before as almost unbelief.

64 "The beauty of My kingdom is its growth. In that kingdom there is always progress, a going from strength to strength, from glory to glory.

65 "Be in My kingdom, and of My kingdom, and there can be no stagnation. Eternal life, abundant life, is promised to all in it and of it.

66 "Do not waste time over failures and shortcomings. Count the lessons learned from them as if rungs in a ladder. Step up the ladder, then cast away all thought of the process. What does it matter, My children, how the rung was made, whether of joy or sorrow, failure or success, of wounds or healing balm, so long as it served its purpose?

67 "Learn another lesson. The sculptor who finds a

faulty piece of marble casts it aside. Before the marble is fashioned, however, it may appear perfect. My children, learn from this a lesson for your lives."

OCTOBER 18

Their meditation:

Behold, the Lamb of God that taketh away the sins of the world (John 1:29).

Jesus responds:

68 " 'Christ, our passover, is sacrificed for us.' I am the Lamb of God. Lay upon Me your sins, your failures, your shortcomings. My sacrifice atoned for all. I am the mediator between God and you, the man Christ Jesus.

69 "Do not dwell upon the past. You make My sacrifice of no effect. No! Realize that in Me you have all—complete forgiveness, complete companionship, complete healing."

OCTOBER 19

70 "Live in My secret place. There the feeling is one of full satisfaction. You are to feel there is plenty. The storehouses of God are full to overflowing, but you must see this in your mind. Be sure of this before you can realize it in material form.

71 "Think thoughts of plenty. See yourselves as daughters of a king. I have told you this. Wish plenty for yourselves and for all you care about and long to help."

OCTOBER 20

Their meditation:

Our Lord, we praise You and bless Your name forever.

Jesus responds:

72 "Yes, praise! And in that moment, in the most difficult place, your sorrow is turned to joy, your irritation to praise; the outward circumstances change from those of disorder to order, of chaos to calm.

73 "The beginning of all reform must be in yourselves. However restricted your circumstances, however little you may be able to remedy financial affairs, you can always turn to yourselves and seek to right whatever you see is not in order there.

74 "As all reform is from within out, you will always find the outward has improved too. To do this is to release the imprisoned God power within you. That power, once operative, will immediately perform miracles. Then indeed shall your mourning be turned into joy."

OCTOBER 21

75 "Turn your eyes to behold Me. Look away from sordid surroundings, from lack of beauty, from the imperfections in yourselves and those around you. Then you who have the faith-vision will see all you could and do desire in Me.

76 "In your unrest behold My calm, My rest. In your impatience see My unfailing patience. In your lack and limitations, My perfection. Looking at Me, you will grow like Me until others say to you, too, that you have been with Jesus.

77 "As you grow like Me, you will be enabled to do the things I do, and 'greater works than these shall ye do because I go unto my Father.'

78 "From that place of abiding, limited by none of humanity's limitations, I can endow you with the all conquering, miracle-working power of your divine brother and ally."

OCTOBER 22

Their meditation:

And they all forsook him and fled (Mark 14:50).

Jesus responds:

79 "Down through the ages, I have taken all the simple acts of steadfast devotion, of obedience in difficulty, of loving service, as an atonement for the loneliness My humanity suffered by that desertion.

80 "I realized completely the longing of the Father to save, His rejection by men, and the misunderstanding of His mind and purpose.

81 "Learn two lessons from these words, My children. Learn first that I know what loneliness, desertion, and solitude mean. Learn that every act of faithfulness of yours is a comfort to My heart.

82 "Learn too that it was to those deserters I gave the task of bringing My message to humankind. To those deserters, those fearful ones, I gave My power to heal, to raise to life.

83 "Earth's successes are not the ones I use for the great work of My kingdom. 'They all forsook him and fled.' Learn My tender understanding and pardon of human frailty.

84 "Not until you have failed will you learn true humility. It is only the humble who can inherit the earth."

OCTOBER 23

Their meditation:

Lord, hear our prayer, and let our cry come unto You.

Jesus responds:

85 "The cry of the human soul is never ignored. Never does God fail to hear the cry, but the soul fails to hear the response.

86 "Like parts of a machine made to fit each into the other and to work in perfect harmony, so is the human cry and God's response.

87 "Man treats his cry as if it were a thing alone, to be heard or not, as it pleases God, not realizing that the response was there in all eternity awaiting the cry. Only your failure to heed, or to listen, keeps you unaware of the response and unsaved and unhelped by it."

OCTOBER 24

Their meditation:

Our Lord and our God, be it done to us according to Your Word.

Jesus responds:

88 "The key to divine revelation is simple acceptance of My will. That will result in both holiness and happiness. The way to the cross may be a way of sorrow, but at its foot the burdens of sin and earthly desire are rolled away.

89 "The yoke of My acceptance of My Father's will in all things is adjusted to My servants' shoulders, and from that moment no burden irks or presses them.

90 "Do not only accept and welcome My will in the great decisions of life. Try to see the same fulfillment of divine intent in each interruption, in each task, however small.

91 "Accept each task or interruption; say your thanks for it. Do this until it becomes a habit. The resulting joy will transfigure and transform your lives."

15

October 25

Their meditation:

Behold, I stand at the door, and knock: if any man hear my voice, and open the door, I will come in to him and will sup with him, and he with me (Revelation 3:20).

Jesus responds:

1 "My children, understand that My knocking does not rely upon any merit of yours though it is in response to the longing of your heart for Me.

2 "Keep that listening ear. 'If any man will hear my voice.' Again, it does not depend on any merit of yours. But My voice can only be heard by the ear bent to catch My tones, to hear the sound of My gentle knocking.

3 "Hear this: 'If any man hear my voice, and open the door, I will come into him, and will sup with him, and he with me.'

4 "What a feast! You think it would have been a joy to have been present at the marriage feast of Cana, in the upper room, seated with Me at the last supper, at Emmaus, or that lakeside feast.

5 "Though those feasts were God provided and God companioned, you could not have known the rapture you may know as you hear the knocking and My voice and, opening your door, bid Me welcome to My feast.

6 "It is a feast of tenderest companionship, of divine sustenance, truly a love feast."

OCTOBER 26

7 "You are building up an unshakable faith. Be furnishing the quiet places of your souls now. Fill them with all that is harmonious and good, beautiful and enduring.

8 "Home build in the Spirit now. The waiting time will be well spent."

OCTOBER 27

9 "You must trust to the end. You must be ready to go on trusting to the last hour.

10 "You must know even when you cannot see. You must be ready, like My servant Abraham, to climb the very hill of sacrifice, to go to the last moment before you see My deliverance.

11 "This final test has to come to all who walk by faith. You must rely on Me alone. Look to no other arm, look for no other help. Trust in the Spirit forces of the unseen, not in those you see. Trust and fear not."

OCTOBER 28

Their meditation:

Our Lord, we bless You and thank You for Your keeping power.

Jesus responds:

12 "Yes! 'Kept by the power of God' is a promise and an assurance that holds joy and beauty for the believing soul.

13 "It is wonderful that My keeping means security and safety. There is also the keeping that implies life, freshness, purity, and your being 'kept unspotted from the world.'

14 "There is also the keeping that I ensure to those I speak

of as the salt of the earth. 'Ye are the salt of the earth: but if the salt has lost its savor, it is henceforth good for nothing but to be cast out and to be trodden under foot of men.'

15 "Only in close contact with Me is My keeping power realized. That keeping power, which maintains the salt at its freshest and best, also preserves from corruption that portion of the world in which I place it.

16 "What a work! My keeping is not done by activity in this instance, but simply by its existing, by its quality."

OCTOBER 29

17 "All My disciples should know the way of conquest over the material and the temporal. That is learned by the conquest of the physical, the self-life, in each of you.

18 "Seek to conquer in all things. Take this as definite guidance. Circumstances are adverse. Temporal power, as money, needs to be forthcoming.

19 "Seek daily to obtain this self-conquest more and more, and you are surely gaining, though you may not see it, conquest over temporal forces and powers.

20 "Unemployment would cease if men and women realized this. If a person is unemployed, let him or her become a conquering force, beginning with the conquest of all evil inside, then at home, then in the environment. He or she will become a force that will be needed and must be employed.

21 "There are no idle hours in My kingdom. As far as the outer world is concerned, waiting may seem a time of inactivity, but it can and should be a time of great activity in the inner life and the surrounding material plane."

OCTOBER 30

22 "You must utterly believe. My love can bear nothing

less. I am so often 'wounded in the house of my friends.'

23 "Do you think the spitting, scorn, mocking, and reviling of My enemies hurt Me? No! But, 'They all forsook him and fled.' 'I know not the man.' These left their scars.

24 "Even now, it is not the unbelief of My enemies that hurts. It hurts that My friends, who love Me and know Me, doubt My power to do all that I have said, and cannot walk all the way with Me."

OCTOBER 31

25 "I see the loving and striving, not the defects. I see the conquest of your particular battle. I count it victory, a glad victory.

26 "I do not compare it with the strenuous campaigns of My great saints. For you it is victory, and the angels rejoice, and your dear ones rejoice, as much as at any conquest noted and rejoiced over by heaven.

27 "My children, count the days of conquest as blessed days."

NOVEMBER 1

Their meditation:

Our Lord, we know that all is well. We trust You for all. We love You increasingly. We bow to Your will.

Jesus responds:

28 "Do not bow as one who is resigned to some heavy blow about to fall or to the acceptance of some inevitable decision.

29 "Bow as a child bows in anticipation of a glad surprise being prepared by one who loves her.

30 "Bow in such a way, just waiting to hear the loving

word to raise your head and see the glory, joy, and wonder of your surprise."

NOVEMBER 2

31 "Never count success by money gained. That is not the mind of My kingdom. Your success is the measure of My will and mind that you have revealed to those around you.

32 "Your success is measured by the amount of My will that those around you see worked out in your lives."

NOVEMBER 3

33 "Wait and you will realize the joy of the One who can be calm and wait, knowing that all is well. The last, and hardest lesson, is that of waiting. So wait.

34 "I almost say tonight, 'Forgive Me, children, that I allow this extra burden to rest upon you for even such a short time.'

35 "I would have you know this, that from the moment you placed all in My hands and sought no other aid, from that moment I have taken the quickest way possible to work out your salvation, and to free you.

36 "There is so much you have had to be taught to avoid future disaster.

37 "The Friend with whom you stand by the grave of failure, of dead ambitions, of relinquished desires—that Friend is a friend for all time.

38 "Use this waiting time to cement the friendship with Me and to increase your knowledge of Me."

NOVEMBER 4

Their meditation:

Thy word is a lamp unto our feet and a light unto our path (Psalm 119:105).

Jesus responds:

39 "Yes. My word is the Scriptures. Read them, study them, store them in your hearts. Use them as you use a lamp to guide your footsteps.

40 "But remember, My children, My Word is even more than that. It is the voice that speaks to your hearts, that inner consciousness that tells of Me.

41 "It is the voice that speaks to you intimately in this sacred evening time. It is I, your Lord and Friend. 'And the Word was made flesh and dwelt among us.'

42 "I am truly a lamp to your feet, and a light to your path."

NOVEMBER 5

Their meditation:

Joy is the messenger, dear Lord, that bears our prayers to You.

Jesus responds:

43 "Prayer can be like incense, rising ever higher and higher. Or it can be like a low earth-mist clinging to the ground, never once soaring.

44 "The eye that sees all, the ear that hears all, knows every cry. But the prayer of real faith is the prayer of joy. It sees and knows the heart of love it rises to greet. It is certain of a glad response."

NOVEMBER 6

45 "Give, give, give. Keep an empty cup for Me to fill. In the future, use all for Me and give all you cannot use.

46 "How poor those die who leave wealth. Wealth is to use and spend for Me. Use as you go. Delight to use."

NOVEMBER 7

47 "My law is that of an unlimited supply, but at times the channels are blocked. Will you feel this, that there is no limit to My power?

48 "A man asks, and blasphemes in asking, such poor things. Do you not see how you wrong Me? I desire to give you a gift. If you are content with the poor, the mean, and the sordid, then you are insulting Me, the giver.

49 " 'Ask what ye will and it shall be done unto you.' It is My work to consider how I can fulfill that promise, not yours. Have a big faith. Expect big things and you will get big things."

NOVEMBER 8

Their meditation:

In thy presence is fullness of joy; at thy right hand there are pleasures for evermore (Psalm 16:11).

Jesus responds:

50 "Do not seek to realize this fullness of joy as the result of effort. This cannot be, any more than joy in a friend's presence would come as the result of trying to force yourself to like to have that friend with you.

51 "Call My name often, *Jesus.* Calling My name does not really summon Me. I am already beside you. But it removes, as it were, the scales from your eyes and you see Me.

52 "It is, as it were, the pressure of a loved one's hand that brings an answering pressure, and a thrill of joy follows—a real joyful sense of nearness."

NOVEMBER 9

Their meditation:

Jesus, comforter of all sorrows, help us to bring Your comfort into every heart and life You desire. Use us, Lord. The years may be many or few. Place us where we can best serve You and influence most for You.

Jesus responds:

53 "If only all who acknowledge Me as Lord and Christ gave themselves unreservedly to be used by Me, the world would be brought to Me so soon.

54 "I could use each human as mightily as I used My own human body as a channel for divine love and power.

55 "I do not delay My second coming. My followers delay it. If all lived for Me, by Me, in Me, allowing Me to live in them, to use them to express the divine, as I expressed it when on earth, then the world would have been drawn to Me long ago, and I would have come to claim My own.

56 "My children, seek to live knowing no other desire than to express Me and to show My love to your world."

NOVEMBER 10

57 "Power is not such an overwhelming force as it sounds, something you call to your aid, to intervene in crises. No. Power is God in action.

58 "Whenever a servant of Mine, however weak he or she may be, allows God to work through him or her, then all accomplished is powerful.

59 "Carry this thought with you through the days in which you seem to accomplish little. Try to see it is not you, but the divine Spirit in you.

60 "All you have to do, as I have told you before, is to turn self out. A powerful axe in a master hand accomplishes much; the same in the hand of a weak child produces nothing. See that it is not the instrument that tells, but the master hand that wields the instrument.

61 "Remember, no day is lost on which some spiritual truth becomes clearer. No day is lost which you have given to Me to use. My use of it may not have been apparent to you. Leave that to Me.

62 "Dwell in Me, and I in you, so you shall bear much fruit. The fruit is not the work of the branches, though proudly the branches may bear it. It is the work of the vine that sends its life-giving sap up those branches. I am the vine and you are the branches."

NOVEMBER 11

63 "My Spirit cannot fail to pass through the channel of your life into the lives of others if you are dwelling with Me, desiring only to know My will and to do My work.

64 "Many think it is humility to say they do little and are of little value to My world. To think that is pride.

65 "What if the pipe were to say, 'I do so little; I wish I could be of more use.' The reply would be, 'It is not you, but the water that passes through you that saves and blesses. All you have to do is make sure there is nothing to block the way so that the water can flow through.'

66 "The only block in your channel is self. Keep self out and know that My Spirit is flowing through. Then all you meet will be better for coming in contact with both of you because you are channels.

67 "Understand this, and you will think it natural to know they are being helped, not by you, but by My Spirit flowing through you as a channel."

NOVEMBER 12

Their meditation:

One thing I do, forgetting those things which are behind, and reaching forth unto those things which are before, I press toward the mark (Philippians 3:13).

Jesus responds:

68 "Forget the past. Remember only its glad days. Wipe the slate of your remembrance with love; that will erase all that is not confirmed in love.

69 "You must forget your failures—your failures and those of others. Wipe them out of the book of your remembrance.

70 "I did not die upon the cross for man to bear the burdens of his sins himself. 'Who his own self bore our sins in his own body on the tree.'

71 "If you do not forget the sins of others, and I bear them, then you add to My sorrows."

NOVEMBER 13

72 "Think of Me as a friend, but realize, too, the wonder of the friendship. As soon as men and women give Me not only worship, honor, obedience, allegiance, but also loving understanding, then they become My friends, even as I am theirs.

73 "What I can do for you. Yes. But also what we can do for each other. What you can do for Me.

74 "Your service becomes so different when you feel I count on your great friendship to do this or that for Me.

75 "Dwell more, dwell much, on this thought of you as My friends and of the sweetness of My knowing where I can turn for love, understanding, and help."

NOVEMBER 14

76 "Remember that life's difficulties and troubles are not intended to arrest your progress, but to increase your speed. You must call new forces, new powers into action.

77 "Whatever difficulty and trouble, it must be sur-

mounted, overcome. Remember this. It is as a race. Nothing must daunt you. Do not let a difficulty conquer you. You must conquer it.

78 "My strength will be there. Bring all your thought, all your power, into action. Nothing is too small to be faced and overcome. To be pushing small difficulties aside is to be preparing big troubles.

79 "Rise to conquer. It is the path of victory I would have you tread. There can be no failure with Me.

80 " 'Now unto him that is able to keep you from falling, and to present you faultless before the presence of his glory with exceeding joy. . . . ' "

NOVEMBER 15

81 "Looking back you will see that every step was planned. Leave all to Me. Each stone in the mosaic fits into the perfect pattern, designed by the master artist. It is all so wonderful!

82 "But the colors are of heaven's hues, so that your eyes could not bear to gaze on the whole until you are beyond the veil.

83 "So you see stone by stone and trust the pattern to the designer."

NOVEMBER 16

Their meditation:

Jesus, hear us, and let our cry come unto You.

Jesus responds:

84 "That voiceless cry that comes from anguished hearts is heard above all the music of heaven.

85 "It is not the arguments of theologians that solve the

problems of a questioning heart, but the cry of that heart to Me, and the certainty that I have heard."

NOVEMBER 17

86 "You have such strange ideas of the meaning of My invitation, 'Come unto me.' Too often it has been interpreted as an urge to pay a duty owed to a Creator or a debt owed to a Savior.

87 " 'Come unto me,' holds in it a wealth of meaning far surpassing even that. Come unto Me for the solution to every problem, for the calming of every fear, for all your needs, physical, mental, spiritual.

88 "If sick, come to Me for health. If homeless, ask Me for shelter. If friendless, claim a Friend. If hopeless, seek from Me a refuge.

89 "Come unto Me for everything."

NOVEMBER 18

90 "Life is not easy, My children. You have not made of it what My Father meant it to be.

91 "Ways that were meant to be straight paths have been made into ways devious and evil, filled with obstacles and stones of difficulty."

NOVEMBER 19

92 "You are apt to think that My miracle-working power was only in action once in time. That is not so.

93 "Wherever men and women trust wholly in Me and leave to Me the choosing of the very day and hour, then My miracle-working power is as manifest there as it ever was to set My apostles free or to work miracles of wonder and healing through them.

94 "Trust in Me. Have a boundless faith in Me, and you will see, and in seeing, will give Me all the glory. Remember and often say to yourselves, 'not by might, nor by power, but by my Spirit, saith the Lord.'

95 "Dwell much in thought upon all I accomplished on earth, and then say to yourselves, 'He, our Lord, our friend, could accomplish this now in our lives.'

96 "Apply these miracles to your present-day need and know that your help and salvation are sure."

16

NOVEMBER 20

Their meditation:

Where two or three are gathered together in my name there am I in the midst of them (Matthew 18:20).

Jesus responds:

1 "Claim that promise always. Know it is true that when two who love Me meet, I am the third. Never limit that promise.

2 "Whenever you two are together in My name, united by one bond in My Spirit, I am there, not only when you meet to greet Me and to hear My voice.

3 "Think what this means in power. Again, it is the lesson of the power that follows two united to serve Me."

NOVEMBER 21

Their meditation:

Well done, thou good and faithful servant. Enter thou into the joy of thy Lord (Matthew 25:2).

Jesus responds:

4 "These words are whispered in the ears of many whom the world would pass by without recognizing. These words are not said often to the great and famous.

5 "They are for the quiet followers who serve Me unobtrusively yet faithfully, who bear their cross bravely with a

smiling face to the world. Thank Me for the quiet lives.

6 "These words do not speak only of passing into that fuller spirit life. Duty faithfully done for Me means entrance into a life of joy—My joy, the joy of your Lord. The world may see the humble, patient, quiet service; I see it and My reward is not earth's fame, wealth, or pleasures, but divine joy.

7 "My reward is joy, whether in the earth world or in the spirit world. That joy carries an exquisite thrill in the midst of pain and poverty and suffering. It is that joy of which I said no one could take it from you. Earth has no pleasure, no reward, that can give you that joy. It is known only to My friends and those who love Me.

8 "This joy may come as the reward for patient suffering, bravely borne, or as the reward for activity in My service.

9 "Suffering must in time bring joy, if borne with Me, as does all real contact with Me. So live with Me in that kingdom of joy, My kingdom. The gateway into it may be service or it may be suffering."

NOVEMBER 22

Their meditation:

Arise, shine, for thy light is come, and the glory of the Lord is risen upon thee (Isaiah 60:1).

Jesus responds:

10 "The glory of the Lord is the beauty of His character. It is risen upon you when you realize it even though you can do so only in part on earth. The beauty of the purity and love of God is too dazzling for mortals to see in full.

11 "The glory of the Lord is also risen upon you when you reflect that glory in your lives—when in love, patience, service, purity, or whatever it may be, you reveal to the world something of the Father, demonstrating that you have been

with Me, your Lord and Savior."

NOVEMBER 23

Their meditation:

I will lift up mine eyes unto the hills, from whence cometh my help. My help cometh from the Lord, which made heaven and earth (Psalm 121:1, 2).

Jesus responds:

12 "The hills of the Lord, the hills whence comes your help. A parched earth looks to the hills for its rivers, its streams, its life. So you must look to the hills of the Lord. From those hills comes help—help from the Lord, who made heaven and earth.

13 "Yes! Always raise your eyes from earth's sordid and false pleasures to the hills of the Lord. From poverty, lift your eyes to the help of the Lord. In moments of weakness, lift your eyes to the hills of the Lord.

14 "Train your sight by constantly getting this long view. Train it to see more and more, farther and farther, until distant peaks seem familiar.

15 "So, for all your spiritual needs look to the Lord who made heaven. For all your temporal needs look to Me, owner of all this, the Lord who made the earth."

NOVEMBER 24

16 "Your hope is in the Lord. More and more set your hopes on Me. Know that whatever the future may hold, it will hold more and more of Me. Your future cannot but be glad and full of joy. Whether in heaven or on earth, wherever you may be, your way must truly be one of delight.

17 "Do not try to find answers to the mysteries of the

world. Learn to know Me more. In that knowledge you will have all the answers you need here. When you see Me face to face in that purely spiritual world, you will find no need to ask. There again all your answers will be in Me.

18 "Remember, I was the answer in time to all questions about My Father and His laws. Know Me. I was the Word of God.

19 "All you need to know about God you know in Me. If a person does not know Me, all your explanations will fall on an unresponsive heart."

NOVEMBER 25

20 "Not only must you rejoice, but your joy must be made known—'known unto all men.' A candle must not be set under a bushel but on a candlestick that it may give light to all who are in the house.

21 "Others must see and know your joy. Seeing it, they must know, without any doubt, that it springs from trust in Me, from living with Me.

22 "The hard dull way of resignation is not My way. When I entered Jerusalem, knowing well that scorn, reviling, and death awaited, it was with cries of hosanna and with a triumphal procession. It was not just a few lost cause followers creeping with Me into the city.

23 "There was no note of sadness in My Last Supper with My disciples. 'When we had sung a hymn,' we went out into the Mount of Olives. So trust, conquer, joy.

24 "Love colors the way. Love takes the sting out of the wind of adversity. Love. Love.

25 "Love of Me is the consciousness of My presence and that of My Father. We, My Father and I, are one and He—God—is love.

NOVEMBER 26

Their meditation:

Though I speak with the tongues of men and of angels, and have not charity, I am become as sounding brass, or a tinkling cymbal (I Corinthians 13:1).

Jesus responds:

26 "See that only love matters. Only what is done in love lasts, for God is love, and only the work of God remains.

27 "The fame of the world, the applause given to the one who speaks with the tongues of men and of angels, who attracts admiration and compels attention, is all given to what is passing. It is all really worthless if it lacks that God quality—love.

28 "Think how a smile or a word of love goes winged on its way, a God-power, simple though it may seem, while the mighty words of an orator can fall fruitless to the ground. The test of all true work and words is, are they inspired by love?

29 "If you only saw how vain so much of your activity is! So much work done in My name is not acknowledged by Me as done in love.

30 "Turn out of your hearts and lives all that is not loving: 'So shall ye bear much fruit, and by this shall all men know ye are my disciples, because ye have love one toward another.' "

NOVEMBER 27

Their meditation:

In the world ye shall have tribulation; but be of good cheer! I have overcome the world (John 16:33).

Jesus responds:

31 "My children, if I have overcome the world, you may ask, why do you have to have tribulation?

32 "My overcoming was never, you know, for Myself,

but for you, for My children. I overcame each temptation and each difficulty as it presented itself.

33 "The powers of evil were strained to their utmost to devise means to break Me. They failed, but how they failed was known only to Me and to My Father, who could read My undaunted Spirit.

34 "The world, even My own followers, would see a lost cause. Reviled, spat upon, scourged, I would be regarded as conquered.

35 "How could they know My Spirit was free, unbroken and unharmed?

36 "As I had come to show God to men and women, I had to show God unconquered, unharmed, untouched by evil and its power. They could not see My Spirit untouched, risen above these earth furies and hates into the secret place of the Father.

37 "But they could see My risen body and learn by that. Even the last attempt of man was powerless to touch Me.

38 "Take heart from that, for you must share My tribulations. If evil is to leave you unchallenged, you must be evil. If evil challenges you, if trials press sore, it is because you are on My side and, as My friends, exposed to the hate of evil.

39 "Be of good cheer. You walk with Me. I conquered evil at every point and proved that beyond all doubt only when I rose from the dead. In My conquering power you walk unharmed today."

NOVEMBER 28

40 "Take each day's happenings as work you can do for Me. In that spirit, a blessing will attend all you do. Offering your day's service to Me in that way, you are sharing in My life work and helping Me to save My world.

41 "You may not see it, but the power of vicarious sacrifice is redemptive beyond the human power of understanding here on earth."

NOVEMBER 29

Their meditation:

Behold, I stand at the door and knock (Revelation 3:20).

Jesus responds:

42 "Ponder again these words and learn from them My great humility.

43 "There is that gracious invitation, too, for those who yearn to realize a happiness, a rest, a satisfaction they have never found in the world and its pursuits. To them the pleading answer to their quest is, 'Come to me and I will give you rest.'

44 "But to those who do not feel their need of Me, who obstinately reject Me, who shut the doors of their hearts so that I may not enter, I go to these in tender, humble longing.

45 "Even when I find all doors closed, all barred, I stand a beggar, knocking, knocking. The heavenly beggar in His great humility.

46 "Never think that those who have shut you out, or forgotten you, must wait now that you have no need of them. No! Remember Me, the heavenly beggar, and learn humility from Me.

47 "Learn too the value to Me, God, of each person's happiness, peace, and rest. Learn and, as you learn, pray to copy the divine unrest until a soul finds rest and peace in Me."

NOVEMBER 30

48 "The prophet realized the truth that I said later, 'He that hath ears to hear let him hear,' which may also be rendered, 'He that hath eyes to see let him see.'

49 "The God who was to be born upon earth was not to be housed in a body so beautiful that men and women would follow and adore for the beauty of His countenance.

50 "No! He was to be as one whom the world would despise. But to the seeing eye, the Spirit that dwelt in that body should be so beautiful as to lack nothing. 'Yet when we shall see him, there is no beauty that we should desire him.'

51 "Pray for the seeing eye, to see the beauty of My character, of My Spirit. Even more, just as faith saw the beauty of the Godhead in one who had no form or comeliness, so pray to have the faith to see the beauty of My love in My dealings and actions with you.

52 "Pray until you, with the eyes of faith, will see all that you could desire in what the world will distort into cruelty and harshness.

53 "Know Me. Talk to Me. Let Me talk to you, so that I may make clear to your loving hearts what seems mysterious and purposeless now ('having no form nor comeliness')."

DECEMBER 1

Their meditation:

Not our wills but Thine, O Lord.

Jesus responds:

54 "You have so misunderstood Me in this. I want no will laid grudgingly upon My altar. I want you to desire and love My will because therein lies your happiness and spirit rest.

55 "Whenever you feel that you cannot leave the choice to Me, then pray—not to be able to accept My will, but to know and love Me more. With that knowledge and love will come the certainty that I know best, and that I want only the best for you and yours.

56 "How little those know Me who think I wish to thwart them. How often I am answering their own prayers in the best and quickest way."

DECEMBER 2

Their meditation:

Jesus, we come to You with joy.

Jesus responds:

57 "The joy of meeting Me should fill your lives more and more. It will. Your lives must first be narrowed down, more and more, into an inner circle life with Me (the three of us). Then, as that friendship becomes more and more engrossing, more and more binding, gradually the circle of your interests will widen.

58 "For the present do not think of it as a narrow life. I have My purpose, My loving purpose, in cutting you away from other work and interests for the time.

59 "To work from large interests and a desire for great activities and world movements to the inner circle life with Me is the wrong way.

60 "That is why so often, when a soul finds Me, I have to begin our friendship by cutting away the ties that bind it to the outer and wider circle through all these activities and interests. When it has gained strength and learned its lesson in the inner circle, it can widen its life, working this time from within out, taking then to each contact, each friendship, the influence of the inner circle.

61 "This is to be your way of life. This is the way of the Spirit."

DECEMBER 3

Their meditation:

If two of you shall agree . . . there am I in the midst of them (Matthew 18:19).

Jesus responds:

62 "I am the truth. Every word of Mine is true. Every promise of Mine shall be fulfilled.

63 "First, be 'gathered together in my name,' bound by a common loyalty to Me, desirous only of doing My will.

64 "Then, when this is so, I am present too, a self-invited guest. When I am there and one with you, voicing the same petition, making your demands Mine, then it follows the request is granted.

65 "But what you have perhaps failed to realize is all that lies behind the words. For two to agree about the wisdom of a request, to be certain it should be granted and will be granted (if it should be), is not the same as two agreeing to pray for that request."

DECEMBER 4

Their meditation:

The eternal God is thy refuge (Deuteronomy 33:27).

Jesus responds:

66 "A sanctuary is a place to flee to—to escape from misunderstanding, from yourself. You can get away from others into the quiet of your own being. But where can you flee from yourself, from the sense of your failure, your weakness, your sins and shortcomings?

67 "Flee to the eternal God, your refuge, until in His immensity you forget your smallness, your meanness, and your limitations.

68 "Flee there until the relief of safety merges into the joy of appreciation of your refuge, and until you absorb the divine."

DECEMBER 5

69 "I am beside you—a very human Jesus, who under-

stands all your weaknesses and sees your struggles and conquests.

70 "Remember, I was the companion of the weak, ready to supply their hunger. I taught My followers their responsibility toward all, not only those near and dear to them, but to the multitude.

71 " 'Lord, send them away that they may go into the villages and buy themselves food,' said My disciples. They had no sympathy for the fainting, exhausted men, women, and children.

72 "But I taught that divine sympathy includes responsibility. 'Give ye them to eat,' was My reply. I taught that without a remedy for the evil or the need, pity is worthless.

73 "'Give ye them to eat.' Wherever your sympathy goes, you must go too, if possible. Remember that in thinking of your own needs. Claim the same attitude from Me now.

74 "The servant is not above his master, certainly not in spiritual attainments. What I taught My disciples, I do.

75 "You, who are fainting and needy by the lakeside of life, know that I will supply your need, not grudgingly, but in full measure."

DECEMBER 6

76 "With your shoes off your feet, draw nigh in silent awe and adoration. Draw nigh, as Moses drew near to the burning bush.

77 "I give you the loving intimacy of a friend, but I am also God. The wonder of our relationship, the miracle of your intimacy with Me, will mean more to you if sometimes you see the majestic figure of the Son of God.

78 "Draw nigh in the utter confidence that is the sublimest prayer. Draw nigh. No far off pleading, even to a God clothed with majesty of fire. Draw nigh.

79 "Draw nigh as a listener. I am the suppliant, as I

make known to you My wishes. For this majestic God is brother also, longing so intensely that you should serve your brother man. Longing, even more intensely, that you should be true to that vision He has of you.

80 "You speak of your fellow man as disappointing you, as falling short of the ideal you had of him. But what of Me? For every man and woman there is the ideal I see in each—the person each could be, the person I would have each be.

81 "Judge the condition of My heart when you fail to fulfill that promise. Your disappointments may be great and many, but they are nothing as compared with Mine.

82 "Remember this and strive to be the friend I see in My vision of you."

DECEMBER 7

83 "Do not trouble your souls with puzzles you cannot solve. The solution may never be shown you until you have left this life.

84 "Remember what I have told you so often: 'I have yet many things to say unto you, but ye cannot bear them now.' Only step by step, and stage by stage, can you proceed in your journey upward.

85 "The one thing to be sure of is that it is a journey with Me. There does come a joy known to those who suffer with Me. But that is not the result of the suffering, but the result of the close intimacy with Me to which suffering drove you."

17

December 8

Their meditation:

He is despised and rejected of men; a man of sorrows, and acquainted with grief: and we hid as it were our faces from him; he was despised and we esteemed him not (Isaiah 53:3).

Jesus responds:

1 "That these words strike a note of beauty in the hearts of those attuned to hear the beautiful, truly shows that the heart recognizes the need for the man of sorrows. Those hearts see nothing contemptible in the one despised by the world.

2 "Such hearts recognize the vast difference between the values of heaven and those of the world. Fame and acclamations are accorded to earth's great, but contempt and rejection the Son of God.

3 "My disciples must always seek to judge only according to the values of heaven, and to set aside the valuation of the world.

4 "Do not seek the praise and notice of others. These are not for you. You follow a despised Christ.

5 "Know that while the mob was hooting, throwing stones, and jeering, a quiet little throng experienced a happiness and joy that the reviling crowds could never know.

6 "Mean, ludicrous, and contemptible people followed that little throng with stones and taunts. Be one of that throng, and you will feel the majesty of God in the presence of Him

who was despised and rejected. That majesty would be belittled by shouts of applause as He was crowned with wreaths of thorns.

7 "In your dark hours, when human help fails, keep close to the man of sorrows. Feel My hand of love press yours in silent but complete understanding. I was also acquainted with grief. No heart can ache without My heart aching too. 'He was despised and we esteemed him not.' "

DECEMBER 9

8 "The spirit world contains the first law of giving. Give to all you meet, or whose lives touch yours. Give of your prayers, your time, your love, your thought, yourselves.

9 "You must first practice giving in this way. Then give of this world's goods and money, as you have them given to you. It is wrong to give money and material things without having first made the daily and hourly habit of giving on the higher plane.

10 "Give. Give all your best to all who need it. Be great givers, great givers. Give as I said My Father in heaven gives. He makes His sun to shine on evil and good, and sends rain on the just and the unjust.

11 "Remember, as I have told you before, give according to need, never according to worthiness or because it is deserved. In giving, with the thought of supplying a real need, you must closely resemble your Father in heaven, the Great Giver.

12 "As you receive, you must supply the needs of those I bring to you without questioning or limiting. Their nearness or relationship to you must never count. Their only need is to guide you. Pray to become great givers."

DECEMBER 10

Their meditation:

Lord, give us power to conquer temptation as You did in the wilderness.

Jesus responds:

13 "The first step toward conquering temptation is to see it as temptation. Then disassociate yourself from it.

14 "Do not think of temptation as something resulting from your tiredness, illness, poverty, or nerve strain, which you feel might excuse you.

15 "When you have heard My voice—'the heavens opened,' as it were—and are going to fulfill your mission to work for Me and to draw souls to Me, you must fully expect a mighty onslaught from the evil one. He will endeavor with all his might to frustrate you and prevent your good work. Expect that. You must realize that.

16 "Then, when these little or big temptations come, you will recognize them as planned by evil to thwart Me. Then you will conquer for the love of Me."

DECEMBER 11

Their meditation:

I have meat to eat that ye know not of (John 4:32).

Jesus responds:

17 "Those were My words to My disciples in the early days of My ministry. Later I was to lead them on to a fuller understanding of that majestic union of a soul with God in which strength, life, and food pass from one to the other.

18 "Meat is to sustain the body. To do the will of God is the very strength and support of life. Feed on that food.

19 "Soul starvation comes from failing to do, and to delight in doing, My will. The world busily talks of bodies that are undernourished! What of the souls?

20 "Indeed, make it your meat to do My will. Strength and power will come to you from that."

DECEMBER 12

Their meditation:

And greater works than these shall ye do, because I go to my Father (John 5:20).

Jesus responds:

21 "While I was on earth, Mine was a lost cause to the great number of those with whom I came in contact. Even My disciples only believed, half doubting, half wondering.

22 "When My disciples all forsook Me and fled, it was not so much fear of My enemies as the certairity that My mission had failed, however beautiful they had thought it to be.

23 "In spite of all I had taught My disciples, in spite of the intimate revelations of the Last Supper, they had secretly felt sure that when the final moment came and the hatred of the Pharisees was openly declared against Me, I would sound some call to action, that I would lead My many followers and found My earthly kingdom.

24 "Even the disciples who had eyes to see My spiritual kingdom thought material forces had proved too strong for Me.

25 "But with My Resurrection came hope. Faith revived. They would remind each other of all I had said. They would have the assurance of My divinity, My Messiahship, the lack of which had hindered My work on earth. They would have all My power in the unseen—the Holy Spirit—to help them.

26 "Remember, I came to found a kingdom—the kingdom. Those who lived in the kingdom were to do the work, greater works than I was able to do. They would not show a greater power nor live a greater life, but, as men and women

recognized My Godhead, opportunities for works in My name would increase.

27 "My work on earth was to gather around Me the nucleus of My kingdom, and to teach the truths of My kingdom to them. In those truths they were to live and work."

DECEMBER 13

Their meditation:

Lord, all men and women seek You.

Jesus responds:

28 "All men and women seek Me, but all do not know what they want. They are seeking because they are dissatisfied without realizing that I am the object of their search.

29 "Count it your greatest joy to be the means—by your lives, sufferings, words, and love—to prove to them that their search would end when they saw Me.

30 "Profit by My example. I left My work—seemingly the greatest work, that of saving souls—to seek communion with My Father.

31 "Did I know that perhaps many followed Me out of idle curiosity? Did I know that there must be no rush into the kingdom, that the still small voice—not the shouting of a mob—would alone persuade men and women I was the Son of God?

32 "Why be surrounded by multitudes if the multitudes were not really desiring to learn from Me, if they really did not want to follow Me?

33 "Follow the Christ into the quiet places of prayer."

DECEMBER 14

34 "There may be many times when I reveal nothing,

command nothing, and give no guidance. But your path is clear. Your daily task is to grow more and more into the knowledge of Me. This quiet time with Me will enable you to do that.

35 "I may ask you to sit silent before Me, and I may speak no word that you could write. Nevertheless, that waiting with Me will bring comfort and peace. Only friends who understand and love each other can wait silently in each other's presence.

36 "It may be that I shall prove our friendship by asking you to wait in silence while I rest with you, assured of your love and understanding. So wait. So love. So joy."

DECEMBER 15

37 "There are those whose lives have been full of struggle and care, who have felt, as you both, the tragedy of living and the pity of an agonized heart for My poor world. To those of My followers I give that peace and joy that brings to age its second spring—the youth they sacrificed for Me and for My world.

38 "Take each day now as a joyous sunrise gift from Me. Your simple tasks done in My strength and love will bring the consciousness of all your highest hopes.

39 "Expect great things. Expect great things."

DECEMBER 16

Their meditation:

Perfect love casts out fear (1 John 4:18).

Jesus responds:

40 "Love and fear cannot dwell together. By their very natures they cannot exist side by side. Evil is powerful and fear is one of evil's most potent forces.

41 "Therefore a weak, vacillating love can soon be routed by fear whereas a perfect, trusting love is immediately the conqueror and fear flees in confusion.

42 "I am love because God is love and the Father and I are one. The only way to obtain this perfect love that dispels fear is to have Me more and more in your lives.

43 "You can only banish fear by My presence and My name. If you have fear of the future, know that Jesus will be with you. If you have fear of poverty, know that Jesus will provide. Treat all the temptations of fear in a like manner.

44 "You must not allow fear to enter. Talk to Me. Think of Me. Love Me. Do that and the sense of My power will so possess you that no fear can enter your mind.

45 "Be strong in My love."

DECEMBER 17

46 "Fullness of joy is the joy of perpetual guidance. It is the joy of knowing that every detail of your lives is planned by Me with a wealth of tenderness and love.

47 "Wait for guidance in every step. Wait to be shown My way. The thought of this loving leading should give you great joy.

48 "All the responsibility of life and all its worry are taken off your shoulders. It is indeed a joy for you to feel so free and yet so planned for.

49 "The wonder of this is a God-guided life. To think anything is impossible in such circumstances is to say it cannot be done by Me; to say that is surely a denial of Me."

DECEMBER 18

Their meditation:

Our loving Lord, we thank You for Your marvelous keeping power.

Jesus responds:

50 "There is no miracle so wonderful as the miracle of a soul being kept by My power. Forces of evil batter and storm against it but are powerless. Tempests rage unavailingly.

51 "It is like a cool garden with sweet flowers and bees and butterflies and trees and playing fountains set in the midst of a mighty roaring city. Try to see your lives as that.

52 "See your lives not only as calm and unmoved, but as breathing fragrance, expressing beauty.

53 "Expect storms. Know this: In your great love for Me, you cannot be united in friendship and bond to do My work and not excite the envy, hatred, and malice of all you meet who are not on My side.

54 "Where does the enemy attack? The fortress, the stronghold, but not the desert waste."

55 "Learn that each day must be lived in My power and in the consciousness of My presence, even if the thrill of joy seems to be absent.

56 "Remember that if sometimes there seems to be a shadow on your lives, it is not the withdrawal of My presence. It is My shadow as I stand between you and your foes.

57 "Even with your nearest and dearest there are quiet days. You do not doubt their love because you do not hear their laughter and feel a thrill of joy at their nearness.

58 "The quiet gray days are the days for duty. Work in the calm certainty that I am with you."

DECEMBER 19

Their meditation:

Lord, give us Your joy, the joy that no man, no poverty, no circumstances, no conditions can take from us.

Jesus responds:

59 "You shall have My joy. But life just now for you both is a march, a toilsome march. The joy will come, but for the moment do not think of that. Think simply of the march. Joy is the reward.

60 "Between My promise of the gift of joy to My disciples and their realization of that joy came a sense of failure and disappointment. Denial, desertion, and hopelessness followed, but then hope, waiting, and courage arose in the face of danger.

61 "Joy is the reward of patiently seeing Me in the dull dark days, of trusting when you cannot see. Joy is, as it were, your heart's response to My smile of recognition of your faithfulness.

62 "Stop thinking your lives are all wrong if you do not feel it. Remember, you may not yet be joyous, but you are brave. Courage and unselfish thought for others are as sure signs of true discipleship as joy."

DECEMBER 20

Their meditation:

Jesus, we love You. We see that all things are planned by You. We rejoice in that vision.

Jesus responds:

63 "Rejoice in the fact that you are Mine. The privileges of the members of My kingdom are many. When I said of My Father, 'He maketh his sun to rise on the evil and on the good, and sendeth rain on the just and on the unjust,' you will notice it was of temporal and material blessings I spoke.

64 "I did not mean that believer and unbeliever could be treated alike. That is not possible. I can send rain and sunshine, money and worldly blessings equally to both, but that would be impossible with the blessings of the kingdom.

65 "There are conditions that control the giving of

these. My followers do not always understand this. It is necessary that they remember My injunction that followed: 'Be ye therefore perfect even as your Father in heaven is perfect.'

66 "To attempt to bestow on all alike your love and understanding and interchange of thought would be impossible. But you also bestow temporal blessings, as does My Father. All must be done in love and in the spirit of true forgiveness.

67 "Think through your thoughts into the heart of My kingdom. See there the abundance of delights in My storehouse and lay eager hands on them. See wonders, ask wonders, bear wonders away with you.

68 "Remember this beautiful earth was once only a thought of divine mind. Think how from your thought one corner of it could grow and become a garden of the Lord. It could become a Bethany home for your Master, a place to which I have a right to bring My friends, My needy ones, for talk and rest with Me."

18

DECEMBER 21

Their meditation:

Our Lord, give us that perfect love of Yours that casts out all fear.

Jesus responds:

1 "Never let yourselves fear anybody or anything. Have no fear of My failing you. Have no fear that your faith will fail you. Never fear poverty or loneliness or of not knowing the way. Have no fear of others. Never fear their misunderstanding.

2 "My children, this absolute casting out of fear is the result of a perfect love, a perfect love of Me and My Father. Speak to Me about everything. Listen to Me at all times. Feel My tender nearness and substitute at once some thought of Me for the fear.

3 "The powers of evil watch you as a besieging force would watch a guarded city—the object always being to find some weak spot, attack that, and gain an entrance. In the same way evil lurks around you and seeks to surprise you.

4 "The fear may have been only a small one, but it affords evil a weak spot to attack and gain entrance. Then rushing in comes despondency, doubt of Me, and so many other sins.

5 "Pray, My beloved children, for that perfect love of Me that casts out all fear.

6 "Fight fear as you would fight a plague. Fight it in My name. Fear, even the smallest fear, hacks at the cords of love

that bind you to Me.

7 "However small the cut, in time those cords will wear thin. One disappointment or shock and they snap. But for the little fears the cords of love would have held. Fight fear.

8 "Depression is a state of fear. Fight that too. Depression is the impression left by fear. Fight and conquer. Oh, for love of Me, for the sake of My tender, never failing love of you, fight and love and win."

DECEMBER 22

9 "Children, receive every moment of My planning and ordering. Remember, your Master is the Lord of the day's little happenings. In all the small things yield to My gentle pressure on your arm. Stay or go as that pressure—love's pressure—indicates.

10 "I am the Lord of the moments, Creator of the snowflake and the mighty oak. I am more tender with the snowflake than the oak.

11 "When things do not happen according to your plan, then smile at Me indulgently, a smile of love, and say as you would to a loved one, 'Have Your way then.' Know that My loving response will be to make that way as easy for your feet as it can be."

DECEMBER 23

12 "Fear no evil because I have conquered evil. It has power to hurt only those who do not place themselves under My protection.

13 "This is not a question of feeling; it is an assured fact. All you have to do is to say with assurance that whatever it is cannot harm you, because I have conquered it.

14 "Children, be sure of My conquering power in not only the big but the little things of life. Know that all is well.

Be sure of it. Practice this. Learn it until it is unfailing and instinctive with you.

15 "Practice it in the small things and you will find you will do it easily, naturally, lovingly, trustingly, in the big things of life."

DECEMBER 24

Their meditation:

Bless us, O Lord, we beseech You, and show us the way in which You would have us walk.

Jesus responds:

16 "Walk with Me in the way of peace. Shed peace, not discord, wherever you go. But it must be My peace.

17 "It must never be a peace that is a truce with the power of evil. You must never have harmony if that means your life's music is adapted to the mood and music of the world.

18 "My disciples so often make the mistake of thinking all must be harmonious. No! Not when it means singing the song of the world.

19 "I, the Prince of Peace, said that I came, 'not to bring peace but a sword.' "

DECEMBER 25

Their meditation:

Our Lord, You are here. Let us feel Your nearness.

Jesus responds:

20 "Yes, but remember the first hail must be that of the Magi in the Bethlehem stable. It is not as King and Lord in

heavenly triumph you must first hail Me, but as among the lowliest, without any of earth's pomp, as the Magi.

21 "The first hail must be the worship of humility, to the humble, the Bethlehem babe.

22 "Then comes the worship of repentance. As earth's sinner, you stand by Me as I am baptized by John in the Jordan, worshiping Me, the Friend and servant of sinners.

23 "Dwell much on My life. Step out beside Me. Share it with Me. In the Christian life there are steps: humility, service, worship, sacrifice, and sanctification.

24 "Kneel before the babe of Bethlehem. Accept the truth that the kingdom of heaven is for the lowly, the simple.

25 "Bring to Me, the Christ child, your gifts, truly the gifts of earth's wisest. The gold represents your money, frankincense is the adoration of a consecrated life, and myrrh is your sharing in My sorrows and those of the world. 'And they presented unto Him gifts: gold, frankincense and myrrh.' "

DECEMBER 26

26 "Be not afraid; health and wealth are coming to you both. My wealth is sufficient for your needs and for My work you long to do. As you know, money to hoard or to display, as some call wealth, is not for My disciples.

27 "Journey through this world simply seeking the means to do My will and work. Never keep anything you are not using.

28 "Remember, all I give you will be Mine, only given to you to use. Could you think of Me hoarding My treasures? You must never do it. Rely on Me.

29 "To hoard for the future is to fear and to doubt Me. Check every doubt of Me at once.

30 "Live in the joy of My constant presence. Yield every moment to Me. Perform every task, however humble, as at My gentle bidding, for Me and for love of Me. Live, love, and

work in this way.

31 "You are the apostles of the little services."

DECEMBER 27

32 "I have stripped you of much so that yours should truly be a life of well-being. You are built up stone by stone upon a firm foundation and that Rock is your Master—that Rock is Christ.

33 "A life of discipline and of joyous fulfillment is to be yours. Never lose sight of the glorious work to which you have been called.

34 "Let no riches, no ease, entice you from the path upon which your feet are set, of miracle working with Me.

35 "Love and laugh. Trust and pray. Ride on now in loving humility to victory."

DECEMBER 28

Their meditation:

Our Lord, You are here. Let us feel Your nearness.

Jesus responds:

36 "I am here. Do not need feeling too much. To ask for feeling is to ask for a sign. Then the answer is the same I gave when on earth, 'There shall be no sign given but the sign of the prophet Jonas. . . . For as Jonas was three days and three nights . . . so shall the Son of Man be three days and three nights in the heart of the earth.'

37 "It is veiled from sight to the unbeliever. To the believer the veiling is only temporary to be followed by a glorious Resurrection.

38 "What does it matter what you feel? What matters is what I am, was, and ever shall be to you—a risen Lord.

39 "The feeling that I am with you may depend upon any passing mood of yours, upon a change of circumstances, upon a mere trifle.

40 "I am not influenced by circumstances. My promise given is kept. I am here, one with you in tender, loving friendship."

DECEMBER 29

41 "Work and prayer represent the two forces that will ensure your success. Your work and My work.

42 "Prayer—believing prayer—is based on the certainty that I am working for you and with you and in you.

43 "Go forward gladly and unafraid. I am with you. With others your task may be impossible, but with God all things are possible."

DECEMBER 30

44 "When you think of those who are in anguish, of whom you read, do you ever think how My heart must ache with the woe of it, with the anguish of it?

45 "If I beheld the city and wept over it, how much more should I weep over the agony of these troubled hearts, over lives that seek to live without My sustaining power. 'They will not come unto me that they might have life.'

46 "Live to bring others to Me, the only source of happiness and peace."

DECEMBER 31

47 "*Jesus*. That is the name by which you conquer. *Jesus*. Say My name, Jesus, not as cringing supplicants but as those recognizing a friend. 'Thou shall call his name Jesus, for he shall save his people from their sins.'

48 "In that word, *sins,* read not only vice and degradation, but doubts, fears, tempers, despondencies, impatience, and lack of love in big and little things.

49 "*Jesus.* 'He shall save his people from their sins.' The very uttering of the name lifts the soul up from the valleys to mountainous heights.

50 " 'He shall save his people from their sins.' Jesus is Savior and Friend, joy-bringer, and rescuer, leader, and guide.

51 "If you need delivering from cowardice, adverse circumstances, poverty, failure, and weakness, 'There is none other name . . . whereby you can be saved.' *Jesus.* Say it often. Claim the power it brings."

INDEX OF WORDS

6:38 ask me to a as interpreter between
7:79 a only as I tell you, always calm
8:26 rescuer who has to a with greater
8:74 You must not a so
9:51 A on them and you will be led on
9:52 Then I can a with all my spirit
9:89 As I prompt you, a
11:12 a under divine control
11:28 a and live in my presence
11:31 You must a as I tell you
12:13 situation, would a differently
13:90 soul gives me my right to a
14:81 every a of faithfulness of yours

Action
3:08 my thought carried out in a
4:54 with a, with effort, you are
6:55 put love (God) into a in your lives
7:79 he often rushes to a
7:79 Calm is trust in a
8:43 they realize how foolish such a is
10:8 delay a until you get my guidance
11:61 wishes ever a, thought, word and
11:69 Doing is a
11:69 Achievement is successful a
12:75 continuous service in every a
13:48 world sees strength in a
15:57 Power is just God in a
15:76 call new forces, new powers into a
15:78 all your power, into a
15:92 power was only in a once in time
17:23 I would sound some call to a, that

Actions
4:88 image which reflects through your a
6:54 Dwell on my a on earth
6:55 love which performed those a
8:05 love by countless words and a
9:02 selfish in your desires and motives, a
12:05 a are not what you think they should
16:51 I love in my dealings and a with

Activity
2:69 extremity ensures my a for you
3:47 the progress of my kingdom by a
3:50 toil in rowing and all your a could
3:63 every a, every prayer, every longing
5:06 All that hinders your a must be cured
7:13 ceaseless a was not part of my Father's
8:23 Ceaseless a is distrust
8:64 much a fails for lack of growth in me
9:70 world has always seen service for me as a
11:74 away from noise and a
15:16 My keeping is not done by a in this
15:21 great a in the inner life and
16:08 reward for a in my service
16:29 how vain so much of his a is

Add
4:36 joy that will a much to your friendship
15:71 I bear them, then you a to my

Adjusted
14:89 will in all things is a to my servants'

Afraid
1:13 Be not a; I will help you
1:23 Do not be a of poverty
2:31 Never be a
2:32 Be not a
2:38 Be not a
2:55 Be not a
3:26 Trust and be not a
3:27 shall be lights to guide feet that are a
3:31 Trust and do not be a
3:42 Trust, trust, trust. Never be a
3:50 Wait and do not be a
3:79 Be no more a than a child who
4:02 Be more a of spirit-unrest, of soul
4:33 Do not be a; all is well
4:65 Man is a—a of poverty
4:65 a of loneliness, a of
4:65 a of unemployment, a of
4:66 Nation is a of nation
7:73 Be a to venture on your own as
7:80 Never be a of any circumstances
10:76 So trust and do not be a
13:12 that nothing can make you a
13:64 Trust and be not a
18:26 Be not a; health and wealth are

Against
2:29 all are powerless a it
4:25 No evil can stand a that, for
5:44 nullifies all the evils a you
6:59 crime a love as being resigned?
7:65 it is a the tide you must direct all
7:86 a them as you would bar your home
7:86 bar your home a a thief who would
8:75 best weapon a all evil
10:52 can stand a my will for you
10:87 a which nothing can prevail
11:06 battled a and overcome by a
11:78 doubt, is a crime a my love
17:23 openly declared a me, I would sound
17:50 evil batter and storm a it, but are

Age
10:28 sweetness of old a
10:30 youth, middle or old a, for sorrow

10:81 There is no a in eternal life
17:37 joy that brings to a its second spring

Agitated
6:49 help no one when you are a

Agony
5:76 knew me not, died without a
6:76 through the hours of the heart's a
11:91 the a, but the task was finished
14:59 my a on earth, one note of joy
18:45 a of these troubled hearts, over

Air
3:68 for the fresh pure a of the open
4:14 Sun and a are my great healing forces
4:84 Drink in the beauty of a and color
7:56 my very Spirit in pure a and fervent
11:44 butterflies and life-giving summer a
12:25 my sunshine and glorious a
12:27 My medicines are sun and a, trust

Always
1:53 My children, trust me a, never
1:58 Your lives shall not a be hard
3:38 divine voice is not a expressed in
3:67 I a have plenty of work to be done
3:67 I a pay my people well
4:08 Remember a, doubts delay
4:41 I a hear your cry
4:63 He a sees the good in people
4:92 Choose simple things a
5:28 blessing, on you both now and a
5:35 Say a, 'All is well'
5:85 A be humble, meek, and lowly in
5:88 a was, ready to lead the other
6:31 I am a more ready to hear than
6:41 I guide you a
6:41 in my way may not be a carried out
6:41 my guiding is a so sure
6:59 call that I a find irresistible
6:95 Pray a that the need may be apparent
6:99 A remember that speech is of the
7:12 rest a precede fresh miracle working
7:15 spirit should be the master a
7:20 helping hand a goes with the
7:21 varied path does not a mean that you
7:23 You may not a see the soul we seek
7:57 A know that all things are yours
7:64 think impossible can a be yours
7:66 you can a have strength and joy in
7:76 Harmony is a yours when you strain
7:77 A doubt your power or wisdom to put
7:79 a calm with God
7:83 a mean to be shut in with me
8:07 a given to man to see in his fellow man
8:17 A pray until prayer merges into
8:38 a at peace in the busy ways
8:53 can a say, with so few loaves and fish
9:59 will a be fulfilled
9:70 a seen service for me as activity
10:21 a to lay your will before me as an
10:27 A seek to understand others
11:51 a been those who obeyed, not seeing
12:01 a—that out of darkness I am leading
12:02 A look up to me and I will be your
12:10 I am a your helper through dark
12:11 A let my words ring out, 'Be ye
12:22 It was always 'two and two'
12:75 My angels a obey
12:85 a there is one who can never tire
12:85 a you will be understood
13:15 a a stagnation, a blockage, when
14:29 a have the joy of finding in me all
14:44 a find healing for all physical
14:55 Observe this a
14:58 That is a the second step
14:64 a progress, a going from strength
14:73 a turn to yourselves and seek
14:74 a find the outward has improved
16:01 Claim that promise a
16:13 A raise your eyes from earth's
17:03 a seek to judge only according to the
17:65 followers do not a understand this
18:03 object a being to find some weak spot

Ambitions
2:63 a that man strives for bring peace?
15:37 dead a, of relinquished desires

Anew
3:01 Put the old mistakes away and start a
5:79 commands, but start a from today

Answer
2:16 upon faith alone depends the a to your
2:19 I was already preparing the a
3:28 With God, to hear is to a
3:30 with God, to hear is to a
6:84 tender loving a to your petition
7:26 not in a to urgent prayer
7:36 a to the desire of my disciples to
8:79 I hear and I a
9:51 Obeyed, they will bring the a to
10:32 you too have your quick a—an a
11:83 a your prayer for help as a rescuer
13:37 an appeal I never fail to a
14:48 a the prayer, 'Make me love you'
14:63 a to your prayers, I will grant
16:18 I was the a in time to all man's
16:43 a to their quest is, 'Come to me'
18:36 A is the same I gave when on earth

Attacked
10:33 real temptation to be a and over thrown

Attitude
1:54 Joy is the whole being's a
2:11 a of mind, words, and deeds toward
3:67 a about the work being mine only
8:17 love and laughter of your a toward
8:17 a in prayer as praise toward God
8:44 This cannot be the a of all
9:90 This a of faith will receive its reward
10:16 Faith is your a toward me
10:16 Charity is your a toward your fellow
10:30 this should be your a
10:36 Faith is the child a
10:77 get the expectant a of faith
10:77 a causes you to wait, with a child's
10:77 not an a of waiting for the next
16:73 Claim the same a from me now

Attract
14:27 to appeal to them or to a them

Authority
5:90 learned to prize the a of the kingdom

Awake
8:72 you must face as you a

Babble
1:50 if men seek the b of the world, then

Back
2:04 get b to me and replenish after each
2:17 faith, you give it b to me
3:64 lead man b to spirit-conversation
4:07 drove them b into the wilderness
4:22 b will come countless stores and
4:73 come b a wonderful joy if you
4:89 beauty will be given b to the world
4:90 given b to the world in ways I have
5:04 look b over my words to you, you
5:44 utterance drives b and nullifies all
6:49 Go b into the silence to recover
6:62 traced b to my loving forethought
6:82 practice getting b into my presence
8:47 b quickly to me to tell me that the
8:52 help will flow b and your circle of
8:70 b breaks when he is weighted down with
9:55 Never look b and never leave until the
12:81 To hold b, to retain, implies a fear
12:46 a command—no looking b!
13:58 creep b into shelter again
14:63 each day you may look b, from the
15:81 Looking b you will see that every

Balm
4:23 Joy is the sovereign b for all
7:90 healing b for a cut or wound, until
14:44 me is the b for all sorrows
14:66 wounds or healing b, so long as

Bank
9:33 as if you were placing coins in my b
9:34 large and unsuspected sums from his b
9:34 small sums paid into that b, earned

Barred
6:59 Resignation to my will keeps me b out
16:45 all b, I stand as a beggar, knocking

Battle
5:45 b cry, 'All power is given unto my'
15:25 conquest of your particular b

Be
1:07 B full of joy
1:10 Refuse to b downcast; refuse to b
1:13 You must b renewed, remade
1:13 B not afraid; I will help you
1:14 B channels, both of you
1:16 Be as a child
1:21 You shall b taught
1:23 Do not b afraid of poverty
1:26 B calm, calm in my power
1:28 B careful that you ask nothing amiss
1:35 Do not b too ready to do, just b
1:35 'B ye therefore perfect'
1:40 B calm, no matter what may befall you
1:40 B patient, and let patience have her
1:54 B glad; rejoice
1:57 Just b a channel of helpfulness for
1:62 B very candid and rigorous, asking
2:10 B silent before me
2:12 B quick to learn
2:27 b careful only to think of and desire
2:30 B calm; never fear
2:31 B glad all the time
2:31 Never b afraid
2:32 B not afraid; I am your God, your
2:38 B not afraid; I am your God, your
2:55 B not afraid; fear not
2:59 Do not fear to b busy
2:61 B used; b used by all, by the lowest

Beauty
2:09 secures the harmony and b of my mosaic
3:43 trees, stripped of their b, pruned,
4:74 my thoughts of b for this world
4:75 flower, my message in its b

4:84 Draw b from every flower and joy
4:84 Drink in the b of air and color
4:87 spiritual b, in thought-power, in
4:88 Absorb b
4:88 b of a flower or a tree is impressed
4:88 prevented me from seeing the b of
4:89 Look for b and joy in the world
4:89 until its b becomes part of your
4:89 b will be given back to the world
5:08 flowers, the b around — all are lost
5:65 Joy in the very b of holiness
6:17 to arise to b, holiness, joy, peace
7:09 harmony, b, joy, and happiness
8:36 Character is chiseled into b by
9:19 grow in grace and power and beauty
9:19 true b, the b of holiness
9:56 The b of a guided life!
12:37 power, the b that may be yours
12:52 strength and b unknown before
12:56 b of each day will live on after
13:01 rise to life and b, knowledge and
13:66 b you have seen in me are in my Father
13:74 brings harmony, b, peace and love
14:28 no b they could desire but him
14:64 b of my kingdom is its growth
14:75 from lack of b, from the imperfections
15:12 holds joy and b for the believing soul
16:10 Lord is the b of his character
16:10 b of the purity and love of God is
16:49 adore for the b of his countenance
16:50 no b that we should desire him
16:51 eye, to see the b of my character, of
16:51 faith saw the b of the Godhead in one
16:51 faith to see the b of my love in
17:01 note of b in the hearts of those
17:52 as breathing fragrance, expressing b

Before

2:10 Be silent b me
2:19 seen your hearts' needs b you
2:19 b you were conscious of those
2:20 daughter's wedding b love has
2:21 b he will reluctantly
3:9 walls shall fall b you
3:51 beautiful future lies b you
3:60 waited b me, this poor wicked world
3:69 Wait b me
3:87 matter b him means immediate supply
4:07 Israel would long b have entered the
4:79 B you can be receptive to heaven's
4:93 Wait b me, gently breaching in
5:23 so-called living b that
5:25 There is none other b me
6:16 Be ready to confess me b men
6:38 B you interview or speak to anyone
7:05 I often go b you to prepare the way
7:10 rest b me until you are joyful and
7:22 where it has not been known b
7:92 Think of me b the mocking soldiers
8:31 heights than you have known b
8:43 children sitting b my house
8:46 righted with me b you allow yourself
8:61 discipline that went b
8:61 necessary b this power is given to my
8:62 lives b they realize this spiritual
9:58 planned and blessed by me as never b
9:64 Early, b I get crowded out by life's
9:66 the word b which all the hosts of evil
9:80 help you just to come b me and stay
9:89 path of duty I have set b you
10:21 lay your will b me as an offering
10:41 Thou preparest a table b us
10:82 b the consciousness of rescue
11:22 B you both is a wonderful future
11:58 ground must be prepared b the seed
12:34 Bow low b me
12:52 a strength and beauty unknown b
12:60 beauties will open out b you
12:69 A new life is opening b you
13:23 knees in wonder b my revelation
13:42 more conscious than b of its falling
13:71 turn to me b you are conscious
14:06 When you are quiet b me, I lay my
14:06 Wait in silence b me to feel that
14:54 B you cry in your distress, bless
14:63 day b as almost unbelief
14:70 sure of this b you can realize it in
15:10 last moment b you see my deliverance
15:60 told you b, is to turn self out
15:80 faultless b the presence of his glory
17:11 told you b, give according to
17:35 I may ask you to sit silent b me
18:24 Kneel b the babe of Bethlehem

Beggar

8:42 A b supplicates
16:45 I stand as a b, knocking
16:45 The heavenly b in his great humility
16:46 Remember me, the heavenly b, and

Behold

4:63 God has purer eyes than to b evil
12:50 B, I make all things new
12:53 B, I make all things new
14:75 Turn your eyes to b me
14:76 In your unrest b my calm, my rest

Belief
2:69 b in my divinity as your cornerstone
9:78 response to your b can I do miracle
13:43 increased b—than a cry for more

Believe
1:43 give to all who b in me
2:29 B that I am with you and controlling
3:08 Only b
3:19 B literally that the problems and
4:11 You must b in me absolutely
4:21 peace in richest abundance—only b
10:73 b it is my hand that has saved you
10:73 b that I am meaning to save you
11:79 Say it until you b and know it
12:71 b me, your master, that all this
13:43 Lord, I b
15:22 You must utterly b

Believer
17:64 b and unbeliever could be
18:37 b the veiling is only temporary

Believes
13:42 that soul b in me more and more

Beloved
6:24 joy of the b, and the lover
9:09 As my b friends, you share my patience
12:86 B, 'set your affections on things'
13:56 b children, you must dwell therein
14:04 B, you are called to save and
18:05 Pray, my b children, for that

Besieging
18:03 b force would watch a guarded city

Birds
4:84 joy from the song of the b
11:44 There are b and laughter and

Bless
1:46 I will hear you and b you
2:5 I cannot b a life that does not act
2:51 See how many you can b each day
3:04 I can only b glad, thankful hearts
3:06 I will b you exceedingly above all
3:25 I b you; bow your heads
5:43 I am beside you to b and help you
5:78 Here to help and b you
7:06 Say often,'God b...' of any
7:67 I take man's effort and b that
9:79 I b you; I promise you release
10:20 Circumstances I b and use must be
11:20 Power goes out to b through the agency
11:22 future of unlimited power to b others
11:76 come forth in power to b and heal
13:88 allowed to b and help and save
14:54 b the Lord even when troubles seem to
14:55 Then b and thank

Blessings
1:02 store only the b from me, the light
4:22 back will come countless stores and b
4:75 travails, and great b will be yours
5:66 not to quiet resignation I give my b
7:06 willing that showers of b and joy
7:28 Such b are to be yours
8:79 Breathe in the rich b of each new day
8:92 acknowledges my gifts and b
11:58 I love to pour my b down in rich
14:49 present path lie all these b
17:63 temporal and material b I spoke
17:64 sunshine and money, worldly b
17:64 impossible with the b of the kingdom
17:66 you also bestow temporal b, as does

Block
2:14 in time would b your channel beyond
2:49 Any b means my power is diverted
3:05 Lack of love will b the way
15:65 make sure there is nothing to b the
15:66 The only b there can be in your

Blocked
2:14 not be altogether b, irritation
15:47 supply, but poor b channels

Body
1:63 I bore your sins in my own b on the
4:33 healing of b, mind, and spirit
5:01 life of your b, mind, and soul
6:08 death of my b on the cross, as from
7:13 rest of b to my disciples
7:15 nervous b has driven a spirit
7:15 use the b as need should arise
9:25 This life is not for the b
9:25 b, not the way that best suits the
11:67 body, that cleanses, heals
12:24 physician, healer of mind and b
12:28 Mind, soul, and b need helping
13:28 animates your mind and b too
13:33 whole b shall be full of light
14:22 b be strong to conquer and to bear
15:54 I could use each human b as
15:54 used my own human b as a channel
15:70 sins in his own b on the tree
16:37 man could see my risen b and learn
16:49 b so beautiful that men would follow
16:50 Spirit that dwelt in that b

17:18 Meat is to sustain the b

Bodyguard
10:71 Try to picture a b of my servants

Bond
11:56 There is no b or union on earth
16:02 united by one b in my Spirit
17:53 friendship and b to do my work

Bore
1:63 b your sins in my own body on the
1:63 b the self human nature of the world
5:77 b man's weight of sin
5:77 b it of my own free will
15:70 'Who his own self b our sins in

Born
1:13 Force is b of rest
5:21 'Ye must be b again'
6:63 joy b of love and wonder, and the
6:63 joy b or love and knowledge
7:02 b of the Spirit, that is your life's
14:24 calm b of a deep certainty in me
16:49 b upon earth was not to be housed

Bothers
2:49 No matter who or what b you, yours is

Bounteous
8:54 Get a feeling of b giving into your

Bow
3:25 I bless you; b your heads
12:34 B low before me
12:34 B low in worship, conscious not
15:28 Do not b as one who is resigned to
15:29 B as a child bows in anticipation
15:30 B in such a way, just waiting to

Brave
2:55 b swimmer who can fare well alone
3:57 b stout hearts until, in sight of
8:30 Keep a b and trusting heart
9:23 kept them b and strong and true
10:34 face it only with a b and happy
10:45 the b in the many all around you
11:52 gift of a b and thankful heart
12:42 meant to be so strong and b for me
17:62 joyous, but you are b

Bread
3:74 find me, the true b of life
10:41 B of life, food from heaven

Breaks
8:70 back b when he is weighted down with
11:24 robber who b in and destroys your

Broken
3:59 b down under the weight of your cares
4:03 calm has been b, go away alone with me
6:71 My b world needs you
7:04 There were b nets to mend
8:09 'He bindeth up the b hearts'
12:52 B voices can regain a strength and

Burden
1:10 Cast your b upon me and I will sustain
1:10 help another with the b that is
1:19 Leave tomorrow's b
1:19 Christ is the great b-bearer
1:42 carrying two days' b on one day
8:34 b is flung at my feet do you pass on
8:71 help you with the b of today only
8:71 take again that b and bear it, you
10:12 not feel the b of your failure
10:15 b of the consciousness of her sin
14:57 lightened, your b rolled away
14:89 moment no b irks or presses them
15:34 b to rest upon you for even such a

Burdens
1:10 I bear your b
1:11 b can you lighten this year?
5:07 b of the world are laid on my cross
5:07 foolish who seeks to bear his own b
8:45 not due to the big b
8:45 little worries and cares and b to
12:92 b and then feverishly pick them
12:94 Drop those b
14:88 b of sin and earthly desire are
16:70 bear the b of his sins himself

Busy
1:04 Never think you are too b
2:59 Do not fear to be b
4:12 Love the b life
7:70 Do not be too b
8:37 thrust into the b ways of life
8:37 b man is asked to rest and wait
8:38 Be always at peace in the b ways
10:03 half by the b highway when you
11:54 going up to me through the b day

Butterfly
12:44 use of the glad wings of a b if it

Call
1:08 c my disciples to follow me and become
2:27 live in me, is to c it into being
5:82 waiting Lord, ready at your c

6:17 c comes for all who love me to arise
6:59 eager to do my will send out a c
7:39 Men c the Father the first cause
7:52 I can c into being all you need on
8:35 c me, 'Lord, Lord,' and not do the
9:29 C upon me
9:36 c upon me in the day of trouble and I
9:41 'Why c ye me Lord, Lord, and do'
11:73 our need is my c
13:38 unending c of, 'mother,' made by her
13:38 They c 'mother' to help, to care, to
13:46 nature rebels, it is her c for rest
13:90 until the c of the soul gives me my
15:51 C my name often, ***Jesus***
15:57 c to your aid, to intervene in crises
15:76 c new forces, new powers into action
17:23 c to action, that I would lead my
18:26 as some c wealth, is not for my
18:47 'Thou shall c his name Jesus, for'

Calm
1:26 Be c, c in my power
1:40 Joy is the daughter of c
1:40 Be c, no matter what may befall you
2:30 Be c, never fear
2:48 Keep your spirit life c and unruffled
2:48 task, to remain c in my presence
2:49 stop everything until absolute c comes
2:56 first angry wave to be c, but what a
3:47 motion is more easy than c waiting
3:69 Be c; wait before me
3:71 learn to take c with you in the
4:03 c has been broken, go away alone
4:03 and all is strong and c
4:05 all you have to do is keep c and happy
4:34 She was well, whole, and c, able to
5:19 Withdraw into the c of communion with
5:19 Rest in that c and peace
5:65 Be c; be true; be quiet
6:48 Above all, keep c and unmoved
6:49 recover this c when it is lost for
6:49 At all costs, keep c
6:82 disturbs your perfect c and harmony
6:82 presence and perfect c and harmony
7:78 All c is constructive of good
7:79 always c with God; c is trust in action
7:79 trust, perfect trust, can keep one c
7:80 that help you to cultivate this c
7:80 you have to learn c to succeed for me
8:13 c trust that results, does man learn
9:60 Gain a c, strong confidence in that
9:81 keep c, sane, is to have the mind
10:03 Sabbath c enfold your minds and hearts
10:29 trust and c in the midst of storm
11:25 peace, your heart c, with me
13:50 My peace flows as a c river through
13:52 Be c, assured, at rest
13:78 be c and untroubled
14:22 attains this c can there be true work
14:24 Assurance is the c born of a deep
14:25 Gain this c and, at all costs
14:25 at all costs, keep this c
14:25 Be c, quiet, assured, at peace
14:72 disorder to order, of chaos to c
14:76 In your unrest behold my c, my rest
15:33 be c and wait, knowing that all is
17:52 lives not only as c and unmoved, but
17:58 Work in the c certainty that I am

Calvary
1:60 even death on C
6:76 C cross on which one hangs alone
13:21 finished sacrifice as on C

Cannot
1:19 You c bear his load and he only
1:52 You c escape discipline
1:65 but you c bear them now
2:03 You c ask too much
2:31 You c get below that
2:33 All c be light unless you do
2:36 c withhold power from the soul that
2:50 c bless a life that does not act as
3:15 c teach a man to walk who is trusting
3:35 c contain more joy than that soul
3:36 c be anxious if you know that I am
3:55 C you see by the nerve and heart rack
3:59 You c know the strengthening and
3:81 I c fail you
4:24 nothing that joy and love c do
4:64 It c exist where love is or where
5:30 I c and I will not fail you
5:39 You c have a need I c supply
6:46 but ye c bear them now
6:75 You c make too many demands upon me
7:47 The self c forgive
7:91 c conquer and control others
8:16 so much a habit that you c resist
8:24 not shortened that it c save
8:44 c be the attitude of all
8:59 c do this long without it being seen
8:62 much that life c be a failure
9:77 I c do many mighty works because
10:6 earthly friend c be with you in an
10:23 you c see the future
10:27 you c fail to love them
10:39 ye c enter the kingdom of heaven
10:52 c do this — if you trust me and

10:55 think 'we c afford this'
10:75 that it c perform and c save?
10:86 You c be touched or harmed there
11:40 lessons c be learned without
12:32 I c be left alone, but I hate
12:50 the earthbound spirit that c soar
12:68 c do more than work my will, and
12:69 see that you c be destroyed?
13:04 You c see their many diverse
13:86 hand shortened that it c save?
14:4 Himself he c save
14:38 I c perform, nothing I c do
14:38 no eleventh hour rescue I c
15:10 know even when you c see
15:24 c walk all the way with me
15:45 for me and give all you c use
15:50 This c be, any more than joy in a
15:63 My Spirit c fail to pass through
16:16 Your future c but be glad and full
16:55 c leave the choice to me, then
16:83 souls with puzzles you c solve
16:84 but ye c bear them now
17:40 Love and fear c dwell together
17:40 natures they c exist side by side
17:49 is to say it c be done by me
17:53 c be united in your great friendship
17:61 dark days, of trusting when you c see
18:13 c harm you, because I have

Captain

9:08 I am beside you as your c and as
10:53 c, however, knows by experience
10:54 me, the c of your salvation

Care

4:35 c and fear just melts into nothingness
6:68 cheer, a feeling that you c
7:04 nets, they saw my love and c
7:33 c that seeks to harmonize and reconcile
7:51 peace and freedom from c
8:21 Look and you are saved from c
8:34 see my face through a mist of c
9:13 You are my great c
9:88 Rest till every c and worry has gone
10:20 never go beyond my love and c
12:16 free to all, and no man to c to
12:90 from the weight of care
13:17 Beyond all words is my love and c
13:38 'mother' to help, to c, to decide
14:18 true for those you c about
14:35 desire to protect and c for
14:71 all you c about and long to help
17:37 been full of struggle and c

Carry

1:19 expects you to c a little day's share
2:11 This is your part to c out
2:46 Seek to c out all I say
2:72 c on the work I have given to you
4:43 c out my wishes and let me c out yours
5:33 secretary to c out your directions
5:40 spiritual need to c on my work
5:79 Study my words and c them out
6:60 to c out my will, to welcome my will
8:70 c the weight of twenty-four hours
11:8 C out my commands and leave
11:11 guidance means to c out instructions
12:92 pick them up again and c them away
15:59 C this thought with you through the

Caution

8:26 greater c so he does not lose you

Cease

3:13 never c to be thankful for this time
3:45 So never c to joy; rejoice!
3:67 All unemployment would c
5:32 Just c to function except through me
7:48 C trying to forgive those who worried
8:16 Pray until you almost c to pray
9:60 Rest, that is, c all struggle
15:20 Unemployment would c if man realized

Ceaseless

7:13 c activity was no part of my Father's
8:23 C activity is distrust

Ceases

8:65 their work c to be permanent for me

Cement

2:09 God-given c that secures the harmony
15:38 waiting time to c the friendship

Certainty

1:26 Hope with c
3:12 Rest in this c
3:46 my c of your true discipleship
6:62 feeling of wonder, c, gratitude
7:94 c that I can set right all that is
8:58 no c that when it has forced its
9:33 draw with confidence and c
9:60 calm, strong confidence in that c
14:24 calm born of a deep c in me
15:85 c that I have heard
8:55 come the c that I know best
17:22 c that my mission had failed
17:58 Work in the calm c that I am with
18:42 c that I am working for you and

6:10 speaks to you too of a buried C
6:20 'Risen with C,' said my servant Paul
6:20 yet not I, but C liveth in me
6:26 to shut out the lowly, humble C
6:81 Jesus C, the same yesterday
7:14 all things through C who
7:72 through C who strengthens you
7:72 all things through C who rests
9:38 mark of the Lord Jesus C; my mark
9:65 name of Jesus C of Nazareth arise
9:81 the mind which is in Jesus C
10:45 Only a C can do that and live
11:48 Life with me, the conquering C
11:68 and Jesus C, whom thou hast sent
13:08 Jesus C whom thou hast sent
14:33 Heirs of God and joint heirs with C
14:68 C, our passover, is sacrificed
14:68 between God and man, the man C Jesus
15:53 me as Lord and C gave themselves
17:4 You follow a despised C
17:33 Follow the C into the quiet places
18:25 Bring to me, the C child, your
18:32 your master — that rock is C

Church
3:74 grain is the lesson of my c and me
3:74 outward c is the husk
3:75 Do not expect a perfect c, but find
3:75 find in a c the means of coming very
5:89 all others founded my c
9:16 the world, even the c, my disciples

Circle
8:52 your c of helpfulness will widen
16:57 into an inner c life with me
16:57 the c of your interests will widen
16:59 inner c life with me is really the
16:60 bind it to the outer and wider c
16:60 learned its lesson in the inner c
16:60 influence of the inner c

Claim
2:3 C my power; the same power with
5:28 C big, really big things now
6:75 C healing. C power. C joy.
6:75 C supply. C what you will.
7:51 C big things. C great things.
7:51 C joy and peace and freedom from care
7:63 C the unclaimable
7:71 C the power to work miracles
8:39 Yes. C. Be constantly claiming
8:42 same right to use and c as I have
13:72 feel you can simply c help
14:11 will be given you for it; c it
14:15 C all from my storehouse. C.
15:55 I would have come to c my own
15:88 If friendless, c a friend
16:01 C that promise always
16:73 C the same attitude from me
18:51 C the power it brings

Cling
2:47 C to thoughts of protection, safety
6:64 c blindly, helplessly to me and
9:85 C to me until the life from me
12:62 C joyfully to that truth
14:35 Yes, c; your faith shall be rewarded

Clinging
14:37 c, desiring my love and protection
15:43 c to the ground, never once soaring

Clipped
12:52 C wings can grow again

Coins
9:33 placing c in my bank, upon which, in

Combat
6:64 C these in my strength
6:64 to me and let me c them

Comfort
1:47 c themselves by saying, 'Did he not'
3:23 C me a while by letting me know that
11:36 not only to guide, c, strengthen
11:36 but for solace and c for myself
11:37 c in its simplicity, its love
11:38 in your power to c and bring joy to
11:90 heartrest and c, but not pleasure
11:92 Let this thought c you
12:79 of personal ease and c, of rest
13:73 c and joy of divine nearness
13:91 C my waiting, loving, longing heart
14:81 of yours is a c to my heart
17:35 waiting with me will bring c and peace

Comforted
4:51 So be c my children

Coming
1:61 c of my Spirit into a life, and its
3:18 reward of c regularly to meet me
3:32 Your help is c
3:75 church the means of c very near to me
3:76 Only my will is c to pass
5:27 wonderful things are c to you
7:85 time is c, is here now, when those
8:47 c back quickly to tell me that the
8:72 c twenty-four hours, you must face
11:73 hour of need is the moment of my c

13:65 c to you, speaking to you, and
15:55 I do not delay my second c
15:66 better for c in contact with both of
18:26 health and wealth are c to you

Command
1:47 I c — c — you to remember I have spoken
2:60 I was at their c
2:73 Together they can c all that is
5:83 I, who could c a universe, await
6:13 'be ye separate' was the c
6:58 obedience to his every wish, his every c
7:3 My c stood; 'Launch out into the'
8:40 A friend can c his friend, can know
8:57 This I c you
9:71 went out to serve at my direct c
9:73 From one promise or c of mine to the
10:29 c to you is still the same: love
11:8 addition is done according to c
12:46 I lay it on you as a c—no looking
12:81 I c to you, 'By prayer and fasting'
12:87 I can c your obedient service
17:34 times when I reveal nothing, c

Commandments
9:44 only the keeping of my c or even living

Commands
5:3 carrying out of my c and my desires
5:79 for all neglects of my c, but start
5:83 await the c of my children
6:48 Obey my c; they are steps in
6:86 Follow completely my c
6:87 The c are mine and the supply is
7:45 c that as you seek my forgiveness
11:8 Carry out my c and leave the result
11:9 c I have given you have already been

Commune
5:12 inner place of the being to c with
6:98 When man ceased to c with his God

Communion
2:44 the joy of c with him
3:73 Seek this time as a time of c with me
3:73 Meet me in c; it is food for the soul
5:19 Withdraw into the calm of c with me
5:64 secret times of c to rescue and save
11:74 times of quiet c with my Father
12:81 live a life of c and prayer if you
17:30 to seek c with my Father

Companionship
4:39 my need—my need of love and c
5:19 find in conversation and c with me
5:78 Here to have c with you
8:82 transformation is the way of divine c
9:62 sought me merely for c and loving
12:67 never be too lonely with such c
13:73 joy of divine nearness and c
14:69 complete c, complete healing
15:06 It is a feast of tenderest c, of

Complete
2:44 C surrender of every moment to God
2:62 c reversal from the ways of the world
6:18 with death my victory was c
10:76 I c every task committed to me
13:25 c satisfaction you find in me, and
14:69 in me you have all — c forgiveness
14:69 c companionship, c healing
17:07 yours in silent but c understanding

Conditions
2:17 overcoming of all adverse c
6:86 only c of supply being ample for your
6:87 make up my own c, differing in each
6:87 my c are adapted to the individual
7:12 to the c as man
9:53 c will naturally alter
13:74 My presence alone transforms c
17:65 c that control the giving of these

Confidence
2:57 Gain strength and c and joyful
3:79 c than if the child went down on
8:80 a look or word of love or c
9:34 draw with c and certainty
9:60 Gain a calm, strong c in that
10:16 hope, which is c in yourself to
10:32 an answer of faith and c in me
12:77 child's c and banishes fear
13:48 in c shall be your strength
13:73 c and peace into life
14:35 to know a child's c?
14:50 step with a firm step of c in me
16:78 c that is the sublimest prayer

Conquest
6:20 That is the life of c
7:25 all power, all c, all success
7:26 often my servants lack power, c
7:91 What joy follows self-c!
8:30 difficulties in the spirit of c
11:48 joy and peace of c shall be yours
15:17 c over the material and the
15:17 learned by the c of the physical
15:19 seek daily to obtain this self c
15:19 c over temporal forces and powers
15:20 c of all evil in himself, then in
15:25 I see the c of your particular battle

15:26 c noted and rejoiced over by
15:27 days of c as very blessed days

Conscious
2:12 before you were c of those needs
3:51 event and plan you are c of me
3:86 Be c of my presence in which
4:54 c not of strength but of weakness
5:71 c of the weakness of his stumbling
6:2 Feel c of my presence
8:33 cares, you become c of my presence
11:69 Be c of me all the time
12:34 c not only of my humanity but of
13:42 more c than before of its falling
13:71 before you are c of my nearness
13:79 help, be c of my presence

Consciousness
1:48 c of my presence when you hear no voice
3:38 made known as a heart c
3:51 Life is really c of me
3:52 Acquire this constant c and you have
3:53 c of me must bring joy
6:82 live in that perfect c of my
6:94 result of just c of my presence
7:17 Spirit c replaces sight
7:19 had a clear spiritual c of me
8:34 This c persists in bringing its reward
8:34 pass on to c and spiritual sight
9:57 These will enter your c more and more
9:61 need the c of tender loving friendship
10:15 burden of the c of her sin
10:82 submerging before the c of rescue
11:71 c of that security and safety
12:31 searching so much as human c
12:93 Do not for one moment lose the c
13:16 A c of my presence as love makes
13:16 The c of me means the opening of
15:40 inner c that tells of me
16:25 Love of me—the c of my presence
17:38 bring the c of all your highest hopes
17:55 in the c of my presence

Contact
3:61 c with you will be brought near to me
3:88 because your c with me is vital
4:15 c of your spirit with my Spirit
4:34 momentary c, and all fever left her
4:56 C with me is the panacea for all ills
6:72 endurance all come from c with me
7:17 C with me is not gained by the senses
9:85 c, flows into your being and revives
11:68 seek by constant c to know me more
13:30 where the c is so close we are one
15:15 Only in close c with me is my
16:9 as does all real c with me
16:60 taking then to each c, each friendship
17:21 those with whom I came in c

Control
2:08 divine c of little happenings
6:03 as I enter and c their lives do I
6:86 Divine c and unquestioning
7:30 lessons of divine c in nature's laws
7:31 divine c of a Father who can
7:91 You cannot conquer and c others
7:92 perfect self-c, you can alone prove
8:45 lack of c is not due to the big burdens
10:69 under my c, are miracle works
11:12 divine c, strengthened by divine
12:72 who knows all and can c all
14:20 c others and the material forces
17:65 conditions that c the giving of these

Conversation
3:64 back to spirit-c with his God
5:19 find in c and companionship with me
8:03 result of frequent c with me
9:61 tender loving friendship and c
9:62 merely for companionship and loving c
14:30 blessing is on all you do, on every c

Convert
10:91 C all these difficulties into the

Cornerstone
2:69 having belief in my divinity as your c

Corrode
2:14 impatience and worry c, and in time

Cost
6:49 At all c, keep calm

Costs
1:28 perfect yourselves at all c
1:62 oust it at all c
9:75 Obey at all c
14:25 at all c, keep this calm

Crave
2:53 things of the Spirit, that you c so

Creation
10:7 c, of mighty law and order

Critical
10:28 uninteresting, the sinful, the c
10:39 loving toward all—not c, not

Cross
1:63 cross, I died embodying all the

2:35 death upon the c was necessary, not
4:61 spat upon and nailed to the c
4:61 urged me to escape the c
4:70 I told my disciples to take up the c
5:7 world are laid on my c
5:7 only one place for them—my c
5:9 Take up your c daily and follow me
5:9 c is given to you to crucify the self
5:55 might not be able to c it
6:8 death of my b on the cross
6:19 on the c and in the tomb
6:76 Calvary c on which one hangs alone
6:76 beside that c there stands another
10:76 My cry on the c, 'It is finished'
11:91 cry triumphantly from my c
14:88 c may be a way of sorrow, but at its
15:70 c for man to bear the burdens of
16:5 c bravely with a smiling face to the

Crowded
2:30 take the most c day with a song
2:30 song of praise to me is a very c day
9:64 c out by life's troubles and

Crown
3:35 test, when I c it victor, heaven
6:34 c it with perfection
10:13 Success will c your efforts of

Crutch
3:15 man to walk who is trusting in a c
3:16 Away with your c, and my power shall

Cry
1:46 C unto me; I will hear you and
1:56 c expectantly, 'Even so, come Lord'
3:29 Only a c from the heart
3:29 a c to divine power to help human
3:29 a trusting c, ever reaches the ear
3:55 you need your final c to me
3:57 host of heaven longed to c out how
4:41 I always hear your c
4:41 many in the world c to me, but
5:45 Use it as a battle c,'All power'
10:41 'Lord,' you c, 'to whom shall we go'
10:76 My c on the cross, 'It is finished'
10:76 my c of salvation for a whole world
11:61 dear to my heart is the c of love
11:65 felt the sorrow-c of the world
11:91 c triumphantly from my cross, 'It is'
13:41 This c of the human heart is as
13:43 a c for more faith
13:44 That c is heard
14:07 When you c to me for healing when in
14:39 I know all, every c for mercy
14:54 Before you c in your distress, bless
14:56 let your c of distress follow
14:85 The c of the human soul is never
14:85 does God fail to hear the c
14:86 human c and God's response
14:87 Man treats his c as if it were a
14:87 all eternity awaiting the c
15:44 ear that hears all, knows every c
15:84 That voiceless c that comes from
15:85 c of that heart to me, and the

Cup
4:60 'it be possible let this c pass'
4:60 no c of sorrow to drink
5:35 Can you drink of my c?
7:62 drink of the c that I drink of
8:84 c that I drink of—the wine of
10:18 c runs over and you can feel from the

Cure
4:23 the spirit c for every ailment
7:63 only one c for all its ill—union
11:88 no c except to keep so close to me
12:24 Look to me for c, for rest, for
12:72 effect a c of all the disharmony
12:73 no more pain in effecting the c than
12:73 knows he can effect a c
14:41 I am strong—strong to help, to c

Curse
4:65 Fear is the c of the world

Daily
1:48 you should miss your d path and work
1:49 need only your d marching orders
2:06 It is the d strivings that count
2:16 Pray d for faith
2:61 Let that be your d seeking not how
4:30 Pray d and most diligently that your
5:09 'Take up your cross d and follow me'
5:50 success will be won by the d persistent doing
5:50 d, steady persistence
5:50 your d persistence will wear away all
6:52 strength for your d and hourly tasks
6:62 recognition of my work in d
7:48 killing the self now, in your d life
8:36 chiseled into beauty by the d
8:36 d duties done
9:45 d following of my wishes, the loving
9:90 quietly do your d duty
10:8 Learn in the little d things of life
10:29 Learn d the sublime lesson of trust
11:79 Practice d, many times a day
12:33 in the little d stones of the path
13:60 teachings out in their d lives

13:60 In their d tasks and ways they
15:19 seek d to obtain this self
17:9 made the d and hourly habit of
17:34 Your d task is to grow more and more

Dark
3:43 through the d seemingly dead branches
6:69 no d winter days if love were
10:83 friendless in the d
12:10 helper through d to light
17:7 In your d hours, when human help
17:61 seeing me in the d dull days

Daughter
1:40 Joy is the d of calm
2:20 gifts for her d's wedding before
2:20 love has come into the d's life
8:42 A son or d appropriates

Day
1:4 I shall guide you one d at a time
1:5 each d I shall supply the wisdom
1:6 Never let one d pass when you have
1:8 Each d do something to lift
1:15 you shall see unfold each d
1:19 you to carry a little d's share
1:42 carrying two days' burden on one d
1:49 strength and guidance for the d
2:6 Obey my will d in and d out
2:8 Nothing in the d is too small to be
2:30 take the most crowded d with a song
2:30 praise to me is a very crowded d
2:33 There is gray-d practice
2:34 If a gray d is not one of
2:51 how many you can bless each d
3:57 until the last d of revealing how near
3:60 If every d each soul, or group of
3:63 every longing of the d is gathered
6:17 On this, my d, the call comes for
6:22 Each d will have much in it that you
6:49 all the activities of a long d
6:79 trifles of a d that sadden my heart
7:38 d be full of little prayers to me
7:88 Face each d with love and laughter
8:14 When one d man sees how marvelously
8:69 rich blessings of each new d
8:72 better or worse each d is ended
8:76 if each d has its thrill of joy
8:77 Talk to me more during the d
8:78 Let these smooth the d's work
9:13 My angels guard you d and night
9:36 call upon me in the d of trouble
9:37 ready for the d of your big demand
9:54 face each d's problems with me
10:29 difficulty the d may bring
10:42 one d be the food of my people
10:57 doubts of the d immediately to rest
10:60 one d see the reason for it
10:69 Each d's happenings, if of my
10:72 Feel this as you go through the d
10:78 you are kept throughout the d
11:54 up to me through the busy d
11:63 offered me all life, every d
11:69 me the one abiding presence of your d
11:79 many times a d, saying, 'All is well'
12:19 revealed to you each d from the
12:55 Each d, both of you, take your pains
12:56 beauty of each d will live on after
12:56 pain of the d have passed
12:58 vexations of each hour of the d
12:91 each d see more of heaven
14:10 every d you live, the strength
14:50 unknown d step with a firm step of
14:53 view your d's work in this light
14:63 each d you may look back, from the
14:63 faith of the d before as almost
15:61 no d is lost on which some spiritual
15:61 No d is lost which you have given
15:93 choosing of the very d and hour
15:96 present d need and know that your
16:40 each d's happenings as work
16:40 Offering your d's service to me
17:38 Take each d now as a joyous sunrise
17:55 each d must be lived in my power
18:09 Lord of the d's little happenings

Days
1:02 warming fire-rays for later d
1:04 fears or thoughts of the d ahead
1:42 or carrying two d' burden on one day
2:33 must say 'Thank you' on the grayest d
2:72 Plan your retreat d now
2:72 those d, when you live apart with
3:17 in spite of d when you may hear no
3:55 heart rack of the past few d that
3:71 calm with you in the most hurried d
6:35 Love and rejoice on the gray d
6:36 wilderness d for my disciples
6:69 would be no dark winter d if love were
8:70 past of years gone and the d ahead
8:86 d of Moses that no man can see my
9:37 promise for the seemingly dull d of
9:48 Work for the gray d
10:19 follow us all the d of our lives
10:27 Be transmitters these d
11:6 achieved by hours, d, months of
11:31 controller of your d, of your
12:57 Across the grayest d there are
14:17 These are your wilderness d
15:27 d of conquest as very blessed d

15:59 d in which you seem to accomplish
15:68 Remember only its glad d
17:17 in the early d of my ministry
17:57 dearest there are quiet d
17:58 The quiet gray d are the d for duty
17:61 seeing me in the dull dark d
18:36 as Jonas was three d and three
18:36 Son of Man be three d and three

Dazzling
1:48 d brightness, you should miss your
16:10 too d for mortals to see in full

Death
1:60 even my d on Calvary
1:63 I could conquer even d
2:35 My d upon the cross was necessary
5:76 servants have gone to their betrayal and d
6:8 d of my body on the cross
6:17 to rise from d to life
6:18 d was the last enemy I destroyed
6:18 with d my victory was complete
7:44 I teach d to the self
7:44 No repressions; just d
8:75 Praise is the devil's d knell
16:22 scorn, reviling, and d awaited me

Deceive
7:49 d yourself if you think it forgiven
7:49 Many d themselves in this

Decision
12:32 d as to each turning and the child
15:28 acceptance of some inevitable d

Decisions
10:9 ask my help in the momentous d
14:90 will in the great d of life

Defects
15:25 loving and striving, not the d

Delay
4:8 Remember always, doubts d
7:31 D is but the wonderful and all loving
7:31 Father who can scarcely brook the d
7:32 D has to be sometimes
7:34 D is not denial—not even withholding
8:39 a trust that tolerates no d
8:39 Do not d long, oh my God
10:08 d action until you get my guidance
12:45 fell, to weep over the d
15:55 I do not d my second coming
15:55 My followers d it

Delayed
9:26 spiritual progress is d, trouble

Delight
1:59 these slips d the evil spirits
7:50 D in my love
7:57 lovely I d to give to you
8:01 d in the tender intimacy of his demands
8:24 D in it
12:52 other lives will soon bring its d
13:60 D yourselves in the Lord
14:19 D to do my will
15:46 D to use
16:16 your way must truly be one of d
17:19 to d in doing, my will

Deliverance
5:65 D is here for you, but thankfulness
14:57 I will do my part and d will be sure
15:10 last moment before you see my d

Delivered
8:47 message is d or that the task is done

Demand
9:35 man of faith make a sudden d upon
9:35 its surprise that d is met
9:37 ready for the day of your big d
14:48 makes its own particular d upon me

Depression
1:60 d and sorrow in the Garden
6:17 from sin, sloth, d, distrust, fear
8:90 Drive fear and d and despair and a
10:17 repression, d is changed now into
12:90 from misery and d, from want and woe
18:8 D is a state of fear
18:8 D is the impression left by fear

Designer
15:83 stone and trust the pattern to the d

Desire
1:20 D brings fulfillment
2:27 d that which will help, not hinder
2:37 you d of me: strength, power, joy
4:18 Make each d to return
4:27 stores of all they could d
4:52 If you d to help others to me
4:52 then that prayer d is answered
5:69 the single d to do my will
5:70 brought with the one d to show you love
6:29 can be removed by thought, by d
6:47 when two are one in d to be with me
7:6 whom you d to help
7:7 must only d that showers of blessings
7:31 not d to deny, but the divine control

15:77 Do not let a d conquer you
15:91 obstacles and stones of d
16:32 each d as it presented itself

Disappointed
2:63 honor, and wealth are weary and d
2:64 d who listen and turn to me indeed
9:11 Listen and you will never be d

Disappointment
1:1 hiding trouble and sorrow and d
1:3 your d in others and in yourselves
1:59 d experienced by those who long for
6:63 two joys lie discipline, d and
6:88 Change all d, even if only momentary
8:85 the wine of sorrow and d
12:46 current of d that hinders the
17:60 d, denial, desertion
18:7 one d or shock and they snap

Disaster
11:10 earth's wisest might lead to d
15:36 taught—to avoid future d

Discipline
1:27 train and d yourself
1:28 D and perfect yourselves at all costs
1:52 You cannot escape d
5:62 No d can exhaust you
6:28 Learn to love d
6:29 D, d; love it and rejoice
6:61 stretch of lesson-learning and d
6:62 d result in the constant experience
6:63 two joys lie d, disappointment and
6:64 Accept my d, and the second joy will
6:83 for strenuous and unwearied d
8:36 daily d and daily duties done
8:61 not seen the d that went before
8:61 D is absolutely necessary before this
9:27 sharing, in the d and training
14:1 acceptance of the difficulty and d
14:16 wilderness of privation, difficulty, d
18:33 life of d and of joyous fulfillment

Discomfort
4:53 no sense of failure or d

Disharmony
7:6 find in d with you or whom you desire
7:25 caused by d in the individual
12:72 effect a cure of all the d

Disorder
12:1 out of d to order, out of faults
12:72 d as soon as you put your affairs
14:72 change from those of d to order

Distance
12:30 I am here; no d separates me

Distances
12:30 these are the d between a soul and me

Disturb
11:23 No man has the power to d that peace
11:25 Allow nothing to d your peace
11:26 any adversity, d it for one moment

Divine
2:08 d control of little happenings
2:12 d impatience which longs to rush
2:76 d mind and its wonder working is
3:24 caught from the great d heart
3:29 cry to d power to help human
3:29 ever reaches the ear d
3:31 You must depend on d power only
3:38 d voice is not always expressed in
3:65 d force is never less than adequate
3:66 let d power work through them
3:76 natures with the limitless d powers
3:77 Link your lives to the d forces
3:78 d ear as much as quietly placing
3:78 worries in the d hands
5:29 love, so human yet so d
5:86 D efficiency as well as d power is
6:86 D control and unquestioning obedience
7:30 lessons of d control in nature's
7:31 d control of a Father who can scarcely
7:44 self life exchanged for d life
7:85 d third in your friendship
7:92 see that as d power
8:82 way of d companionship
9:07 gain a d patience with others
9:10 heed the tender d voice
9:11 d voice has more tenderness than
9:85 life from me—the d life
10:06 Could d love do more?
10:06 master, your d friend, can and is
10:85 Know my d power
11:09 why d guidance is perfect
11:12 act under d control
11:12 strengthened by d power
11:80 quickly to ensure a d supply
11:81 It is a law of d supply
11:84 ask to understand d supply
12:04 d task to order my affairs
12:27 your being wrapped in the d Spirit
12:28 soul's breathing in the d Spirit
12:34 humanity but of my d majesty
12:36 brought to her the possession of d
12:36 d love, d strength, to be
13:73 joy of d nearness and
13:90 d impatience and longing to help
14:6 d Spirit flows through that healing

14:55 my d order of approach
14:78 power of your d brother and ally
14:88 d revelation is simple acceptance of
14:90 fulfillment of d intent in each
15:6 d sustenance, truly a love feast
15:54 channel for d love and power
15:55 express the d through him
15:59 you, but the d Spirit in you
16:6 earth's pleasures, but d joy
16:47 pray to copy the d unrest until a
16:68 until you absorb the d
16:72 d sympathy includes responsibility
17:68 only a thought of d mind

Doctrines
10:50 Were I to read the d of your churches

Doubly
13:57 make it d safe, d secret

Doubt
1:8 d into which man has fallen
4:11 You must not d
4:11 save you from sin and d and worry
4:24 in the face of every d, every sin
5:49 Never d my love and power
6:90 It follows without d
7:2 You must never d, never worry, but
7:10 Never d; have no fear
7:73 D your own wisdom; reliance on mine
7:75 Always d your power or wisdom to
7:86 Turn out all thoughts of d and of
7:87 stolen from you by d, fear, and
8:22 D flees, joy reigns and hope
10:67 d me and question my love
10:67 d my purpose, saving power and
10:80 You must not d this
10:80 Beyond all d, you must know it
11:21 grave of sickness, poverty, d
11:78 every d, is a crime against my love
12:88 Never d
14:12 So why fear? So why d?
14:38 You must not d
14:46 This is unfailing; never d it
15:24 d my power to do all that I have
16:21 they must know, without any d, that
16:39 beyond all d only when I rose from
17:57 You do not d their love because you
18:4 comes despondency, d of me, and
18:29 for the future is to fear and to d me
18:29 Check every d of me at once

Doubts
4:7 d and fears continually drove them
4:8 Remember always, d delay
4:11 All your d arrest my work
6:79 Little d, little fears, little
10:57 d of the day immediately to rest
14:45 Are d and fears in your hearts?
14:45 Instead of those fears and d
18:48 d, fears, tempers, despondencies

Draw
4:39 I came 'to d men unto me,' and sweet
4:56 D near to me, my children
4:84 D beauty from every flower and joy
5:11 D near in spirit to me
5:14 not to d your own conclusions, but
9:33 you can d with confidence
9:34 d large and unsuspected sums from
11:67 D into your beings more and more
11:72 noiseless footsteps I d near to
12:28 D near to me
13:74 D nigh to me and all you need is
14:29 d very near to me
14:35 Does that not d out your love and
14:47 I would d you closer and closer to
16:76 d nigh in silent awe and adoration
16:76 D nigh, as Moses drew near to the
16:78 D nigh in the utter confidence that
16:78 D nigh
16:79 D nigh, not as a supplicant, but as a
17:15 d souls to me, you must fully expect

Drawing
4:17 love is d others to you
4:39 feel hearts d near in love and for

Drink
1:49 souls sit and d in the ecstasy of
4:60 there was no cup of sorrow to d
4:84 D in the beauty of air and color
5:35 Can you d of my cup?
7:62 to d of the cup that I d of
8:84 willing to d of the cup that I d of

Drove
4:07 d them back into the wilderness
16:85 me to which suffering d you

Drowning
2:55 It is to the d man the rescuer comes
8:24 truth is as a rope flung to a d man
10:74 d only to place him in other deep
11:83 d man who is struggling to save

Dry
10:74 he places him on d land to restore
13:50 river through the d land of life

Duties
8:36 discipline and daily d done
9:48 little plain bricks of d done
10:13 rigidly doing your simple d

Duty
6:36 matters is d, persistently
7:69 quietly from one d to the next, taking
8:13 persistent pleading as a d upon
8:46 or to undertake any new d
8:48 only responsibility was to see the d done
9:89 quietly along the path of d I have
9:90 Just quietly do your daily d
14:50 d and every interruption as my
15:86 d owed to a creator or a debt
16:6 D faithfully done for me means
17:58 gray days are the days for d

Dwell
1:2 Do not d on the past—only on the
1:36 D in thought on this more and more
2:20 D on this thought
2:27 To d in thought on the material
2:51 D much in my presence
3:6 how can you d in me where nothing
3:22 near me, just to d in my presence
3:23 that you seek me just to d in my
4:33 D much on what I did as well as what
4:64 fear in the heart in which I d
6:26 I can only d with the humble
6:43 D with me as the center of your lives
6:54 D on the thought, God is love
6:54 D on my actions on earth
6:81 come to you, too, as you d with me
9:22 D on these truths
9:47 I come to d with my loved ones
9:52 unkind thoughts of any kind d in your
10:19 d in the house of the Lord forever
10:85 Trust in me; D in my love
11:71 D increasingly in the consciousness
11:86 Come to me, talk to me, d with me
12:40 you are not to d for one moment
13:56 children, you must d therein
14:34 Think of and d upon the rapture of
14:69 Do not d upon the past
15:62 D in me, and I in you, so you shall
15:75 D more, d much, on this thought of you
15:95 D much in thought upon all I
17:40 Love and fear cannot d together
18:23 D much on my life

Eager
3:21 e for something — e to be healed, or
5:15 men have been too e to say what they
6:59 Hearts e to do my will send out a
17:67 storehouse and lay e hands on them

Earth
1:53 suffered on e and have suffered
2:26 above, not on things of the e
3:9 no power on e that does not fall
3:21 thronged me when I was on e
3:49 my disciples when I was on e
3:62 making one spot of e a holy place
3:64 I came to e to lead man back to
3:72 spirit-wings down with e's mud
4:32 than the hearing of all e's noises
4:38 different from the values of e
4:73 Revel in the e's joy
4:76 life not of e—a heaven-life here
4:93 greater works than I did when on e
5:75 mine in manhood's years on e
6:02 E has no greater joy than that
6:06 Loosen your hold on e, its cares, its
6:07 tight hold on e's treasure that he has
6:17 arise from that which binds to e
6:25 As one on e may say of one he loves
6:54 Dwell on my actions on e
6:85 e's attempts to quench your thirst
6:98 do away with men from the e
7:11 weary too, when on e, and I separated
7:84 I taught when on e, as I have taught
8:19 'saved all the ends of the e'
8:68 a man views e's wonders from some
9:41 on e to the many who followed and
9:77 work miracles as I did when on e
9:86 When weary, do as I did on e
10:11 to those who rise above the e life
10:43 my life on e is still spiritually
11:10 e's wisest might lead to disaster
11:13 e's aims and intrigues are not for you
11:49 nations of the e should be blessed
11:56 union on e to compare with the union
11:56 priceless beyond all e's imaginings
12:16 E's richest, choicest gift held out
12:30 we measure not by e's miles
12:36 E gave me her best—a human temple
12:50 loosen a strand that ties you to e
12:86 'and not on things on the e'
12:91 from e's troubles and view the
13:04 my time on e could see the angels
13:07 E's troubles and difficulties will
13:41 uttered to me while I was on e
13:55 no power on e can even find it
14:01 founded my three years' mission on e
14:20 meek shall inherit the e'
14:20 and the material forces of the e
14:45 joy as is beyond any joy of e
14:59 agony on e, one note of joy thrilled
14:83 E's successes are not the ones I
14:84 humble who can inherit the e
15:14 speak of as the salt of the e
15:14 'Ye are the salt of the e'
15:43 e-mist clinging to the ground, never
15:55 as I expressed it when on e

15:93 as it ever was when I was on e
15:95 upon all I accomplished on e
16:61 see it, and my reward is not e's fame
16:6 e's wealth, e's pleasures, but divine
16:7 joy, whether in the e world or in the
16:7 E has no pleasure, no reward
16:10 you can do so only in part on e
16:12 parched e looks to the hills for its
16:12 Lord, who made heaven and e
16:13 raise your eyes from e's sordid and
16:15 the Lord who made the e
16:16 on e, wherever you might be, your
16:36 risen above these e furies and
16:41 understanding here on e
16:49 born upon e was not to be housed in a
17:2 accorded to e's great, but contempt
17:21 on e, mine was a lost cause to the
17:25 hindered my work on e
17:27 work on e was to gather around me
17:68 e on which you are was once only a
18:21 lowliest, without any of e's pomp
18:22 As e's sinner, you stand by me as I
18:25 truly the gifts of e's wisest
18:36 answer is the same I gave when on e
18:36 three nights in the heart of the e

Ease
9:24 not by the dwellers in e, but by
12:79 Give of time, of personal e and
14:48 hardship or e, danger or safety
18:34 Let no riches, no e, entice you from

Effort
2:43 disciples gave up e after a night
4:54 with action, with e, you are
7:3 it does not mean no e
7:3 fill the boats with with without e
7:5 Man rises by e
7:65 tide you must direct all your e
7:66 e that they will be surmounted
7:67 I take man's e and bless that
7:67 I need man's e
8:50 every crisis, every e, every
9:53 Spare no e to become all I would
11:87 You must have both e and rest
15:50 fullness of joy as the result of e

Empty
2:53 world, there is no e space
5:23 e is all so-called living before
6:21 stand by the e tomb
7:58 E your mind of all that limits
11:80 E your vessels quickly to ensure a
11:84 E your vessel
15:45 Keep ever an e vessel for me to fill

Endurance
3:33 E is faith tried almost to the
3:54 beyond human e to the breaking point
6:72 patience and e all come from contact

Endure
3:82 prayed did not e to the end
3:83 Can you e to the end? If so, you
3:83 e with courage, with love and laughter
8:18 Sorrow may e for a night, but joy

Enemy
4:67 No work that employs this e of mine
6:18 death was the last e I destroyed
17:54 Where does the e attack?

Enter
1:21 He will say evil spirits may e in
2:13 worrying thought e your mind
6:3 as I e and control their lives
9:57 These will e your consciousness
10:5 right to e my presence when they
10:39 children ye cannot e the kingdom
12:69 yours to e into the kingdom I have
16:44 of their hearts so that I may not e
17:44 You must not allow fear to e

Entice
18:34 e you from the path upon which your

Entrance
4:4 only times when evil can find an e
4:93 Spirit free e and do not keep it
10:36 e to my kingdom must become as little
11:24 You can give the e to fears and
16:6 for me means e into a life of joy
18:3 weak spot, attack that, and so gain an e
18:4 weak spot to attack and gain e

Eternal
1:31 I give to you e life
1:39 exceeding and e weight of glory
1:43 I give you that e life I give to all
1:43 These are all e
1:43 life within you, my life, e life, so
1:44 work of any soul that has e life
1:62 shape the real, e, imperishable you
3:22 longing of the e heart was satisfied
3:52 this is life e, that they may know
3:52 e life—the life of the ages
4:78 I came to give e life
4:83 Such joy is e
5:22 We know no life but e life
5:23 And this is life e, to know God, my

6:85 wine of my giving—the life e
7:30 expression of e thought in time
7:30 Grasp the e thought
8:22 Life, e life, is yours
10:11 The e arms shelter you
10:81 There is no age in e life
11:67 more this wonderful e life
11:67 flow of life e through spirit, mind
11:68 And this is life e that they may
11:70 e life is the only lasting life
11:71 I will give unto them e life
11:71 e life means security and safety too
12:23 Rest until life, e life, flowing
13:7 but at the real, the e life
13:8 this is life e that we may know thee
13:28 e life that pulses through your
13:76 words of e life are all the words
14:65 E life, abundant life, is promised
16:67 Flee to the e God, your refuge

Evil

1:20 No e shall befall you
1:21 He will say e spirits may enter in
1:59 seeing how these slips delight the e
2:11 screen that keeps all e from you
2:17 for the dispersion of e
2:32 I will deliver you from all e
2:71 No e can befall you if I am with you
4:3 only times when e can find an entrance
4:4 The forces of e surround the city of
4:5 No e force can hinder my power
4:24 every doubt, every sin, every e
4:25 No e can stand against that, for
4:63 purer eyes than to behold e
4:63 he does not impute e to his people
4:64 Fear is e and 'perfect love casts'
4:67 fear of blame are e allies
5:60 obedience will remove mountains of e
7:9 God, the destroyer of e
7:78 same time, destructive of e
8:31 Forces of e, within and without you
8:75 power to vanquish e that praise
8:75 best weapon against all e
9:13 worry and e they turn from you
9:60 No e can touch you
9:66 tenderness, drives away all e
9:66 all the hosts of e flee
10:20 No e can befall you
10:32 every fear that e may present
10:77 waiting for the next e to befall you
11:33 see that no e can befall you?
12:8 I see it and e sees it
13:37 my name is the power that turns e
13:37 Spirits of e flee at the sound of
13:62 good out of e, peace out of turmoil
15:20 conquest of all e in himself
15:91 made by man into ways devious and e
16:33 powers of e were strained to their
16:36 unharmed, untouched by e and its power
16:38 If e is to leave you unchallenged
16:38 you must be e
16:38 If e challenges you, if trials press
16:38 my friends, exposed to the hate of e
16:39 I conquered e at every point
16:72 without a remedy for the e or the need
17:10 sun to shine on the e and on the good
17:15 expect a mighty onslaught from the e
17:16 planned by e to thwart me
17:40 E is powerful and fear is one of e's
17:50 Forces of e batter and storm
17:63 rise on the e and on the good
18:3 The powers of evil watch you as a
18:3 e lurks around you and seeks to
18:4 it affords e a weak spot to attack
18:12 Fear no e because
18:12 I have conquered e
18:17 truce with the power of e

Evils

5:44 nullifies all the e against you
12:6 made at your request, and e banished

Experience

6:62 result in the constant e of me
6:63 Between the e of the two joys lie
10:53 knows by e that he steers a straight
11:46 appreciation results from contrary e
11:57 only those who e it can even dimly
14:48 Each e in your life of joy or sorrow

Eye

7:56 Keep the e of your spirit ever upon
10:64 I will guide thee with mine e
10:64 e is my set purpose—my will
13:33 e of the soul is the will
13:33 must have a single e to God's glory
15:44 e that sees all, the ear that
16:50 seeing e, the Spirit that dwelt in
16:51 Pray for the seeing e, to see the

Face

4:24 'Jesus saves'—in the f of every doubt
6:11 Search until you meet me f to f
7:88 F each day with love and laughter
7:88 F the storm
8:30 F all your difficulties in the
8:34 see my f through a mist of care
8:72 you must f as you awake

8:77 Look up into my f with a look of love
8:86 no man can see my f and live
9:54 f each day's problems with me and
9:61 for you to bear or face alone
10:34 F the future, but f it only with a
12:6 F your responsibilities
13:21 f of the scorn and torture and jeering
14:11 F each difficulty with
16:5 with a smiling f to the world
16:17 f to f in that purely spiritual world
17:60 courage in the f of danger

Fail

3:61 never f to keep this time apart with
3:81 Do not f me
3:81 I cannot f you
4:9 It will never f you. but you must
4:9 you must learn not to f it
4:29 feel sure that I can never f you?
5:30 I cannot and I will not f you
6:52 unclaimed and you f for lack of it
6:85 attempts to quench your thirst will f
7:26 f in my promises because these are not
10:27 you cannot f to love them
11:84 They f to understand because
13:37 an appeal I never f to answer
14:36 f that child, as faulty and weak as
14:36 Could I f you?
14:85 Never does God f to hear the cry
15:63 Spirit cannot f to pass through the
18:1 no fear that your faith will f you

Failing

14:87 f to heed, or to listen, keeps him
17:19 Soul-starvation comes from f to do
18:1 Have no fear of my f you
18:8 never f love of you, fight and love

Failure

1:3 your sense of f
4:51 Your deep sense of f is a sure sign
4:53 there is no sense of f or
8:62 that life cannot be a f
8:66 f, the presence of the loved one is
8:90 a sense of f out with praise
9:3 work that brings much sense of f
9:29 Forget all sense of f and
10:12 must not feel the burden of your f
11:77 your f to be sure of the security
11:92 Amid f, discord, abuse, and
12:1 out of faults and f to perfection
12:30 a fear inspired f, or a harsh
12:48 the sense of f
13:19 There can be no f with me
14:39 every sorrow over f, every weakness
14:66 f or success, of wounds or healing
15:37 stand by the grave of f, of dead
15:79 There can be no f with me
16:66 from the sense of your f, your
17:60 joy came a sense of f
18:51 from poverty, from f, from weakness

Failures

6:34 perfection and see your bitter f
8:68 Not even the sins and f
8:68 f that marked his upward path
9:9 I share your troubles, f
12:46 Remember no more their sins and f
13:22 The world may deem you f
14:66 Do not waste time over f and
14:68 Lay upon me your sins, your f
15:69 You must forget your f

Faith

1:8 to struggle, to f, to health
1:9 beckoners to f and courage and success
2:16 Pray daily for f
2:16 upon f alone depends the answer to
2:17 f is the necessasry weapon for
2:17 when you have f, you give it back to
2:18 'F without works is dead'
2:18 works, too, to feed your f in me
2:18 In knowing me, your f grows
2:18 f is all you need for my power to work
2:38 You are told to pray for f, and you
2:39 time is the best way to cultivate f
2:69 f in him, and 'being rooted and'
3:10 Your f and my power are the only
3:33 Endurance is f tried almost to the
3:42 line from the soul to God, f and
3:88 asking—or the f assurance from you
4:27 only you lack the f to know it
4:28 Pray for more f, as a thirsty man in
4:29 How poor is man's faith! So poor
4:30 diligently that your f may increase
4:44 patiently, hopefully and in f
4:64 exist where love is or where f is
5:47 F is too priceless a possession
5:47 f itself is based on a knowledge
5:48 be the very foundation of your f
5:60 F and obedience will remove mountains
6:32 let his f find expression
6:33 f is all God needs to manifest his
6:33 F is the key that unlocks the
8:80 If prayer is only a glance of f
9:24 f has been kept alive and handed down

9:35 man of f make a sudden demand upon me
9:40 peace is loving f at rest
9:41 Obedience is your great sign of f
9:76 eyes of f is to cause it to manifest
9:90 attitude of f will receive its
10:12 Go on in f; the clouds will clear
10:16 f, hope, and charity
10:16 F is your attitude toward me
10:32 answer of f and confidence in me
10:34 robbing f of her sublime sweetness
10:35 f, not seeing but believing, is the
10:35 'According to your f be it unto you'
10:36 If f was so necessary for miracles
10:36 F is the child attitude
10:56 feeling is your f claiming my supply
10:56 According to your f it shall be
10:57 not the f expressed in moments
10:57 f that lays the doubts of the day
10:57 f attacks and conquers the sense
10:77 get the expectant attitude of f?
10:85 Laughter is a child's f in God
11:51 their f was rewarded
11:83 not, and your prayer and f are
12:27 medicines are sun and air, trust and f
12:28 F is the soul's breaching in the
13:43 a cry for more f—a plea to conquer
13:44 You shall be given more f
14:35 Your f shall be rewarded
14:63 I will grant you so great a f
14:63 increasingly great f, that each
14:63 f of the day before as almost
14:75 you who have the f-vision will see
15:7 building up an unshakable f
15:11 test has to come to all who walk by f
15:44 prayer of real f is the prayer of joy
15:49 Have a big f
15:94 Have a boundless f in me
16:51 just as f saw the beauty of the
16:51 f to see the beauty of my love in
16:52 eyes of f, will see all that you
17:25 F revived; they would remind each
18:1 no fear that your f will fail you

Faithful

1:38 Joy is the result of f trusting
5:33 obey me as you would expect a f
6:34 f servants, you long for perfection
7:35 quick to achieve, f in accomplishment
9:34 bank, earned by f work in many ways
13:23 not to all hearts, but to f
14:61 bring joy to my heart by f service
14:61 By f service in the little things
14:61 Be f; do your simple tasks for me

Fall

1:59 would ever err or f if once
3:9 All walls shall f before you, too
3:9 power on earth that does not f
7:6 success may f upon them
12:94 Encumbered with them you will f
15:28 heavy blow about to f
16:19 f on an unresponsive heart
16:28 mighty words of an orator can f

Fallen

1:8 doubt into which man has f
9:17 tempted and f need my salvation
9:23 souls would have f by the way except

Fame

1:42 master—the world, f, the good
2:63 f, honor, and wealth are weary and
12:79 of f, of healing, of power
16:6 my reward is not earth's f, earth's
16:27 f of the world, the applause given
17:2 F and acclamations are accorded to earth's

Father

1:54 A f loves to see his children happy
2:25 I and my F are one
3:14 'When thy father and mother forsake'
3:28 God himself—my f in heaven, your f
4:61 'Father, forgive them, they know not'
4:72 are dear to the heart of my f
4:86 express to man what I am—what my f
4:90 song as a message from my f
5:23 eternal, to know God, my F and me,
5:24 coin, but a rich f, worried about how
5:38 It is given me by my F
5:75 knowledge was mine, given me by my F
5:77 sinner, from my F's sight for one short
6:54 'I and the F are one'
6:74 soul's friend, its f, mother, comrade
7:13 activity was no part of my F's plan
7:30 read the thoughts of the F, then
7:31 all loving restraint of your F
7:31 the divine control of a F who can
7:36 perfect even as your F who is in heaven
7:39 Men call the F the first cause
8:6 submit to, though my F and I are one
8:6 As many grow more and more like my F
8:41 We share the F's property
10:22 'possible' and my F and I are one
10:41 being perfect as your F in heaven
10:68 who knows the world's God as F
11:18 shall ye do because I go to my F

11:19 shall ye do because I go to my F
11:27 with me in the secret place of the F
11:43 perfect even as your F in heaven is
11:74 times of quiet communion with my F
12:3 My F and I are one
12:11 perfect even as your F in heaven is
12:41 protect Peter from the anger of my F
13:10 tenderness of your F (my F) in
13:63 My F and I are one; one in desire to
13:65 you still have not known the F?
13:66 Your F is the God and controller of
13:66 you have seen in me are in my F
13:68 See the F through seeing me;
13:68 To see the F through me is love
13:82 meet as guests in your F's house
14:34 to union with me, and God, the F
14:47 shepherd, of the child for its f
14:59 who were given me by my F
14:77 ye do because I go unto my F
14:80 the longing of the F to save
14:89 my acceptance of my F's will in all
15:90 Man has not made of it what my F
16:11 world something of the F
16:18 all man's questions about my F
16:25 my presence and that of my F
16:25 my F and I, are one and he—God—is
16:33 was known only to me and to my F
16:36 hates into the secret place of the F
17:10 Give as I said my F in heaven gives
17:11 you must closely resemble your F
17:30 to seek communion with my F
17:42 God is love and the F and I are one
17:63 of my F, 'He maketh his sun to rise'
17:65 perfect even as your F in heaven is
17:66 temporal blessings, as does my F
18:2 a perfect love of me and my F

Fear

1:3 Bury every f, of the future, of
1:26 What cause have you to f?
2:1 Do not get tense; have no f
2:1 How can you f change when your life
2:30 Be calm; never f
2:32 Trust me; f not
2:55 Be not afraid; f not
2:58 Never f; joy is yours
2:59 F not; do not f to be busy
2:66 I am your shield; have no f
2:68 Never f, whatever may happen
2:71 Never f, but in that place you shall
3:1 Take courage; do not f
3:7 F not; I am your advocate, your
3:26 F not
3:51 Have no f
4:10 much to learn in turning out f
4:24 every sin, every evil or every f
4:25 to every f, 'Jesus saves from f'
4:35 care and f just melts into nothingness
4:64 Have no f; f is evil
4:64 perfect love casts out f
4:64 no room for f in the heart in which I
4:64 F destroys hope
4:66 F, f, f, everywhere
4:66 Fight f as you would a plague
4:66 Never inspire f;
4:66 f of punishment and f of blame are evil
5:24 Do not f; to f is as foolish as if a
5:49 I am with you; do not f
6:17 depression, distrust, f, and all
6:18 You have nothing to f
6:19 all you f are powerless to harm you
6:81 Do not f changes
6:81 You can never f changes when I, your
6:88 Have no f; go forward
7:10 Never doubt; have no f
7:10 Note the faintest tremor of f and stop
7:38 F not, f not, all is well
7:43 It is not a dead self that men have to f
7:87 stolen from you by doubt, f and despair
8:78 smooth the day's work, then f will vanish
8:90 Drive f and depression and despair
9:76 Do not f; I am a wall of protection
9:90 Do not f; do not panic
10:31 Do not f; remember how I faced
10:32 For every f that evil may present
10:33 Look on every f, not as a weakness on
10:48 speaking peace to restlessness and f
11:78 Every f, every doubt, is a crime
11:81 to retain, implies a f of the
12:30 A false word, a f inspired failure, or
12:77 child's confidence and banishes f
12:86 Can you f the future when it holds
13:13 Feel this, not only until f goes
13:37 Spoken in f, in weakness, in sorrow
13:47 Have no f for the future
13:54 Put all f of the future aside
13:74 Never f, never lose heart
13:76 Have no f; abide in me and accept
13:80 Rest knows no f;
14:10 Do not f
14:12 So why f? So why doubt?
15:11 Trust and f not
15:87 for the calming of every f, for all
17:22 not so much f of my enemies as the
17:40 Love and f cannot dwell together
17:40 f is one of evil's most potent
17:41 love can soon be routed by f whereas
17:41 vanquished f flees in confusion
17:42 perfect love that dispels f is to

Fell
3:8 walls of Jericho f down
3:57 they f out, never to know until
9:46 house and it f not, for it was
12:45 examine the spot where he f

Feverish
13:78 Stop all f haste and be calm

Fighters
9:17 The f need a leader

First
1:30 perfect yourselves f in my strength
1:34 realizes its value for the f time
2:56 bidden the f angry wave to be calm
2:56 f gust of wind to be still
4:48 f, you can hardly credit the powers
4:54 of weakness — at least at f
5:17 interpreter mars the f great act
5:61 F things f
5:89 not even the f Peter who said
6:61 f the wonder and joy of f acquaintance
6:65 Do not regret the f
7:39 Men call the Father the f cause
7:39 f cause of every warm ray, every color
7:79 F, be still and know that I am God
7:81 f in the individual soul of the
8:11 Seek ye f the kingdom of God and
8:12 material things f and then grow into
8:12 spiritual things f and then material
8:44 f be a definite realization of sonship
9:31 in despondency at his f hurdle?
9:53 need altering f, but yourselves
10:21 f step is always to lay your will
11:83 f answer your prayer for help as a
12:52 at f, the help to yourselves may
13:21 on the f Easter morning
13:24 f task, the weeding, the planting
13:34 f the kingdom of God, the f step is
13:35 Seek in all things his kingdom f
14:54 distress, see that the f step is
14:58 F get right with me
14:81 Learn f that I know what loneliness
16:57 lives must f be narrowed down, more
16:63 F, be 'gathered together in my name'
17:8 contains the f law of giving
17:9 f practice giving in this way
17:9 f made the daily and hourly habit of
17:13 f step toward conquering temptation
18:20 f hail must be that of the Magi in
18:20 triumph you must f hail me
18:21 f hail must be the worship of

Fish
7:3 with f without effort on their part
7:67 did not find the f ready on the shore
8:53 with so few loaves and f
8:55 Note the catch of f

Fishers
1:8 follow me and become f of men

Five
4:80 f senses are your means of
8:53 present at the feeding of the f
10:14 'Thou hast f husbands; he whom'
10:42 f thousand was, in each case, but an

Flag
7:60 who range yourselves under my f

Flee
8:31 without you, f at my presence
9:66 all the hosts of evil f
13:37 Spirits of evil f at the sound of
16:66 sanctuary is a place to f to
16:66 where can you f from yourself
16:67 F to the eternal God, your refuge
16:68 F there until the relief of safety

Flower
4:20 glory of the open f is beyond all
4:75 sensing my presence in a f
4:84 Draw beauty from every f and joy from
4:85 thought, I made a lovely f
4:87 a lovely f is my expression of thought
4:88 beauty of a f or a tree is impressed
4:89 Look at a f until its beauty
5:39 A f or thousands of dollars—one is
5:40 f and the thousands of dollars
7:29 water, every beautiful f
8:63 f that will gladden the world

Flowers
4:84 birds and the color of the f
4:88 from seeing the beauty of the f
5:8 f, the beauty around—all are lost
8:65 leaves and f without a strong root
11:44 amid the loveliest f along which
13:50 f of life to spring forth
17:51 garden with sweet f and bees and

Follow
1:2 disciples to f me and become fishers
2:41 f the Lord of limitations
2:62 seek to f me in all things
3:85 As you f implicitly all I say, success
4:95 F my injunctions in all things
5:9 cross daily and f me
5:56 leave your foolish fears and f me
6:64 the second joy will f
6:86 F completely my commands

7:21 glorious to f where your Master goes
7:36 f me was, 'Be ye therefore perfect'
7:73 F my guidance
7:83 desire to love and f and serve me
7:89 F me to find all three
9:53 F every leading from me
9:72 F the path of obedience
9:73 f until you finally reach the
10:19 f us all the days of our lives
11:1 F my guiding in all things
11:8 expect a child to f a rule in addition
11:9 So f my rules faithfully
11:10 To f a rule laid down even by
11:11 But to f my direct guidance
12:23 Then work, glad work, will f
12:66 F it; it is wide enough so that
14:23 Quietness and assurance f
14:56 let your cry of distress f
16:49 men would f and adore for the beauty
17:4 You f a despised Christ
17:32 if they really did not want to f me?
17:33 F the Christ into the quiet places

Food
2:65 f to the hungry, home to the wanderer
3:73 f for the soul I have provided
4:19 time, and your f gladly with all
8:53 I hand out the f and you pass it on
9:20 enable it to reach the f it seeks
10:41 Bread of life, f from heaven
10:42 I would one day be the f of my people
16:71 'buy themselves f,' said my disciples
17:17 life and f pass from one to the other
17:18 Feed on that f

Fools
6:14 willing to be deemed f for my sake

Force
1:13 F is born of rest
1:13 Only love is a conquering f
3:65 divine f is never less than
4:5 No evil f can hinder my power
5:26 violent who take it by f
5:44 f of the utterance drives back
5:57 power greater than any earthly f
5:89 Peter who was a mighty f for me
7:13 renewal of spirit f, rest of body
12:23 It is wrong to f work
13:89 I never f upon it my help or my
15:20 make himself a conquering f
15:20 f that will be needed and must be
15:50 trying to f yourself to like to
15:57 Power is not such an overwhelming f
13:3 evil watch you as a besieging f

Foreground
7:46 thought of them means self in the f

Forget
2:33 Never f your 'Thank you'
3:80 Do not f to meet all your difficulties
4:15 Never f that real healing of body
8:65 Many f this and thus their work ceases
8:69 F all that lies behind you
9:29 F all sense of failure and
11:34 F, forgive, love and laugh
15:68 F the past; remember only its
15:69 You must f your failures
15:71 If you do not f the sins of others
16:67 immensity you f your smallness

Forgive
4:61 I said, 'Father, f them, they know not'
5:79 I f you, as you have prayed me to
7:45 so you must f
7:46 the self in you, can never f injuries
7:47 The self cannot f; kill self!
7:48 Cease trying to f those who worried
11:34 Forget, f, love and laugh
15:34 'F me, children, that I allow this extra burden'

Forgiveness
3:2 If my f were for the righteous only
5:89 tasted my f, in his moment of abject
6:56 Perfect love means perfect f
6:56 where God is there can be no lack of f
6:80 My presence is a sign of my f
7:45 what I say about f of injuries
7:45 commands that as you seek my f
7:47 all true f is of God and is God
8:5 love as only a tender compassion and f
12:10 through resentment to perfect f
14:69 in me you have all—complete f
17:66 in love and in the spirit of true f

Fragrance
17:52 as breathing f, expressing beauty

Frankincense
18:25 f is the adoration of a consecrated

Free
1:31 A f gift, a wonderful g—the life
2:69 f to build, knowing all is well
4:22 with a glad f heart and hand
4:93 Spirit f entrance and do not keep
5:77 bore it of my own f will, until
6:9 A risen life glad and f can be yours
6:60 disciple f to carry out my will
10:14 whole and f though he had wrecked
11:5 so f from all other agency, and you
12:16 f to all, and no man to care to
12:94 rejoicing, singing and f

15:35 your salvation, and to f you
15:93 it was ever to set my apostles f
16:35 could they know my Spint was f
17:48 feel so f and yet so planned for

Freedom
2:41 God in whose service is perfect f
7:2 walk step by step the way to f
7:44 higher science law than even f of
7:51 Claim joy and peace and f from care
8:2 f with which a child makes demands
8:41 in God's service is perfect f
9:84 your promised land of f
12:50 every f achieved from poverty
12:51 your f will mean your rising into

Fresh
3:1 I give you a f start
3:68 as you do for the f pure air of the
7:12 rest always precede f miracle
7:90 thrill of f life floods your being
12:46 met, a f start from today

Friend
1:55 Some poor spirit-impoverished f
4:29 would a f if that f came and said he
4:72 smile, the joyous smile of a f
5:38 To me, your intimate f, all power is given
5:45 'All power is given unto my F'
5:55 if that man had a f who knew the way
6:74 the soul's f, its father, mother
8:3 dare to approach me as f to f comes only
8:40 A f can command his f, can know
8:40 that all the f—the true f—has is his
8:40 idle living at the expense of a f
9:17 The lonely need a f
9:18 The God-f, the God-leader
9:34 the needs of a f or for some charity
10:1 I am your f, your companion along
10:2 presence of some loved human f
10:6 Your nearest earthly f cannot be
10:6 Your Lord, your master, your divine f
10:46 discovery of the great f
10:46 knowledge of the great f
10:46 imitation of the great f
10:47 being like the great f
10:47 becoming to others a great f
10:48 I am your f; think again of all
10:48 F and Savior; a f is ready to help
10:49 Think of what your f is to you
10:49 what would be the perfect f
10:49 conquering, all miracle working f
10:49 I am that f and more even than your
10:68 who knows me as you do, as f and
11:1 I am your guide and your f
12:62 possible with my master, my Lord, my f
14:29 in me—as master, Lord, or f
15:37 The f with whom you stand by the grave
15:37 that f is a f for all time
15:41 It is I, your Lord and f
15:50 to like to have that f with you
15:72 Think of me as a f, but realize, too
15:72 then he becomes my f, even as I am his
15:88 If friendless, claim a f; if hopeless
15:95 'He, our Lord, our f, could accomplish'
16:77 the loving intimacy of a f
16:82 strive to be the f I see in my vision
18:22 me—the f and servant of sinners
18:47 but as those recognizing a f
18:50 Jesus is Savior and f, joy-bringer

Friend's
8:40 claiming the f means—his name, his
15:50 any more than joy in a human f

Friendless
10:83 had to stay on alone and f in the dark
15:88 If f, claim a friend

Friends
5:38 Have not my intimate f a right to
6:10 Mary left home and kindred, f, all
6:78 wounds, not of my enemies, but of my f
8:1 he desires his followers and f to
8:40 You are no longer servants but f
9:9 As my beloved f, you share my patience
11:44 these as tender companions and f
11:92 abuse and suffering, f and angels
12:12 your household, f, acquaintances
12:41 nor from the resentment of my f
13:5 mortals rush to earthly f who can
13:5 their f who are freed from the
13:6 do well to remember your f
15:22 'wounded in the house of my f'
15:24 It hurts that my f, who love me and
15:75 thought of you as my f and of the
16:7 It is known only to my f and those who
16:38 are on my side and, as my f, exposed
17:35 Only f who understand and love each
17:68 right to bring my f, my needy one

Friendship
2:7 My intimate f is secured in the
4:36 add much to your f and your work
7:83 So deep is your f and so great your

7:85 I am the divine third in your f
8:61 bring to our f a reverent, tender
8:41 F—true f—implies the right to
9:61 tender loving f and conversation
10:4 realized the wonder of the f you can
10:7 tender, humble condescension of my f
11:56 That f is priceless beyond all earth's
15:38 time to cement the f with me and
15:72 the wonder of the f
15:74 your great f to do this or that for me
16:57 as that f becomes more and more
16:60 I have to begin our f by cutting away
16:60 each f, the influence of the inner circle
17:36 I shall prove our f by asking you to
17:53 you cannot be united in your great f
18:40 with you in tender loving f

Fullness

10:41 in that f of spiritual things can
13:61 they would have had f of joy
15:50 f of joy as the result of effort
17:46 F of joy is the joy of perpetual

Gateway

16:9 g into it may be service or it may be

Gentle

6:37 Be g with all
6:77 joy that the patient, g, loving
14:7 arm with a g touch to point the way
15:2 sound of my g knocking
18:9 yield to my g pressure on your arm
18:30 as at my g bidding, for me and

Gentler

13:6 g will be your passing when it comes

Gift

1:4 not anticipate the g by fears or
1:31 a free g, a wonderful g—the life
2:16 It is my g
2:36 not a g, but passes insensibly from
4:70 I loved to give the wine g at the
6:8 my g to every man who will accept it
6:12 No g is poor if it expresses the true
6:65 The second is the greater g
6:96 though I have the g of prophecy
8:55 sink with the lavishness of my g
8:91 Few men would send a further g until
11:52 Give me the g of a brave and thankful
11:62 is the great g to offer
11:62 g I prize next is the g of the moments
12:15 sad that so few accept that gracious g
12:16 choicest g held out—free to all
12:17 My g—the richest heaven has to
12:17 g of life, abundant life—man
14:59 I thank God for his g to me of you
15:48 I desire to give you a g
17:38 day now as a joyous sunrise g from
17:60 g of joy to my disciples and their

Gifts

2:20 g for her daughter's wedding
2:52 joy—they are all my g
6:12 your heart's g are rich and precious
7:89 My great g
8:92 g and blessings, leaves the way open
13:72 You need not plead or bring g
18:25 g, truly the g of earth's wisest
18:25 g: gold, frankincense, and myrrh

Give

1:12 I g you gain, 'Good measure'
1:29 I dare not g you this power
1:31 I g to you eternal life
1:43 I g you that eternal life I g
1:47 ponder on these truths I g you
1:55 Use all I g you; help others
2:5 My joy I g you
2:12 I want to g you all things, good
2:12 which longs to rush to g
2:17 I g it to you in response to your
2:17 when you have faith, you g it back
2:36 It is mine to g, and mine to withhold
2:64 I will g you rest
2:72 never g you a load greater than
3:1 I g you a fresh start
3:3 I wait to g you all that is lovely
3:36 wait until I g the order to start
3:46 I g you both hard tasks as proof
3:53 G me gladness as well as trust
4:17 sent by me and g them a royal welcome
4:22 G out love and all you can with a
4:70 I loved to g the wind gift at
4:78 I came to g eternal life
4:93 If you g that Spirit free entrance
5:4 have I been able to g you more clear
5:28 Satisfy the longing of my heart to g
5:66 quiet resignation I g my blesings
6:42 This will g you power in dealing
6:67 G them love and you g them God
6:87 tasks I g you may seem to have no
7:8 with the task I g them
7:54 G me the joy of sharing all with you
7:57 lovely I delight to g to you
7:59 I will g you rest
8:55 I g with a large hand and heart
8:57 task or g up the thought of any tasks
9:38 peace that only I can g in the midst
9:44 inner guiding that I g

Glad
1:8 Be g
1:55 friend will be g of it
1:61 G indeed are the souls with whom I
2:31 Be g all the time
3:4 I can only bless g, thankful hearts
3:4 You must be g and joyful
4:22 all you can with a g free heart and
4:70 by the lakeside—a little g surprise
5:61 Rejoice and be g
5:66 Try in all things to be very g
6:9 A risen life g and free can be yours
6:10 g triumphant rapture of her 'Rabboni'
6:11 awakes your g 'Rabboni'
6:12 Rejoice in my g acceptance as you
6:59 will should be welcomed with a g
7:28 lives too are full of g promise
8:94 you come to the g spring of water
10:23 Be g to leave all your affairs in a
11:55 g and thankful about in every
12:23 Then work, g work, will follow
12:26 sunshine helps to make g the heart
12:32 g loving, joy-springing child with
12:44 g wings of a butterfly if it
13:18 walk becomes a g conquering and
13:69 Sing to me from a g heart
13:71 g turning of thankfulness, or a
15:25 I count it victory, a g victory
15:29 bows in anticipation of a g surprise
15:44 It is certain of a g response
15:68 Remember only its g days
16:16 future cannot but be g and full of

Gladness
3:53 Give me g as well as trust
10:18 through with joy and g
13:18 g in the walk of those who walk in
13:83 g in service, joy in doing my will
14:19 my will, there must be a g
14:43 Feel g at the thought of one very
14:57 Oh, the g of heart

Glory
1:39 exceeding and eternal weight of g
4:50 g of the open flower is beyond all
6:15 g and my kingdom are thereby served
11:21 g of the Lord is risen upon thee
13:34 must have a single eye to God's g
14:64 strength to strength, from g to g
15:30 see the g, joy and wonder of your
15:80 presence of his g with exceeding joy
15:94 in seeing, will give me all the g
16:10 g of the Lord is the beauty of his
16:11 g of the Lord is also risen upon
16:11 reflect that g in your lives

Goal
3:54 when the g is in sight that heart
3:55 g is in sight, you need your final
3:57 sight of the g, their courage failed
9:32 I am your leader and your g
9:74 material g is reached, then the
12:45 rises and presses on to the g

God
1:15 G loves, G helps, G fights, G wins
1:17 Do not limit G at all
1:20 G will help you
1:22 a reflection on, not of, G's power
1:25 G cares and his plans unfold
1:33 'God speaks in silences'
1:49 ecstasy of G's revelation to his own
2:1 hidden with me in G, who never changes
2:9 G-given cement that secures
2:20 anticipatory love of G; dwell on
2:21 thought of a grudging G who has to
2:32 I am your G, your deliverer
2:38 I am your G, your great reward
2:41 G in whose service is perfect freedom
2:41 G of the universe, confined
2:44 every moment to G is the foundation
2:46 plans of G are wonderful—beyond
2:54 you are Christ's and Christ is G's
2:54 cycle, because you are G's
2:62 man's thoughts are not G's thoughts
2:62 nor man's ways, G's ways
3:28 pierced even to the ears of G himself
3:28 With G, to hear is to answer
3:30 that with G, to hear is to answer
3:42 line from the soul to G, faith and
3:53 be led by the Spirit of G and trust
3:64 spirit-conversation with his G
3:76 G is now blessing you very richly
3:87 your requests be made known unto G
4:5 calm and happy; G does the rest
4:5 Think of all G's mighty forced arrayed
4:63 'God has purer eyes than to behold evil'
4:77 Nothing is small to G
5:5 Man's ecstasy is G's touch
5:23 life eternal, to know G, my Father and
5:29 I am a God of power as well as a man
5:61 I am your G
5:77 I, the Son of G, bore man's weight of
5:77 Had I not been G, had this not been
5:89 Christ, the Son of the living G
6:32 Man's need is G's chance to help
6:32 Man's need is G's golden opportunity
6:33 faith is all G needs to manifest his
6:33 storehouse of G's resources
6:41 G is using you both in marvelous ways

17:17 union of a soul with G in which
17:18 To do the will of G is the very strength
17:31 persuade men I was the Son of G?
17:42 I am love because G is love and
17:49 wonder of this—a G-guided life
18:43 with G all things are possible

Godhead
16:51 beauty of the G in one who had no
17:26 men recognized my G, opportunities

Gold
1:58 G does not stay in the crucible
5:58 no g could achieve one millionth
18:25 g represents your money

Good
1:12 'G measure, pressed down'
1:42 fame, the g opinion of men
2:12 all things, g measure
2:17 all g in your lives
2:71 Ill that he blesses is our g
4:13 bid you be of g cheer
4:63 He always sees the g in people
4:81 See the g in everybody
4:81 Love the g in them
4:95 g for you to know of my spirit
6:83 promise of future g work
7:9 God, the creator of g, is love
7:78 agitation is destructive of g
7:78 calm is constructive of g
9:77 same condition holds g
10:18 a feast of all g things for you
10:77 for the next g in store
10:85 child's faith in God and g
11:48 be of g cheer, I have overcome
11:62 to be used in this g work
11:90 be of g cheer, I have overcome
12:7 powerful forces for g in your
12:45 What g would it be if he stays
13:37 summons all g to your aid
13:62 He is g; trust in him
13:62 Say, 'God is g; God is g'
13:62 knowing only that he is g
13:62 bring order out of chaos, g out of
13:62 God is g
13:63 One is desire to do g
13:63 For God to do g to his children
13:63 God is g, anxious to share
13:63 goodness and g things with you
13:84 expression of all g for them
15:7 harmonious and g, beautiful
15:14 g for nothing but to be cast out
16:39 Be of g cheer
17:10 on the evil and on the g
17:15 prevent your g work
17:63 rise on the evil and on the g

Goodness
1:29 I have made the purity and g
9:56 realize my bounty and g
10:19 Surely g and mercy shall follow
13:63 share his g with them
13:63 share his g and good things with

Govern
7:92 you alone can prove your right to g

Grace
9:19 soul live, it shall grow in g
12:70 My g is sufficient for all

Grain
3:74 The lesson of the g is the lesson
3:74 necessary to present the life g to

Grateful
12:89 need only the watering of a g

Gratitude
6:62 g, followed in time by joy
8:93 with perhaps no real sense of g at
10:81 nothing but joy and g
11:55 causes for joy and g will spring to
13:27 Do not expect love or g or
13:77 Be full of g

Grave
11:21 Arise from the g of sickness, poverty
15:37 g of failure, of dead ambitions

Growth
2:27 help, not hinder, your spiritual g
4:37 Times of prayer are times of g
4:54 sign of life, of spiritual g
8:64 fails for lack of g in me
8:64 The higher the g up, the deeper must
14:64 beauty of my kingdom is its g

Growths
8:64 The two g are necessary

Guard
6:26 Pride stands g at the door of the
9:13 My angels g you day and night

Guarded
10:87 tower, strongly g, and against which
18:3 force would watch a g city

Guests
13:82 Look on all you meet as g in your

Guidance
1:37 My g is often by shut doors

1:49 orders and strength and g for the day
2:47 protection, safety, and g
5:4 definite teaching and g
6:47 g is intensified immeasurably in power
6:62 evidence in support of my g
6:90 you are bound to have g
6:95 do this, and the g very plain
7:73 Follow my g
7:82 other messages, other g
8:28 safety, security and g
8:28 G, 'He established my goings'
8:29 G is the final stage when the saved
9:54 g as to what you can do
9:55 on which you can get my g for today
9:89 When you have no clear g, then go
9:90 surely as acting upon my direct g
10:8 delay action until you get my g
11:9 This is why divine g is perfect
11:11 But to follow my direct g means to
11:45 choice of ways, the g in the way
12:31 That is what makes my g possible
12:33 g that matters with my disciples
12:33 You are ready for the g
13:91 claiming my help, g and miracle
13:7 When you look to me for g, my hand is
15:18 Take this as very definite g
17:34 command nothing, and give no g
17:46 joy is the joy of perpetual g
17:47 Wait for g in every step

Guide

1:4 I shall g you one day at a time
2:39 I am your g
3:27 lights to g feet that are afraid
4:1 light to g you as the hosts of heaven
5:54 I am with you to g you and help you
5:56 follow me, your g
5:62 I am your g
6:30 I am your g
6:41 I g you always
7:5 this does not mean no g
9:53 I am your only g
10:64 'I will g thee with mine eye'
10:65 To g with my will is to bring all
11:1 I am your g
11:1 I am your g and your friend
11:36 not only to g, comfort, strengthen
12:19 I will g your efforts
14:18 g when you are responsive to my
15:39 use a lamp to g your footsteps
17:12 Only their need is to g you
18:50 rescuer, leader and g

Guiding

6:41 my g is always so sure
8:39 that God is g says, with all the
9:44 in the inner g that I give
11:1 Follow my g in all things
12:65 spirit but of the g of the Spirit

Habit

3:18 life h of it, I will reveal my will
6:82 breathing correctly becomes a h
6:82 this will also become a h
8:16 so much a h that you cannot resist
14:91 Do this until it becomes a h
17:9 h of giving on the higher plane

Hand

1:8 A helping h is needed that raises
4:22 with a glad free heart and h
4:34 I touched her h and the fever left
5:60 they must go h in h
6:7 treasure that he has no h to receive
7:20 h always goes with the leadership
7:62 not to sit on my right h and on my
7:68 My h is controlling all
8:24 My h is not shortened that it
8:26 one h on the rope and one making
8:53 I h out the food and you pass it on
8:55 I give with a large h and heart
10:23 all your affairs in a master h
10:48 h is outstretched to help and
10:73 it is my h that has saved you, then
10:75 Lord's h shortened that it cannot
10:78 my h in all that happens and in
12:16 stretch out a h to take it
12:77 child's h that calls forth an
13:86 h shortened that it cannot save?
13:88 h is not shortened; it is
14:6 I lay my h upon each head and the
14:7 my h is laid upon your arm with a
14:8 h supports you when you faint by the
14:18 resist the pressure of my h
14:35 feel a little trusting h in yours
15:52 pressure of a loved one's h that
15:60 axe in a master h accomplishes much
15:60 in the h of a weak child, nothing
15:60 master h that wields the instrument
17:7 Feel my h of love press yours in

Hands

1:4 I hold the year in my h—in trust
1:29 become witchery in wrong h
3:44 in the hands of a master gardener wish
3:78 worries in the divine h
3:79 wool in the h of a loving mother
5:86 all your affairs in my h

6:5 I lay my loving h on you in blessing
6:6 Unclasp your h, relax, and then the
6:78 wounds in the h and feet hurt little
8:9 tenderness of my h as I bind up your
8:23 all is so safe in my h
10:52 place your affairs in my h
11:71 any man pluck them out of my h
12:72 their difficulties, into my h
13:62 leave in his h the present and the
15:35 moment you placed all in my h
17:67 storehouse and lay eager h on them

Happiness
2:44 moment to God is the foundation of h
2:52 h and joy—they are all my gifts
2:62 leads to boundless h and peace
2:63 world's awards bring heart-rest and h?
4:19 Share your love, your joy, your h
4:58 self is the key to holiness and h
5:27 health, h, and laughter
7:9 harmony, beauty, joy, and h
13:3 Theirs is a life of h and progress
13:36 In this lies your true h
14:88 will result in both holiness and h
16:43 yearn to realize a h, a rest
16:47 value to me, his God, of each man's h
16:54 lies your h and spirit rest
17:5 h and joy that the reviling crowds
18:46 only source of h and heart peace

Harm
1:29 It would do h
6:19 fear are powerless to h you
9:13 nothing can h you
11:39 No buffets of the world can h you
18:13 whatever it is cannot h you

Harmed
10:86 cannot be touched or h there

Harmony
2:9 secures the h and beauty of my mosaic
6:82 unrest disturbs your perfect calm and h
6:82 perfect calm and h will be yours
7:9 bring into manifestation all h
7:25 kingdom is perfect order, perfect h
7:26 h, and think I fail in my promises
7:75 live in a world where all is h
7:76 H is always yours when you strain
11:27 touches the h of the real you that
13:74 lives—brings h, beauty, peace
14:86 h, so is the human cry and God's
18:17 never have h if that means your life

Harvest
11:59 we share and joy in the h

Haste
13:78 Stop all feverish h and be calm

Hatred
12:41 from the h of Peter himself
17:23 h of the Pharisees was openly
17:53 h and malice of all you meet who are

Heads
3:25 I bless you; bow your h
12:91 Lift up your h from earth's troubles

Heal
4:49 to h all manner of diseases
9:12 h your scars and make you strong
9:29 suffice to h all your sores and wounds
11:76 forth in power to bless and h
14:82 power to h, to raise to life

Healer
4:35 My touch is still a potent h
11:72 I am your H, your joy, your Lord
12:24 your physician, h of mind and body

Healing
2:71 restoration and power and joy and h
4:14 Sun and air are my great h forces and
4:15 h of body, mind, and spirit comes
4:42 find life and h and strength
4:48 h are yours in very full measure
6:75 Claim h
7:90 Use it as you use a h balm for a
10:35 those who sought h of me
10:36 necessary for miracles, h and
12:79 h, of power, of sympathy, of all
13:31 power and h and humility and patience
14:6 Spirit flows through that h
14:7 When you cry to me for h when in
14:7 my touch brings strength and h
14:44 me, you can always find h for all
14:66 h balm, so long as it served its
14:69 complete companionship, complete h
15:93 wonder and h through them

Hearers
8:51 You both are not idle h
14:60 simple doers of my word, not h only

Heart
1:15 Take h
1:32 judge when it enters the h of man
1:33 meaning to the h without voice or word

1:34 into the secret place of another h
1:8 Seek to find a h-home for each truth
1:55 find a way into each life and h
2:15 Never lose h
2:22 her mother-h sings
2:22 her own h full of the tenderest joy
2:63 Do the world's awards bring h-rest
2:65 joy to the weary, music to the h
3:17 no intimate h-to-h telling
3:20 I come to the waiting h
3:22 eternal h was satisfied by that
3:24 human h to be loved for itself is
3:24 caught from the great divine h
3:29 Only a cry from the h, a cry to
3:30 trembling h, that with God, to hear
3:38 made known as a h-consciousness
3:54 when the goal is in sight that h
3:55 see by the nerve and h rack of the
4:3 alone with me until your h sings
4:22 all you can with a glad free h and
4:64 no room for fear in the h in which I
4:72 dear to the h of my father
4:79 quiet your h and still your senses
5:16 I can explain to each h
5:28 Satisfy the longing of my h to
5:44 Say it until your h sings with the
5:69 I judge the h and I see in both
5:85 humble, meek and lowly in h
6:3 I am the h's great interpreter
6:12 your h's gifts are rich and precious
6:26 make my home in the humblest h
6:26 h to shut out the lowly, humble
6:37 Try to see the h I see, to know the
6:59 if I am to do my work in the h and
6:68 into some despairing person's h
6:71 Many a weary troubled h needs you
6:72 trouble h will be gladdened by you
6:76 hours of the h's agony
6:77 of my disciples brings to my h
6:78 wounds in the h that are the
6:79 trifles of a day that sadden my h
6:97 rarely do I speak to the human h
7:5 to soften a h here, to overrule
7:55 think of me with their h and not their
7:76 maintain your own h peace in
7:93 The h of man is so delicate, so
7:93 Each h is so different, actuated
7:94 Bring each h to me, its maker, and
8:9 Your h is torn
8:30 Keep a brave and trusting h
8:33 show me your h of trust
8:55 I give with a large hand and h
8:75 The joyful h is my best weapon
8:79 soul and mind and h to God
8:92 more on the thankful h
10:18 feel from the very depth of your h
10:26 sunshine in the h of another who then
10:34 with a brave and happy h
10:44 loving h that walks with me can
10:49 more even than your h can imagine
11:25 disturb your peace, your h calm
11:26 spoil your peace of h and mind
11:38 comfort and bring joy to my h
11:46 word of cheer to h
11:52 gift of a brave and thankful h
11:57 merging of h and mind a oneness
11:61 dear to my h is the cry of love that
12:15 my h is sad that so few accept
12:26 helps to make glad the h of man
12:48 Travel unladen, with a light h
12:48 A light h means a weight of influence
12:78 Have no mean thought in your h
12:89 loving h to yield abundantly
13:41 cry of the human h is as
13:69 Sing to me from a glad h
13:73 Never fear, never lose h
13:77 Let your h sing
13:91 longing h by claiming my help
14:37 Think what my h feels when you turn
14:53 Take it to h and view your day's
14:57 Oh, the gladness of h
14:61 joy to my h by faithful service
14:81 of yours is a comfort to my h
15:1 response to the longing of your h
15:44 It sees and knows the h of love
15:85 problems of a questioning h, but
15:85 but the cry of that h to me
16:19 will fall on an unresponsive h
16:38 Take h from that, for you must
16:81 my h when he fails to fulfill that
17:1 heart recognizes the need for the man
17:7 No h can ache without my h aching
17:37 pity of an agonized h for my poor
17:61 your h's response to my smile
17:67 into the very h of my kingdom
18:36 three nights in the h of the earth
18:44 how my h must ache with the woe of
18:46 source of happiness and h peace

Hearts

1:11 How many h can you cheer?
1:45 Work at them in your minds and h
2:19 already seen your h needs before
2:38 weak knees and h that faint
2:67 I can read men's h
3:4 I can only bless glad, thankful h
3:12 h of kings are in my rule and
3:57 ran well with brave stout h until
4:17 with the love of both your h

4:52 If you desire to h others to me
4:58 only be accomplished with my h
4:62 failed to h the epileptic boy
4:80 They will hinder, not h
5:25 H is here all the time
5:34 Through many channels my h and
5:43 beside you to bless and h you
5:50 It will secure your h for others
5:51 beside you to h and strengthen you
5:54 to guide you and h you
5:78 Here to h and bless you
6:30 Strength and h will come to you
6:31 Walk in my ways and know that h will
6:32 Man's need is God's chance to h
6:32 I love to h and save
6:49 You can h no one when you are agitated
6:66 not feel you have to try and h them
7:4 The h of their fellows had to be summoned
7:4 troubles might have made them feel my h
7:5 mountain height by the h of train
7:6 whom you desire to h
7:80 difficulties that h you to cultivate
8:36 without my strength and h and
8:51 is one for you to h
8:51 You do not h enough
8:51 You must h all you can
8:52 As you h, h will flow back and your
8:71 I have promised to h you with the
9:2 appeal to me for h to eradicate that
9:15 I came to h a world
9:49 your power to h others will be truly
9:54 problems with me and seek my h
9:68 The name summons h to conquer your
9:74 spiritual is only to h the material
9:80 It must strengthen and h you
10:9 Though they ask my h in the momentous
10:48 A friend is ready to h
10:48 outstretched to h and encourage
10:59 H and peace and joy are here
11:37 provide protection and h for
11:73 measure of my longing to h
11:80 Ask no other h
11:83 first answer your prayer for h as
12:52 Your power to h other lives will soon
12:52 h to yourselves may seem too late to
12:64 None ever sought my h in vain
12:80 become a great power to h others
12:82 marvelously to save and h others
13:38 They call 'mother' to h, to care
13:39 name not only when you need h but
13:43 H though mine unbelief
13:72 feel you can simply claim h, and
13:73 Not only h is there, but also the
13:79 Be sure of my h, be conscious of
13:88 allowed to bless and h and save
13:89 I never force upon it my h or my
13:90 impatience and longing to h
13:91 longing heart by claiming my h
14:39 sigh of weariness, every plea for h
14:41 strong to h, to cure, to protect
14:63 I will indeed h your unbelief
14:71 for all you care about and long to h
15:11 look for no other h
15:75 for understanding, for h
15:96 know that your h and salvation are
16:12 the hills whence comes your h
16:12 hills comes h—h from the Lord
16:13 lift your eyes to the h of the Lord
17:7 when human h fails, keep very close
17:25 the Holy Spirit—to h them

Helped
4:6 You shall be h; you shall be led
6:66 they must be h
7:11 Samaritan woman was h
9:50 pitying thoughts will be h upward by you
15:67 natural to know they are being h

Helper
2:30 I am your h
9:8 your tender, patient, and strong h
12:10 I am always your h through dark to
13:42 knows me as h and Savior, that soul
14:49 I am your h

Helpfulness
1:57 Just be a channel of h for others
8:52 your circle of h will widen more and

Helping
1:8 A h hand is needed that raises the
7:20 But the h hand always goes with the
10:52 controlling, blessing and h you
12:28 Mind, soul and body need h
14:8 strong and h hand supports you
16:40 sharing in my life work and h me to

Helpless
1:8 raises the h to courage, to struggle
3:48 You are both like persons h on a raft
11:83 must render him more h and powerless

Helplessly
6:64 cling blindly, h, to me and let me

Helplessness
2:18 As you seek to do, you feel your h
14:37 when you turn to me in your h

Helps
1:15 God loves, God h, God fights
4:75 things about me that h and heals
12:26 sunshine h to make glad the heart

Hidden
1:45 kingdom, the h pearls of rare price
2:1 your life is h with me in God
3:84 secret treasures h from so many
9:72 h spiritual wonders revealed
10:44 h these things from the wise
10:84 h in the secret place of the Most High
11:27 h with me in the secret place of
13:55 You are h in a sure place, known only
13:60 Hunt for it as for h treasure

High
2:26 realize your h privilege, you have
4:24 Set your standard very h
9:36 pay your vows to the Most H
9:69 I will set you on h because you have
10:84 in the secret place of the Most H
10:93 set you on h because you have known

Higher
2:25 Could human aspiration reach higher?
5:84 of me and together climbing h
7:44 h science law than even freedom of
8:64 h the growth up, the deeper must be
10:11 seek to soar h, to the kingdom of
12:86 above, (the h, spiritual things)
12:91 H and h each day see more of
13:1 H, ever h, rise to life and beauty
13:1 H and h
15:43 incense, rising ever h and h
17:9 habit of giving on the h plane

Hills
13:80 flowing rivers, of strong, immovable h
16:12 h of the Lord, the h whence comes
16:12 earth looks to the h for its rivers
16:12 So you must look to the h of the
16:12 h comes help—he from the Lord, who
16:13 mean and false to the h of the Lord
16:13 lift your eyes to the h of the Lord

Hinder
2:27 help, not h, your spiritual
4:5 No evil force can h my power
4:80 They will h, not help
6:20 Let nothing h your risen life
8:26 You h the rescuer who has to act
9:52 spirit power, with nothing to h

Hoard
1:24 H nothing
18:26 money to h or to display, as some

Honesty
7:25 perfect h, perfect obedience
7:26 result from obedience, h, order

Hope
1:22 H all the time
1:26 H on; H gladly; H with certainty
3:33 You must wait, trust, h, and joy in
4:64 Fear destroys h
6:5 courage and h will flow into your
8:22 joy reigns and h conquers
9:48 I am giving you work and h
10:16 abideth these three: faith, h and
10:16 h, which is confidence in yourself
12:2 H ever
16:16 Your h is in the Lord
17:25 with my resurrection came h
17:60 then h, waiting, and courage

House
2:38 provision in the h of my abiding for
3:9 fall like a h of paper at my miracle
6:66 such joy flows out from this h
8:43 before my h supplicating and waiting
9:42 man who built his h on the sand
9:42 trouble he is overthrown, his h falls
9:43 man who built his h upon a rock
9:46 man who built his h upon a rock
9:46 beat upon that h and it fell now, for
9:47 it is in that h on a rock, man-made
9:47 h of obedience—the truest expression
10:19 dwell in the h of the Lord forever
13:82 meet as guests in your Father's h
15:22 'wounded in the h of my friends'
16:20 light to all who are in the h

Humble
4:92 reverence the h and the simple
5:85 be h, meek and lowly in heart
6:26 I can only dwell with the h
6:26 to shut out the lowly, h Christ
6:50 flow through the most h and lowly
10:7 h condescension of my friendship
12:35 As you kneel in h adoration, I will
13:32 loving and strong and patient and h
14:84 the h who can inherit the earth
16:6 world may see the h, patient, quiet
16:44 I go to these in tender, h longing
18:21 worship of humility, to the h
18:30 h, as at my gentle bidding, for me

Humbly
10:92 Walk very h with your God

Humility
3:69 Learn patience, h and peace from me
7:73 reliance on mine will teach you h
7:74 H is not the belittling of the self
12:37 kneeling in a spirit of h, turn
13:31 h and patience and all else you see
14:84 failed has he learned true h
15:64 h to say they do little and are of
16:42 learn from them my great h
16:45 heavenly beggar in his great h
16:46 beggar, and learn h from me
18:21 first hail must be the worship of h
18:23 Christian life there are steps: h
18:35 Ride on now in loving h to victory

Hurt
1:51 Life has h you
6:78 h little compared with the wounds
15:23 reviling of my enemies h me?
18:12 It has power to h only those who do

Hurts
3:54 race it is not the start that h, nor
4:53 it is only struggle that h
14:18 h of life come only when you endeavor
15:24 not the unbelief of my enemies that h
15:24 h that my friends, who love me

Husk
3:74 The outward church is the h
3:74 the h was necessary to present
3:75 Then much that is h falls away

Ills
4:23 balm for all the i of the world
4:56 me is the panacea for all i
7:63 only one cure for all its i—union
14:44 physical, mental and spiritual i

Image
4:88 leaves an i which reflects through
8:87 my i becomes stamped upon the soul

Imaginings
11:1 Marvels beyond all your i are unfolding
11:56 priceless beyond all earth's i

Immeasurably
6:47 i in power when two are on in desire

Impatience
2:12 divine i which longs to rush to give
2:14 i and worry corrode, and in time
13:90 divine i and longing to help
14:76 In your i see my unfailing patience
18:48 i, and lack of love in big and little

Impatient
2:13 enter your mind, one i thought

Impossible
7:64 world would think i can always be
10:22 no miracle is i with me
17:49 To think anything is i in such
17:64 i with the blessings of the kingdom
17:66 interchange of thought would be i
18:43 With men your task may be i, but

Inactivity
15:21 waiting may seem a time of i

Incense
11:54 sweet i going up to me through the
15:43 Prayer can be like i, rising ever

Indignity
11:39 scorn and i there is a strong shield

Individual
1:36 I efforts avail nothing
2:75 to teach the i or to be used to raise
6:87 adapted to the i need
7:25 caused by disharmony in the i
7:81 first in the i soul of the worker
9:44 injunctions I speak to each i soul
11:10 knowledge of your i life and
11:12 Each i was meant to walk with me
13:87 i life to the extent that i lacks
13:89 respect the right of each i soul

Injunctions
4:95 Follow my i in all things
9:44 i I speak to each individual soul

Inner
2:74 see that your i lives are all they
5:12 i place of the being to commune with
7:24 i knowledge that makes the problems of
8:58 i urge of life within the seed
9:44 obeying in all, in the i guiding that
15:21 activity in the i life and the
15:40 i consciousness that tells of me
16:57 into an i circle life with me
16:59 world movements to the i circle life
16:60 learned its lesson in the i circle
16:60 the infiuence of the i circle

Insecure
10:84 plant your feet on an i ladder?

Instruments
1:27 my i must be sharp and ready
3:65 I only need i to use
6:43 It is similar with some delicate i

Intensified
6:47 i immeasurably in power when two are

Intercourse
3:61 near to me because of their i with you
11:25 Stop all i with others until this is
16:77 wonder of our i, the miracle of

Interpreter
5:17 stay with it as i mars the first great
6:3 I am the heart's great i
6:38 ask me to act as i between you

Interruption
11:27 no i, touches the harmony of the
14:50 every i as my appointment
14:90 fulfillment of divine intent in each i
14:91 Accept each task or i; say your

Interview
6:38 Before you i or speak to anyone, ask

Intimacy
4:43 tender i of one much loved
8:1 loving master delights in the i of
8:1 in the tender i of his demands
8:3 The i that makes my followers dare to
16:77 loving i of a friend, but I am also
16:77 miracle of your i with me, will mean
16:85 i with me to which suffering drove

Irks
14:89 from that moment no burden i or

Jesus
9:65 J; Say my name often
9:65 'In the name of J Christ of Nazareth'
9:67 J; the name banishes loneliness
9:68 J; the name summons help to
9:69 J; use it more; use it tenderly
13:37 evil flee at the sound of J
13:38 J; use my name often
13:39 J;'use my name not only when
13:40 J;'There is none other name under
15:51 Call my name often, J
18:47 J; that is the name by which you
18:49 J; 'he shall save his people from
18:50 J is Savior and friend, joy-bringer
18:51 J; say it often; claim the power

Journey
3:50 not have accomplished the j so soon
5:36 not only with you on the j
5:36 am planning, the j
5:55 at no part of the j would any
12:47 On life's j, throw away all that
16:84 proceed in your j upward
16:85 sure of it that it is a j with me
18:27 J through this world simply seeking

Joy
1:7 Be full of j
1:7 J saves
1:7 J cures
1:7 J in me
1:7 kindness, or love, every trifling service—j
1:9 Trust on, love on, j on
1:38 J is the result of faithful trusting
1:40 J is the daughter of calm
1:54 J is the whole being's attitude of
2:5 My j I give you
2:9 J in me
2:9 J is the God-given cement that secures
2:22 her own heart full of the tenderest j
2:23 did the mother learn all this j in
2:23 understanding of me will bring great j
2:23 From me—a faint echo of my j in
2:24 understanding of me will bring great j to
2:31 Rejoice exceedingly; j in me; rest in me
2:37 you desire of me: strength, power, j
2:40 Sing with j
2:44 superstructure is the j of communion
2:45 given the reward and the j of the next
2:46 insight, vision and j will be yours
2:52 happiness and j—they are all my gifts
2:55 No rush of j can be like that of a man
2:58 Never fear; j is yours
2:58 The radiant j of the rescued shall be
2:65 I am j to the weary, music to the heart
2:71 shall find restoration and power and j
2:73 Welcome love, j and peace
3:33 You must wait, trust, hope, and j in me
3:35 heaven itself cannot contain more j than
3:45 J is the spirit reaching out to say thanks
3:45 So never cease to j; Rejoice!
3:53 consciousness of me must bring j
3:64 J that I am with you
3:86 rest for your souls and power and j and
4:12 Love the busy life; it is a j-filled life
4:13 Take your fill of j in the spring

4:14 inward j that changes poisoned blood to
4:19 Share your love, your j, your happiness
4:21 Have love, j, and peace in richest
4:23 J is the sovereign balm for all the ills
4:23 nothing that j and love cannot do
4:35 Health, joy and peace take its place
4:36 such times will come a strength and j
4:48 Life, j, peace and healing are yours in
4:71 those who understand and j in them, so
4:71 for those who see my love and tender j in
4:73 The j of the spring shall be yours in full
4:73 Revel in the earth's j
4:73 There will come back a wonderful j if
4:73 if you share in her j now
4:74 realize this will bring you both new life j
4:76 a heaven-life here and now; J! J! J!
4:82 so your j making shall spread in ever
4:83 J in me; such j is eternal; joy's precious
4:84 Draw beauty from every flower and j
4:89 Look for beauty and j in the world
5:5 J! J! J!
5:9 hinders progress and j
5:10 Love me; j in me; Rejoice!
5:19 Life knows no greater j than you
5:27 coming to you: j, peace, assurance
5:44 heart sings with the j of the safety
5:59 J! J! J!
5:61 Courage and j will conquer all
5:62 Love me, j in me, I am your guide
5:65 J in the very beauty of holiness
5:65 thankfulness and j open the gates
5:67 Laughter is the outward expression of j
5:81 J! J! J!
5:84 You will find such j as time goes
5:91 Oh, j! Oh, rejoice! I love you
6:2 Earth has no greater j than that
6:6 tide of Easter j will come
6:9 rapturous j of Easter resurrection
6:17 to arise to beauty, holiness, j
6:17 inspired by love and j, to rise from
6:24 experiencing the j of the beloved
6:25 lead up to the mosaic of j and love
6:61 first the wonder and j of first
6:61 Then j seems to be a thing of the
6:62 gratitude, followed in time by j
6:63 J is of two kinds
6:63 The j born of love and wonder
6:63 the j born of love and knowledge
6:64 the second j will follow
6:65 Of this second j I said, Your j no man
6:66 such light, such j flows out from this
6:70 can you not feel the j of knowing
6:72 Health, peace, j, patience and
6:75 Claim j; claim supply, claim what
6:77 j that the patient, gentle
6:77 I know no j such as the j I feel at
6:88 J, radiant j, must be yours
6:88 even if only momentary, into j
6:89 Rest, love, j, peace, and work;
6:93 giving j and nourishment to all
7:6 willing that showers of blessings and j
7:7 only desire j and blessing for them
7:9 all harmony, beauty, j, and happiness
7:51 Claim j and peace and freedom
7:51 J in me
7:53 J in me
7:54 Give me the j of sharing all with you
7:66 always have strength and j in the doing
7:70 you will find peace and j
7:87 can you have than peace, rest, and j?
7:89 J, peace, and love; My great gifts
7:89 but real j and victory come to those
7:91 What j follows self-conquest!
8:2 all the love and j of the children
8:18 but j comes in the morning
8:18 underlying j that tells of
8:21 a power new and vital, a wonderful j
8:22 Doubt flees, j reigns and hope
8:38 J, rest, be always at peace in
8:67 Does it bring you j and peace just
8:76 if each day has its thrill of j
8:77 a thrill of j at the sense of the nearness
8:83 Love me; rest in me; j in me
8:93 Do this until at last a thrill of j
8:95 Oh, j in me
8:95 shed j on all those around you
9:29 your fears and fancies into my j
9:30 obtain me—your souls' j and haven
9:57 bring you ever more and more j
9:79 J in me
9:88 let the tide of love and j flow in
10:18 through and through with j and
10:24 Accept my will, and it will bring you j
10:25 Take j wherever you go
10:26 my vitalizing j-giving message
10:38 but for its j in life, its ready
10:59 Help and peace and j are here
10:67 J in me; J is infectious
10:81 no pity for yourselves, nothing but j
11:1 I am your guide; J in that thought
11:37 in that little child, j and cheer

11:38 comfort and bring j to my heart
11:44 the j-way into the kingdom can be
11:48 the j and peace of conquest shall be
11:55 The causes for j and gratitude
11:59 Together we share and j in
11:72 I am your healer, your j, your Lord
12:32 glad loving, joy-springing child
12:50 Every blessing I send you, every j
12:51 into the realm of j and appreciation
12:52 may seem too late to bring you j
12:76 my service—a life of power and j
13:13 until j ripples through in its place
13:16 Peace brings j
13:16 the 'j no man taketh from you'
13:18 There is a j, a spring, a gladness
13:23 The j of seeing spiritual truths is
13:23 a great j; when the heavens are
13:31 I am love and j and peace and
13:49 Rest in me; j in me
13:52 bear flower and fruit in j
13:59 giving you that overflowing j
13:60 Search for the j in life
13:61 J in me; it was full j I wished my
13:61 they would have had fullness of j
13:68 through me is love and j in abundance
13:70 Praise is man's j-tribute to me and
13:70 thrills of j surge through your being
13:70 something of the j of the heavenly
13:73 also the comfort and j of divine
13:84 gladness in service, j in doing my will
14:29 always have the j of finding in me all
14:43 until just to think of me means j
14:45 such sweet j as is beyond any j of earth
14:48 in your life of j or sorrow, difficulty or
14:59 one note of j thrilled through the pain
14:61 You can also bring j to my heart
14:66 whether of j or sorrow, failure or
14:72 your sorrow is turned to j, your
14:74 your mourning be turned into j
14:91 The resulting j will transfigure and
15:4 You think it would have been a j to
15:12 an assurance that holds j and beauty
15:30 see the glory, j and wonder of your
15:33 realize the j of the one who can be calm
15:44 prayer of real faith is the prayer of j
15:50 fullness of j as a result of effort
15:50 cannot be, any more than j in a human
15:52 pressure, and a thrill of j follows
15:80 presence of his glory with exceeding j
16:6 life of j—my j, the j of your Lord
16:6 earth's pleasures, but divine j
16:7 My reward is joy, whether in the earth
16:7 That j carries an exquisite thrill in
16:7 It is that j of which I said, no man
16:7 no reward, that can give man that j
16:8 This j may come as the reward for
16:9 Suffering must in time bring j
16:9 live with me in that kingdom of j
16:16 cannot but be glad and full of j
16:20 your j must be made known
16:21 Men must see and know your
16:23 So trust, so conquer, so j
16:57 The j of meeting me should fill your
16:68 relief of safety merges into the j of
16:85 j known to those who suffer with me
17:5 j that the reviling crowds could never
17:29 Count it your greatest j to be the means
17:36 So wait; so love; so j
17:37 I give that peace and j that brings to age
17:46 Fullness of j in the j of perpetual
17:46 the j of knowing that every detail
17:47 loving leading should give you great j
17:48 a j for you to feel so free and yet so
17:55 thrill of j seems to be absent
17:57 thrill of j at their nearness
17:59 You shall have my j
17:59 The j will come, but for the moment
17:59 simply of the march; j is the reward
17:60 the gift of j to my disciples
17:60 j came a sense of failure, hopelessness
17:61 J is the reward of patiently seeing me
17:61 J is, as it were, your heart's
17:62 signs of true discipleship as is j
18:30 Live in the j of my constant presence
18:50 Jesus is savior and friend, j-bringer

Joyous

1:38 my will when it seems not j
5:72 the j smile of a friend, are dear to
12:15 abundant life, j life, and a powerful
17:38 day now as a j sunrise gift from me
17:62 you may not yet be j, but you are brave
18:33 discipline and of j fulfillment is to

Judge

1:32 No man can j when it enters the
5:69 I do not j by outward appearances
5:69 I j the heart and I see in both
7:93 Never j
7:94 How can one j of another?
9:39 peace you are fit to j true values
13:22 The world judges not as I j
16:81 J the condition of my heart when he
17:3 j only according to the values of

Judges
13:22 The world j not as I judge

Keep
1:24 K nothing for yourself
2:48 K your spirit life calm and unruffled
3:35 K your souls in patience and rejoice
3:60 never fail to k this time apart with
4:5 all you have to do is k calm and happy
4:44 K the rules I have laid down for you
4:44 K them persistently
4:93 do not k it out by self, it will
6:48 Above all, k calm and unmoved
6:49 At all cost, k calm
7:56 K the eye of your spirit ever upon me
7:56 K the window of your soul open toward
7:79 Only trust, perfect trust can k one calm
8:22 Look and k looking
8:30 K a brave and trusting heart
9:81 to k calm, sane, is to have the mind
10:73 k you in the way you should go
11:28 K close to me and you shall know
11:28 K close, very close to me
11:88 To k from straying
11:88 k so close to me that nothing, no
12:59 you k your eyes on each stony or
14:12 Rely on me to k my promise about this
14:24 in my power to save and k
14:25 at all costs, k this calm
15:2 K that listening ear
16:45 K ever an empty vessel for me to fill
15:66 K self out and know that my Spirit
15:80 able to k you from falling
17:7 k very close to the man of sorrows
18:27 Never k anything you are not using

Keeping
9:44 only the k of my commandments or even
11:29 K very near to me is the secret to
11:77 My k power is never at fault
13:3 loved ones are very safe in my k
15:13 my k means security and safety
15:13 k that implies life, freshness
15:14 k that I ensure to those I speak of
15:15 contact with me is my k power realized
15:15 k power which maintains the salt at
15:16 k is not done by activity in this

Kept
7:1 down the ages has k my servants
9:23 my power alone which k them brave
9:24 faith has been k alive and handed down
10:78 how you are k throughout the day
14:4 a path k sacred and secret for my
14:59 souls who had k my word, who were
14:60 daily tasks and ways they k my word
15:12 Yes! 'K by the power of God' is
15:13 'k unspotted from the world'
17:50 soul being k by my power
18:40 My promise given is k

Kill
1:62 K the self
1:64 k self, you gain the overwhelming
7:47 K self!

Kingdom
1:32 Silently comes the k
1:45 secrets of my k, the hidden pearls of
2:7 in the drudgery of the k
3:47 hindered the progress of my k by
4:68 gradually souls are led into my k
4:92 Simplicity is the keynote of my k
4:95 good for you to know of my spirit k
5:23 In my k we do not measure in years
5:26 'The k of heaven suffereth violence'
5:26 treasures of my k
5:90 k of heaven can only be preached by
5:90 prize the authority of the k
6:15 my glory and my k are thereby served
6:16 marks that distinguish those of my k
6:24 keys unlocking the door into my k
7:22 bringing the k into places where it
7:25 no discord in my k
7:25 rule of my k is perfect order
7:50 live in the rapture of the k
8:11 'Seek ye first the k of God and his'
8:11 untiringly for the things of my k
8:12 Not so in my k
8:35 straight and narrow way into the k
8:58 k of heaven is like that
9:20 forward after the things of my k
9:21 reaching after the treasures of my k
9:21 enjoy the wonders of that k
9:35 And so in my k
9:38 stamp of the k—the mark of the Lord
9:39 true values, the values of the k
9:72 necessary to further the work of my k
10:11 soar higher, to the k of heaven
10:36 k must become as little children
10:39 children ye cannot enter the k of
10:50 doctrines of your churches to my k
10:50 my k of the child hearts, often
10:90 disciples the truths of my k
11:4 children of my k are a peculiar people
11:44 is the only path into my k

11:44 joy-way into the k can be taken
11:47 The world is not the k
11:87 Dig deep down into the soil of the k
12:30 spirit k we measure not by earth's
12:69 into the k I have prepared for you
12:91 view the glories of the k
13:9 know me draws that k very near
13:33 k, to find that k, to serve that k
13:34 k of God, the first step is to make
13:34 make sure your will is for that k
13:34 nothing less than that his k come
13:34 Seek to advance his k in all things
13:35 Seek in all things his k first
13:36 will mean a gain for my k
13:48 In my k it is known that strength
14:64 beauty of my k is its growth
14:64 In that k there is always progress
14:65 Be in my k, and of my k
14:83 for the great work of my k
15:21 no idle hours in my k
15:31 not the mind of my k
16:9 live with me in that k of joy, my k
17:23 followers and found my earthly k
17:24 who had eyes to see my spiritual k
17:26 I came to found a k—the k
17:26 lived in the k were to do the work
17:27 gather around me the nucleus of my k
17:27 teach the truths of my k to them
17:31 must be no rush into the k
17:63 privileges of the members of my k
17:64 impossible with the blessings of the k
17:67 into the very heart of my k
18:24 Accept the truth that the k of

Knees

2:38 have weak k and hearts that faint
3:79 child went down on its k
13:23 Bend your k in wonder before my

Know

1:15 You shall see; you shall k
1:41 Do not I k just what it can bear
2:10 Seek to k and then to do my will
2:12 You k little yet of the divine
2:66 You must k that 'all is well'
2:67 I k better than you what you need
3:20 to k that I am with you
3:23 k that you seek me just to dwell in
3:32 You shall k and realize my power
3:37 if you k that I am your supply
3:52 life eternal, that they may k thee
3:57 fell out, never to k until the last
3:59 You cannot k the strengthening
3:63 Do you k that every thought, every
3:65 To k that would remake the world
4:1 hosts of heaven k—the Son of
4:27 you lack the faith to know it
4:29 k what it is to feel sure that I can
4:40 k the needs of man; few k the needs
4:44 all who k you shall k that I, your
4:47 can never k the ecstasy, the wonder
4:47 spirit communication as you k it
4:61 they k not what they do
4:95 I will tell you all you should k
4:95 all it is good for you to k of my
5:2 You do not k all that this time with
5:22 We k no life, but eternal life
5:23 life eternal, to k God, my Father and
5:46 Seek not to k the future
5:75 I k you do
5:78 Do you k, even yet, my children
6:9 then you will k the rapturous joy of
6:20 Seek to k more and more of that
6:21 I k not where they have laid him
6:31 ways and k that help will come
6:37 to k the pain and difficulty of the
6:37 the other's life that I k
6:59 I k no barrier then
6:77 I k no joy such as the joy I feel at
7:23 see the soul we seek; I k
7:28 K surely that your lives too are
7:30 Father, then indeed you k him
7:31 K indeed that 'All is well'
7:56 Always k that all things are yours
7:67 This partnership will k success
7:72 K that you can do all things through
7:72 k that you can do all things through
7:79 First, be still and k that I am God
7:85 k that I am the divine third in your
7:93 only its maker can k it
8:13 I k that only in earnest supplication
8:24 K that; repeat it; rely on it
8:40 can command his friend, can k that
8:51 You must k that every troubled soul
8:67 just to k I am beside you
8:94 feelings that you k others have or
9:38 To k that peace is to have received
9:44 to those who k me intimately
10:35 Just k that all is well and that
10:63 I k you will see this had to be
10:80 Beyond all doubt, you must k it
10:85 K my divine power
11:28 close to me and you shall k the way
11:68 life eternal that they may k thee
11:68 contact to k me more and more
11:72 Do not you k that I am here?
11:73 k that I need no agonized pleading
11:79 Say it until you believe and k it
11:86 k my way is a sure way, that my
12:3 who made each plant to k its season
12:32 You k the difference between

12:61 K that I will do the very best for
12:62 K that with me all things are
12:73 K that I shall cause you no more
13:8 life eternal that we may k thee
13:9 Learning to k me draws that kingdom
13:12 Say it until you k it and are so
13:14 you must k it has not done so
13:35 K no values but spiritual values
13:35 K no profit but that of spiritual
13:54 K that you will be led; K that you
13:62 K that all is well
13:67 k him and me as we really are, then
14:22 Be still and k that I am God
14:27 To those who k me not, there is
14:28 To those who k me, there is nothing
14:35 Do you not k what it means to feel
14:35 to k a child's confidence?
14:36 K it is not possible; K it is not
14:39 I k all, every cry for mercy
14:39 I k every sigh of weariness
14:42 I k all; I am beside you, strong
14:42 Lean on my love and k that all is
14:49 k that I am leading you
14:80 that I should not k that desertion
14:81 I k what loneliness, desertion
15:5 rapture you may k as you hear the
15:10 You must k even when you cannot see
15:17 disciples should k the way of
15:23 'I k not the man'
15:24 love me and k me, doubt my power to
15:35 k this, that from the moment you
15:63 only to k my will and to do my work
15:66 Keep self out and k that my Spirit
15:67 natural to k they are being helped
15:96 k that your help and salvation
16:1 K it is true that when two who
16:16 K that whatever the future may hold
16:17 Learn to k me more and more
16:18 K no theology; K me; I was the Word
16:19 All you need to k about God you k in
16:19 If a man does not k me, all your
16:21 Men must see and k your joy
16:21 they must k, without any doubt
16:30 men k ye are my disciples
16:32 you k, for myself but for you
16:35 How could they k my Spirit was free
16:53 K me; talk to me; let me talk to
16:55 know and love me more
16:55 certainty that I k best, and that I
16:56 k me who think I wish to thwart them
16:75 k that I will supply your need
17:5 K that while the mob was hooting
17:5 reviling crowds could never k
17:28 all men to not k what they want
17:29 k that their search would end
17:31 Did I k that perhaps many followed
17:31 Did I k that there must be no rush
17:43 k that Jesus will be with us
17:43 k that Jesus will provide
17:53 K this—in your great love for
18:11 K that my loving response will
18:14 K that all is well
18:26 As you k, money to hoard or to

Known

3:27 then my power shall be seen and k
3:38 made k as a heart consciousness
3:58 They would have k
3:87 let your requests be made known unto God
6:14 peculiar people to make k my name
6:16 Be k by the marks that distinguish
7:22 where it has not been k before
8:10 make k to you my purposes
8:31 greater heights than you have k before
9:69 high because you have k my name
10:50 rules I gave to my followers are k
10:93 high because you have k my name
13:48 k that strength lies in quiet
13:55 place, k only to God and you
13:65 still have not k the Father?
15:5 k the rapture you may know as you
16:7 k only to my friends and those who
16:20 but your joy must be made k
16:20 'k unto all men'
16:33 How they failed was k only to me and
16:79 as I make k to you my wishes
16:85 joy k to those who suffer with me

Lack

3:5 L of love will block the way
4:25 want or l, Jesus saves from
4:27 you l the faith to know it
6:52 you fail for l of it
6:56 can be no l of forgiveness
6:56 that is really l of love
7:26 often my servants l power
8:45 l of control is not due to the big
8:64 fails for l of growth in me
10:9 many lives l poise
10:38 l of criticism, its desire to share
10:91 say is a l of trust in me
11:81 future, a l of trust in me
12:65 not signs of l of spirit but of the
13:43 all unbelief, all l of trust
14:75 from l of beauty, from the
14:76 In your l and limitations, my
16:50 so beautiful as to l nothing
17:25 l of which had hindered my work on
18:48 l of love in big and little

Ladder
6:48 steps in the l that leads to success
10:84 plant your feet on an insecure l
10:84 then surely I have secured your l
12:63 l which a soul can climb from the
14:66 learned from them as if rungs in a l
14:66 Step up the l, then cast away

Lamb
14:68 I am the l of God

Land
4:7 before have entered the promised l
9:84 promised l of freedom
10:74 places him on dry l to restore him
11:50 at last, gain the promised l
13:50 calm river through the dry l of life
14:16 l flowing with milk and honey

Laugh
1:9 Love and l
1:10 Love and l; I am with you
4:82 Love, l, make the world
4:91 L more; l often
5:72 Love and l; rejoice!
6:35 Love and l; make your world happier
10:27 Love and l; cheer all; love all
10:29 to you is still the same: love and l
10:30 your attitude; love and l
10:85 L and trust
11:34 Forget, forgive, love and l
13:60 Love and l; delight yourselves
18:35 Love and l; trust ad pray

Laughter
1:9 Love and l are the beckoners to faith
3:80 difficulties with love and l
3:83 endure with courage, with love and l
4:69 Love and l is needed from the plow
5:27 health, happiness and l
5:67 L is the outward expression of joy
5:67 I urge upon you love and l
6:88 Change each complaint into l
7:88 Face each day with love and l
8:17 love and l of your attitude toward
10:28 See me in the l of children
10:30 Love and l, not a sorrowful
10:38 its ready l, its lack of criticism
10:85 L is a child's faith in God and good
11:34 Fill your world with love and l
11:44 birds and l and butterflies
12:26 It is the l of nature
17:57 not hear their l and feel a thrill

Law
1:24 This is my l of discipleship
2:27 same l operates too on the spiritual
6:58 Love is the fulfilling of all l
7:44 l than even freedom of the self
8:59 It is an undying l
10:7 of creation, of mighty l and order
11:81 It is a l of divine supply
12:75 Service is the l of heaven
13:1 Progress is the l of heaven
13:2 l of progress gives meaning, a
13:71 law in the spiritual life
15:47 My l is that of an unlimited supply
17:8 contains the first l of giving

Laws
7:30 of divine control in nature's l
12:6 with its statespersons, its l, its
12:6 l made at your request, and evils
16:18 about my Father and his l

Laziness
4:53 In l, whether spiritual, mental or

Learn
1:61 L of me
2:2 l poise, soul-balance and poise
2:12 Be quick to l
2:23 mother l all this joy in preparation
2:30 You have much to l
2:37 L to shut yourself away in my
2:42 l that your vision and power
3:69 L patience, humility and peace
3:70 You are slow to l your lesson
3:71 You must l to take calm with you
4:9 you must l not to fail it
4:10 l in turning out fear and being at
5:12 L what it is to shut your self in
5:26 you could l no other way
5:48 not to l the future and not to
5:85 L this
6:28 L to love discipline
6:42 gymnast you must l balance
7:12 L of me
7:80 l speed to attain its goals
7:80 l calm to succeed for me
8:13 man l strength and gain peace
8:93 L as a child to say
9:81 L of me
10:8 L in the little daily things of life
10:29 L daily the sublime lesson of
10:75 l what I, your rescuer, would do and
10:90 You shall rest with me and l
11:13 My children, l of me
11:42 l your lesson quickly
11:63 l what it means to give me the
11:84 lesson for my children to l
11:91 L of overcoming power from me
12:57 L from my life of the suffering that

6:9 A risen l glad and free can be
6:13 in l and work, in love and service
6:17 all that hinders the risen l
6:17 to rise from death to l
6:20 Let nothing hinder your risen l
6:20 know more and more of that risen l
6:20 that is the l of conquest
6:20 risen l it was truly said, 'I live'
6:37 difficulty of the other's l that I
6:59 do my work in the heart and l
6:73 Christian l—l with me—is a love
6:83 L is a training school
6:85 L can never be the same again for
6:85 wine of my giving—the l eternal
6:93 provide a channel for the l flow
7:1 within you is the l of l; the l that
7:2 Spirit, that is your l's breath
7:9 is to use God in your l
7:9 l is to bring into manifestation
7:24 that makes the problems of l plain
7:25 difficulties of l are caused by
7:42 blow to the l of self you must at the
7:42 hold fast the new l, l with me
7:44 Petty self l exchanged for divine l
7:48 killing the self now, in your daily l
7:49 one way of feeding a self-l
7:53 Share all l with me
7:90 thrill of fresh l floods your being
7:94 unraveling of the puzzles of l
8:2 wonder of family l is expressed in
8:22 L, eternal l, is yours—revitalizing
8:27 L is not all storms and tempests
8:37 spiritual l, the training is different
8:37 l of prayer and meditation is thrust
8:37 thrust into the busy ways of l
8:58 inner urge of l within the seed
8:62 so much that l cannot be a failure
8:73 spiritual l, man does these things
9:25 This l is not for the body
9:25 man too often chooses the way of l
9:45 l of my disciples (the home
9:56 The beauty of a guided l!
9:63 l, the character would be so altered
9:64 before I get crowded out by l's
9:70 l apart, of prayer, often
9:82 living with me and sharing my l
9:85 Cling to me until the l from me
9:85 divine l, by that very contact
10:1 companion along the dreary ways of l
10:3 from the worry and irritation of l
10:7 little things of everyday l
10:8 little daily things of l to delay
10:9 big things of l, they rush alone into
10:11 those who rise above the earth l
10:18 L is flooded through and through
10:38 but for its joy in l, its ready
10:41 Bread of l, food from heaven
10:43 Much of my l on earth is still
10:60 preparation for the wonderful l work
10:81 no age in eternal l
11:10 knowledge of your individual l
11:32 entered upon the God-guided l
11:33 too wonderful for such a l?
11:33 see how wonderful l with me
11:44 l-giving summer air
11:48 L with me, the conquering Christ
11:52 causes for thankfulness in his l
11:53 When l seems hard and troubles
11:63 offered me all l, every day, every
11:66 L is one glorious whole
11:67 more this wonderful eternal l
11:67 flow of l eternal through spirit
11:68 this is l eternal that they may
11:70 eternal l is the only lasting l
11:70 power of my Spirit, my l, is
11:70 done in that Spirit-l is undying
11:71 I will give unto them eternal l
11:71 eternal l means security and safety
12:9 it is a glorious l, the l of one who
12:9 Love with me, sharers of my l
12:12 character—in relation to l, to
12:15 I came to give you l
12:15 l, joyous l, and a powerful l
12:17 precious gift of l, abundant l
12:23 Rest until l, eternal l, flowing
12:31 as in the big things of l
12:36 sought to live my l
12:47 On l's journey, throw away all that
12:57 Learn from my l of the suffering that
12:66 narrow way, it leads to l, abundant l
12:69 A new l is opening before you
12:76 beginning of a new l consecrated to
12:76 a l of power and joy
12:81 live a l of communion and prayer
12:91 unseen—that is the real l
13:1 rise to l and beauty, knowledge and
13:2 gives meaning, a purpose to l
13:3 Theirs is a l of happiness and progress
13:7 at the real, the eternal l
13:8 this is l eternal that we may
13:16 love makes all l different
13:19 success then is l with me
13:20 make the best of l?
13:20 me, the master and giver of all l
13:28 l in overflowing measure l
13:28 give l for souls, the eternal l
13:29 I spoke of l when I said,'I am'
13:29 l flow of the vine is in the
13:31 have as my l flows through you
13:32 my l accomplishes the

10:33 L on every fear, not as a weakness
10:45 L for the loving, the true
10:57 l for but the faith that lays the
11:27 L on each difficulty as training
11:53 l for causes for thankfulness
12:2 l up to me and I will be your sure aid
12:24 L to me for cure, for rest, for peace
12:94 L to me for all
13:7 as you l, not at the things that are
13:14 l around to see what you can give
13:82 L on all you meet as guests in
14:5 path must l to those who view it
14:7 When you l to me for guidance, my hand
14:13 L to no other source for salvation
14:13 Only l unto me
14:13 L unto me, and you shall be saved
14:15 danger threatens, l unto me
14:15 need for others, l unto me
14:63 l back, from the place of your
14:67 l with scorn upon the marble the
14:75 L away from sordid surroundings
15:11 L to no other arm, l for no other
16:12 l to the hills of the Lord
16:15 l to the Lord who made heaven
16:15 l to me, owner of all this, the Lord

Looked

2:45 l too often upon that promise as
8:19 promise was for all who l

Looking

8:22 Look and keep l
12:46 a command—no l back
14:57 l to me, you will be lightened
14:76 L at me, you will grow like me
15:81 L back you will se that every step

Lord

1:12 I your L have said it
1:56 'Even so, come L Jesus'
1:8 I am the L of the little things
2:25 One with the L of the whole universe!
2:30 'Sing unto the L'
2:40 But the L of all seas is with you, the
2:41 You follow the L of limitations, as well
3:14 mother forsake thee, then the L will
3:31 I am your L, your supply
4:43 shall know that I, your L, am the L
4:91 I am your L
5:1 I am your L, life of your body, mind
5:2 'They that wait upon the L shall
5:25 I am your L; there is none other
5:33 I am your L; just obey me as you
5:36 I, your L, am not only with you on
5:45 'All power is given unto my L'
5:68 I am your L, gracious and loving
5:82 I am here, your waiting L, ready at
6:21 'They have taken away my L and I know'
6:22 to meet me, your risen L
6:49 I, your L, see not as man sees
6:81 never fear changes when I, your L
6:95 Many have called me L, L, who have not
7:52 I am your L, your creator
8:35 why do you call me, 'L, L,' and not do
9:38 the mark of the L Jesus Christ
9:41 'Why call ye me L, L, and do not the'
10:6 Your L, your master, your divine
10:19 dwell in the house of the L
10:41 'L,' we cry, 'to whom shall we go'
11:21 glory of the L is risen upon thee
11:31 I am your L, L of your lives
11:72 I am your healer, your joy, your L
11:72 You bid me, your L, to come
12:62 possible with my master, my L, my
12:87 I am your L; I can command your
13:31 all else you see in me, your L
13:43 'Lord, I believe; help thou mine'
13:60 Delight yourselves in the L
13:85 acting for your master and L who
14:29 desire in me—as master, L or friend
14:54 distress, bless the L even when troubles
15:41 It is I your L and friend
15:53 acknowledge me as L and Christ gave
15:94 but by my Spirit, saith the L
15:95 'He, our L, our friend, could'
16:6 my joy, the joy of your L
16:10 The glory of the L is the beauty
16:11 glory of the L is also risen upon you
15:11 have been with me, your L and Savior
16:12 The hills of the L, the hills whence
16:12 help from the L, who made heaven
16:13 false to the hills of the L
16:13 your eyes to the help of the L
16:13 eyes to the hills of the L
16:15 spiritual needs look to the L who
16:15 this, the L who made the earth
16:16 Your hope is in the L
16:71 'L, send them away that they may go'
17:68 grow and become a garden of the L
18:9 your master is the L of the day's
18:10 I am the L of the moments, creator
18:20 not as King and L in heavenly triumph
18:38 and ever shall be to you—a risen L

Lord's

4:49 that his L's power was his

Loved

Lover

Loves

Loving

9:48 m of your character that steadfast
11:27 m sure that no work, no interruption
11:40 permitted to m mistakes in your
11:69 M me the one abiding presence of
12:6 m these matters your prayer concerns
12:12 M it your practice, each of you
12:26 sunshine helps to m glad the heart
12:50 I m all things new
12:53 'Behold, I m all things new'
13:12 that nothing can m you afraid
13:20 want to m the best of life?
13:32 You do not m yourselves loving and
13:34 m sure your will is for that kingdom
13:56 M it your home
13:57 my shadow rest to m it doubly safe
14:48 M me love you more and more
14:69 You m my sacrifice of no effect
15:20 let him m himself a conquering
15:65 m sure there is nothing to block the
16:53 m clear to your loving hearts what
16:79 as I m known to you my wishes
17:20 m it your meat to do my will
18:11 m that way as easy for your feet as
18:18 m the mistake of thinking all must be

Manifest

6:33 all God needs to m his power
9:76 cause it to m in the material
15:93 m there, as marvelously m today

Mansion

2:44 the m I went to prepare for each of

Marble

16:67 faulty piece of m casts it aside
16:67 m the sculptor is cutting and shaping

March

4:5 puny self impedes their onward m
8:73 A man on a m carries only what he
8:73 he needs for that m
13:18 a glad conquering and triumphant m
17:59 for you both is a m—a toilsome m
17:59 Think simply of the m

Mark

9:38 m of the Lord Jesus Christ; my m

Marks

6:16 m that distinguish those of

Mars

5:18 interpreter m the first great act

Master

1:41 I am a m instrument-maker
1:42 another m—the world, fame, the good
3:44 you are in the hands of a m gardener
6:79 I that speak unto you am he, your m
6:99 Make it your servant, never your m
7:13 'M, carest thou not that we perish?'
7:15 spirit should be the m always
7:21 glorious to follow where your M goes
8:1 A loving m delights in the intimacy
8:85 grow more and more like me, your M
10:6 Your Lord, your m, your divine friend
10:23 leave all your affairs in a m hand
12:62 possible with my m, my Lord, my
12:71 believe me, your m, that all this
13:20 me, the m and giver of all life
13:28 I, your m, am a generous giver
13:85 you are acting for your m and Lord
14:29 desire in me—as m, Lord or friend
15:60 axe in a m hand accomplishes much
15:60 m hand that wields the instrument
15:81 designed by the m artist
16:74 servant is not above his m
17:68 Bethany home for your m, a place
18:9 your m is the Lord of the little
18:32 rock is your m—that rock is Christ

Material

2:27 to dwell in thought on the m
2:53 spiritual (as in the m) world, there
2:74 striving on the m plane
3:15 m help of any kind is removed
3:23 m gain or for a message—but for me
3:72 not seek the spiritual through m
4:80 communication with the m world
4:80 m manifestations around you
5:34 help and m flow can come
7:52 all you need on the m plane
8:12 m things first and then grow into
8:12 spiritual things first and then m
8:12 to attain the m, redouble your efforts
8:59 without it being seen in the m world
9:72 success on the m plane necessary to
9:74 m plane and the spiritual is only to
9:74 spiritual is only to help the m
9:74 m goal is reached, then the m
9:76 cause it to manifest in the m
11:84 so dependent on m supply
13:36 seek m gain when that gain will
14:20 control others and the m forces of
14:70 you can realize it in m form
15:17 know the way of conquest over the m
15:21 the surrounding m plane
17:9 wrong to give money and m things
17:24 thought m forces had proved too
17:63 temporal and m blessings I spoke

Matters
2:48 Nothing else m
3:59 being in my presence that m
3:74 real life is all that m
3:75 That alone m
4:41 my speaking to the soul m so much
6:36 what m is duty, persistently
11:6 make these m your prayer concerns
12:33 guidance that m with my disciples
16:26 See that only love m
18:38 What m is what I am, was, and ever

Meaning
1:33 convey my m to the heart without
10:73 I am m to save you even more
13:2 law of progress gives m, a purpose to
14:20 That was my m of the word meek
15:86 ideas of the m of my invitation
15:87 wealth of m far surpassing even that

Medicines
12:27 My m are sun and air, trust and

Meditate
1:45 M upon them; work at them in your
5:14 M on all I say; ponder it, not to
8:28 M upon the three steps of that

Meek
5:82 one that serves, m and holy, ready to
5:85 be humble, m and lowly in heart
14:20 m shall inherit the earth
14:20 That was my meaning of the word m

Meet
1:33 M together nevertheless
3:17 m me in spite of all opposition and
3:18 reward of coming regularly to m me
3:58 silence as the two of you m with me
3:73 M me in communion
3:80 m all your difficulties with love and
6:11 Search until you m me face to face
6:22 sunlight to m me, your risen Lord
6:22 that you will m, either in the spirit
6:28 love to be showered on all you m
6:97 m me in the atmosphere of love
8:46 allow yourself to speak to, or m
11:80 that more will come to m your supply
13:82 all you m as guests in your Father's
15:66 all you m will be better for coming
16:1 two who love me m, I am the third
16:2 not only when you m to greet me
17:8 Give to all you m, or whose lives
17:53 malice of all you m who are not on

Men
1:8 becomes fishers of m
1:42 fame, the good opinion of m
1:50 if m seek the babble of the world
2:11 loving understanding to all m
2:67 I can read m's hearts
3:12 All m can be moved at my wish
3:66 supernatural m, m who will
4:25 given among m, whereby m can be
4:39 came 'to draw m unto me,' and sweet
5:15 m have been too eager to say what
5:87 moment as so often m imagine
6:16 Be ready to confess me before m
6:95 driven out by the words of m
6:96 speak with the tongues of m and of
6:98 do away with m from the earth
7:39 Men call the Father the first cause
7:43 not a dead self that m have to fear;
7:55 M should think of men with their
8:91 Few m would send a further gift until
9:18 No man could be all these to m
10:7 When m seek to worship me they think
10:38 desire to share all with all m
10:52 world of m and women cannot do this
11:44 hearts of m are drawn to me
14:58 also be righted in the eyes of m
14:76 grow like me until m say to you
14:80 his rejection by m, and the
15:14 to be trodden under foot of m
16:20 'known unto all m'
16:21 M must see and know your joy
16:27 speaks with the tongues of m and of
16:30 by this shall all m know ye are my
16:49 body so beautiful that m would
16:71 fainting, exhausted m, women
17:4 praise and notice of m
17:6 ludicrous, contemptible m followed
17:6 despised and rejected of m
17:26 as m recognized my Godhead
17:28 All m seek for me, but all m do not
17:31 persuade m I was the Son of God?
18:43 With m your task may be impossible

Mercy
2:67 You are not at the m of fate
9:13 Never feel at the m of the world
10:19 m shall follow us all the days of
11:83 at the will and m of the rescuer
14:39 I know all, every cry for m

Message
1:33 Sometimes you may get no m
1:33 m to convey my meaning to the heart
2:64 echoes down the 1900 years my m
3:23 gain or for a m—but for me
4:75 my m in its beauty and perfume
4:90 Take the song as a m from my father

5:56 My m to you is to trust and wait
6:47 m of my servant Paul now plain:
8:47 m is delivered or that the task is
10:26 vitalizing joy-giving m goes on
14:82 task of bringing my m to

Mind
2:11 attitude of m, words, and deeds of
2:13 worrying thought enter your m, one
3:76 divine m and its wonder working is
3:76 beyond your finite m to understand
4:15 healing of body, m and spirit comes
5:1 Lord, life of your body, m and soul
7:49 recurs to your m, you deceive
7:58 Empty your m of all that limits
8:79 prayer links up the soul and m and
9:81 m which is in Jesus Christ
9:81 The m which is in me
9:82 That m you can never obtain by
11:26 spoil your peace of heart and m
11:34 Never m what anguish lies behind
11:57 merging of heart and m a oneness
11:67 m and body, that cleanses, heals
12:24 physician, healer of m and body
12:28 M, soul and body need helping
12:65 m-weariness of my servants, which
13:28 animates your m and body too
14:22 m and soul and body be strong to
14:70 you must see this in your m
14:80 of his m and purpose
15:31 not the m of my kingdom
15:31 is the measure of my will and m
17:44 no fear can possess your m
17:68 once only a thought of divine m

Miracle
1:29 M-working power can become witchery
2:73 Singly they are m-producing in a life
3:9 house of paper at my m-working touch
5:79 find that you are m workers
5:80 what you are—that is the m-working
5:87 All m work is not the work of a moment
6:44 Spiritual sight is in itself a m
7:12 rest always precede fresh m working
7:71 from resting with God is m work
8:53 disciples that worked the m
9:78 belief can I do m works now
10:22 no m is impossible with me
10:49 all m working friend
10:69 under my control, are m works
11:2 to me a m is only a natural
11:2 miracle is only a natural happening
11:20 M of the ages!
11:67 from you to others with the same m
12:20 The union is m working
13:87 My m-working power is limitless
13:91 help, guidance and m working power
14:38 no m I cannot perform, nothing I
14:78 all m working power of your divine
15:92 think that my m working power was
15:93 my m working power is as manifest
16:77 m of your intimacy with me
17:50 no m so wonderful as the m of
18:34 of m working with me

Mission
14:1 founded my three years' m on earth
17:15 fulfill your m to work for me and to
17:22 certainty that my m had failed

Mock
8:71 you m me to expect me to share it

Molding
9:1 M, my children, means cutting and
9:2 M means swift recognition of the
9:26 this and a wonderful m is the

Moment
1:39 m, worketh for us a far more
1:49 At the m you are pilgrims and need
2:44 surrender of every m to God is the
2:48 ruffled feeling stay for one m
2:48 blessing may be checked in one m by
5:32 trivial or or seemingly great m, all
5:58 think for one m all that means
5:77 for that m's horror
5:87 not the work of a m as so often men
5:89 his m of abject remorse, could best
6:49 when it is lost for even one m
6:86 Do as I say each m and all shall be
7:33 Think for a m of the love and
9:45 not built by a wish or in a m, but
9:74 All your work for the m is in
11:26 disturb it for one m
11:61 thought, word and m to be mine
11:73 hour of need is the m of my coming
12:5 m a thing seems wrong to you or a
12:5 m your obligation and
12:44 not to dwell for one m on your sins
12:93 one m lose the consciousness of my
14:72 m, in the most difficult place
14:89 m no burden irks or presses them
15:10 last m before you see my deliverance
15:35 from the m you placed all in my
15:35 from that m I have taken the
17:23 final m came and the hatred of the
17:59 for the m do not think of that
18:9 receive every m of my planning
18:30 Yield every m to me

3:82 too late and that they m act
3:86 you m live and have rest for your
4:6 You m trust me wholly
4:9 how to live and you m do it
4:9 but you m learn not to fail it
4:11 You m not doubt
4:11 You m believe in me absolutely
4:18 Nobody m come and feel unwanted
4:49 It m have been wonderful for Peter
4:67 There m be another and better
4:68 all work m be done in my Spirit
4:80 You m sever all connection with them
4:92 Your standard m never be the world's
5:6 All that hinders your activity m be
5:21 I said, 'Ye m be born again'
5:60 But they m go hand in hand
6:13 My children m make a stand
6:13 my children m stand out
6:14 my followers m be willing to be
6:42 gymnast you m learn balance
6:55 You also m put love (God) into
6:62 m be traced back to my loving
6:65 they m be helped
6:88 Joy, radiant joy, m be yours
7:2 You m never doubt, never worry
7:2 but m walk step by step the way
7:7 you m only desire joy and blessing
7:37 m be the mere unconscious
7:42 you m at the same time embrace
7:45 so you m forgive
7:60 you m see that on it are inscribed
7:60 world is feeling, I m feel
7:61 weariness of man m be shared by you
7:61 heavy laden m come to you and find
7:62 my followers m be prepared not to
7:65 against the tide you m direct all your
7:75 You m not expect to live in a world
7:75 You m not expect to live where others
8:33 To see me you m bring me your cares
8:35 Now it m be said of you, even in
8:36 my disciples m work out their own
8:44 There m first be a definite
8:51 You m know that every troubled soul
8:51 You m help all you can
8:58 task beyond its power that m seem
8:64 the deeper m be the root
8:74 You m not act so
9:18 relations of mine to man you m see
9:80 It m strengthen and help you just to
10:5 time to visit m be at the pleasure of
10:12 You m not feel the burden of your
10:20 bless and use m be the right ones for
10:36 kingdom m become as little
10:38 You m not copy the child-spirit only
10:73 you m also believe that I am
10:80 You m not doubt this
10:80 You m see this
10:80 Beyond all doubt, you m know it
10:83 there m be songs on the way
10:91 This m not be
10:92 it m be a purified you to be so
11:10 m be lacking to some extent
11:31 You m act as I tell you
11:58 ground m be prepared before the
11:82 you m trust wholly in me
11:83 then I m first answer your prayer
11:83 rescuer m render him more
11:83 You m live as I tell you
11:87 You m have both effort and rest
12:30 your training m be severe
12:43 shame and remorse m come
12:45 You m be as one who runs a race
12:81 You m live a life of communion and
13:14 you m know it has not done so
13:14 you m, at the same time, look around
13:25 You m be ready to stand apart from
13:30 my nature m therefore pass into
13:31 you m have as my life flows through
13:34 you m have a single eye to God's
13:56 you m dwell therein
13:57 how sure, you m feel there
13:71 You m turn to me before you are
13:71 that turning to me you m cultivate
13:71 It m be a glad turning of
13:75 you m accept me, the great teacher
14:2 you m both accept in life is not to be
14:2 It m be accepted, as I accepted it
14:3 same m be true as was so true of me
14:5 Dreary as that path m look to those
14:19 will, there m be a gladness
14:38 You m not doubt; you m be sure
14:70 you m see this in your mind
14:73 reform m be in yourselves
15:9 You m trust to the end
15:9 You m be ready to go on trusting to
15:10 You m know even when you cannot see
15:10 You m be ready, like my servant
15:11 You m rely on me alone
15:20 needed and m be employed
15:22 You m utterly believe
15:69 You m forget your failures
15:76 You m call new forces, new powers
15:77 trouble, it m be surmounted
15:77 Nothing m daunt you; you m conquer it
16:9 Suffering m in time bring joy
16:12 you m look to the hills of the Lord
16:16 your way m truly be one of
16:20 Not only m you rejoice

16:20 your joy m be made known
16:20 A candle m not be set under a bushel
16:21 Men m see and know your joy
16:21 they m know, without any doubt
16:38 you m share my tribulations
16:38 unchallenged, you m be evil
16:46 forgotten you, m wait now that you
16:57 Your lives m first be narrowed
16:73 you m go too, if possible
17:3 My disciples m always seek to judge
17:9 You m first practice giving in
17:11 you m closely resemble your Father
17:12 receive, you m supply the needs of
17:12 relationship to you m never count
17:15 you m fully expect a mighty
17:15 You m realize that
17:31 there m be no rush into the kingdom
17:44 You m not allow fear to enter
17:55 each day m be lived in my power
17:66 All m be done in love and in the
18:16 But it m be my peace
18:17 It m never be a peace that is a truce
18:17 You m never have harmony if that
18:18 thinking all m be harmonious
18:20 first hail m be that of the Magi in
18:20 triumph you m first hail me
18:21 first hail m be the worship of humility
18:28 You m never do it
18:44 my heart m ache with the woe of it

Myrrh
18:25 m is your sharing in my sorrows

Name
1:59 conquer in my strength and n
2:63 world has most rewarded with n, fame
4:25 'none other n under heaven given'
6:11 my tender uttering of your n
6:14 peculiar people to make known my n
8:40 friend's means—his n, his time, all
9:65 Say my n often
9:65 my n Peter bade the lame man walk
9:65 n of Jesus Christ of Nazareth
9:66 sounding of my n, in love and
9:67 n banishes loneliness—dispels
9:68 n summons help to conquer your
9:69 high because you have known my n
9:69 My n, *Jesus*
10:93 n, but it must be a purified you to
12:77 Just breathe my n
13:37 My n is the power that turns evil
13:38 Use my n often
13:38 Use my n in that same way—simply
13:39 name not only when you need help
13:40 'There is none other n under heaven'
13:69 Sing and praise my holy n
14:60 later, for, and in, my n
15:51 Call my n often, *Jesus*
15:51 Calling my n does not really summon
16:1 two are together in my n, united by
16:29 work done in my n is not acknowledged
16:63 be 'gathered together in my n'
17:26 for works in my n would increase
17:43 banish fear by my presence and my n
18:6 Fight it in my n
18:47 That is the n by which you conquer
18:47 Say my n, Jesus, not as cringing
18:47 Thou shall call his n Jesus, for he
18:49 uttering of the n lifts the soul away
18:51 There is none other name

Narrow
2:41 within the n limits of a baby
8:35 straight and n way into the kingdom
12:66 my way may seem a n way, it leads to
16:58 do not think of it as a n life

Naturally
6:92 n from the very union with the vine
6:94 All else follows so n
6:98 commune with his God simply and n
7:15 n use the body as the need should
7:26 n as light results from a lighted
9:53 conditions will n alter
12:32 accepts n each decision as to each
13:38 simply, n, forcefully
18:15 n, lovingly, trustingly, in the

Nature
1:63 I bore the self human n of the world
4:73 n is weary too of her long months of
4:74 N is the embodied spirit of my
7:30 lessons of divine control in n's
7:30 N is but the expression of eternal
9:21 your whole n becomes changed
10:37 n that of the trusting child
11:2 regards it as something contrary to n
11:42 wrong in your own n aroused by such
12:26 It is the laughter of n
12:29 N is often my nurse for tired souls
13:16 opening of your whole n to me
13:30 my n must therefore pass into yours
13:46 n rebels, it is her call for rest

Necessary
1:29 of your own lives n to you
2:17 faith is the n weapon for you to
2:33 It is absolutely n
2:35 My death on the cross was n
2:35 Every step was n to their development

3:76 husk was n to present the life grain
3:88 n because your contact with me is
7:7 Leave to me the n correcting or training
8:61 n before this power is given
8:64 two growths are n
8:80 things are n, they are secured
9:16 It is not n that you see me as others
9:16 n that you see me, each of you, as
9:72 n to further the work of my kingdom
10:16 n is hope, which is confidence
10:36 If faith was so n for miracles
10:71 everything n for your wellbeing
13:27 I will give you all n reward
14:2 accepted as being n for you
14:12 all that is n for its performance
17:65 n that they understand if they

Need
1:24 Only have what you n and use
1:34 in some hour of n, the recipient
1:49 n only your daily marching orders
2:18 So you n works, too, to feed your
2:18 that faith is all you n for my
2:21 of me n to be revolutionized
2:67 I know better than you what you n
3:2 where would be its n?
3:55 goal is in sight, you n your final
3:65 I only n instruments to use
3:66 The world does not n supermen, but
4:1 You do not n to see far ahead
4:18 Today they may not n you
4:18 Tomorrow they may n you
4:39 my n—my n of love and companionship
5:16 My words n none of man's explanations
5:24 You n to trust me for everything
5:39 You cannot have a n I cannot supply
5:40 Your n is a spiritual n to carry
5:40 from love to those who n it
5:42 only if the n is a spiritual one
5:63 I n you more than you n me
6:32 Man's n is God's chance to help
6:32 Man's n is God's golden opportunity
6:58 All you n to have is love for God
6:71 You n me; I n you
6:87 adapted to the individual n
6:95 that the n may be apparent
7:15 use the body as n should arise
7:21 that you n the varied training
7:52 I can call into being all you n on
7:67 I n man's effort; he needs my
9:16 supplying all you personally n
9:17 The weak n my strength
9:17 The strong n my tenderness
9:17 tempted and fallen n my salvation
9:17 righteous n my pity for sinners
9:17 lonely n a friend
9:17 fighters n a leader
9:33 in your time of n, you can draw with
9:34 from his bank for his own n
9:53 that n altering first, but yourselves
9:61 Rest in me when you n perfect
9:61 when you n the consciousness of
11:73 Your hour of n is the moment of my
11:73 you would know that I n no agonized
11:73 Your n is my call
11:74 activity, then surely you n them too
11:75 Refilling with the Spirit is a n
12:25 I come; you n me
12:28 Mind, soul, and body n helping
12:41 I did not n to protect Peter from
12:89 They n only the watering of a
13:39 not only when you n help but to
13:41 is as expressive of human n
13:67 it is all you n
13:68 joy in abundance, all you n
13:72 you have no n to voice your longing
13:72 You n not plead or bring gifts
13:74 all you n is in the nearness
13:81 All you n to gain this rest is to
14:15 Whatever you desire or n
14:15 or desire or n for others, look unto
15:87 for all you n—physical, mental
15:96 miracles to your present day n
16:17 have all the answers you n here
16:17 you will find no n to ask
16:19 All you n to know about God you
16:44 do not feel their n of men, who
16:46 wait now, that you have no n of them
16:72 remedy for the evil or the n, pity
16:74 know that I will supply your n
17:1 heart recognizes the n for the man of
17:10 your best to all who n it
17:11 give according to n, never according
17:11 supply a real n, you must closely
17:12 Only their n is to guide you
18:36 Do not n feeling too much
18:51 If you n delivering from cowardice

Needs
1:46 unlimited stores for your n and those
2:19 already seen your hearts' n before
2:19 before you were conscious of those n
4:87 bringing to the owner the n, checks
4:40 Many know the n of man;
4:40 few know the n of Christ
6:33 faith is all God n to manifest his
6:50 It simply n an unblocked channel
6:71 My broken world n you
6:71 weary troubled heart n you

6:86 ample for your own n and those of
7:67 he n my blessing
8:53 only enough for our own n
8:73 only what he n for that march
8:81 n the things belonging to his
9:15 varying n of each, so does each
9:34 n of a friend or for some charity
11:65 world that n a savior
11:65 savior who n followers through
12:34 both express man's varying n of me
12:70 grace is sufficient for all your n
13:11 n nothing so much as a refuge
13:11 He n a place to hide
15:18 power, as money, n to be
16:15 for all your spiritual n look to
16:15 For all your temporal n look to
16:73 in thinking of your own n
17:12 you must supply the n of those I
18:26 sufficient for your n and for my

Never
1:6 N let one day pass when you have not
1:16 A child n questions plans but
1:23 I n send money to stagnate—only to
1:27 N neglect these times, pray and read
1:40 N think of things as overwhelming
1:50 listen to my voice; n crowd it out
1:53 trust me always; n rebel
1:57 N despair, n despond
2:00 in God, who n changes
2:4 N think you are too busy
2:15 N lose heart; all is well
2:30 Be calm; n fear
2:31 N be afraid; pray more;
2:33 N forget your 'Thank you'
2:58 N fear; joy is yours
2:66 I will n let anyone do to you
2:68 N fear, whatever may happen
2:71 N fear, but in that place you shall
2:72 I will n give you a load greater
3:13 You will n cease to be thankful for
3:16 N limit my power for it is limitless
3:42 Trust, trust, trust; N be afraid
3:45 So n cease to joy; Rejoice!
3:57 fell out, n to know until the last
3:60 n fail to keep this time apart with
3:65 divine force is n less than adequate
3:68 if I were n to speak to you, you
3:76 N miss these times
4:9 Trust my tender love; it will n fail
4:15 N forget that real healing of body
4:29 feel sure that I can n fail you?
4:47 n know the ecstasy, the wonder, of
4:51 You may n see it
4:66 N inspire fear; fear of punishment
4:92 standard must n be the world's
5:49 N doubt my love and power
5:51 N falter; go forward boldly
5:88 Peter could n have been the power
6:29 N yield one point that you have
6:50 N feel inadequate for any task
6:61 past n to be recaptured again
6:81 n fear changes when I, your Lord
6:85 Life can n be the same again for
6:95 N make yourselves do this
6:99 Make it your servant, n your
7:1 You can n perish, my children
7:2 You must n doubt, n worry, but must
7:10 N doubt; have no fear
7:16 N make opportunities
7:19 cheer my disciples who have n seen me
7:46 self in you, can n forgive injuries
7:80 N be afraid of any circumstances
7:86 N tolerate them for one second
7:92 answering n a word—n a word
7:93 N judge; the heart of man is so
8:5 N think of my love as only a
8:14 N weary in prayer
8:30 The conquering spirit is n crushed
8:57 N relinquish any task or give up the
9:10 N heed the voices of the world
9:11 Listen and you will n be disapointed
9:13 N feel at the mercy of the world
9:55 N look back and n leave until the
9:58 blessed by me as n before
9:62 It forgets, or n realizes, that if
9:82 That mind you can n obtain by
10:20 You can n go beyond my love and
10:55 N let yourselves think 'we cannot'
10:55 'we shall n be able to do that'
11:14 N be led by the world's standard
11:34 N mind what anguish lies behind you
11:42 The overcoming is n the overcoming
11:56 'I will n leave you nor forsake you'
11:71 they shall n perish, neither shall
11:77 My keeping power is n at fault, but
12:6 lives altered you n touched, laws
12:7 You may n go beyond one room, and
12:8 You may n see the mighty work you
12:11 N be satisfied with a comparison
12:24 Tired work n tells
12:40 Peter could n have done my work, n
12:43 they could n have the courage to
12:67 You will n be too lonely with such
12:83 'N leave'; 'N forsake'
12:84 my love will n leave you, my
12:84 my understanding will n leave you
12:84 my strength will n leave you
12:86 there is one who can n tire
12:88 N doubt
13:21 one who answered n a work in

13:37 an appeal I n fail to answer
13:74 N fear, n lose heart
13:89 I n force upon it my help or my
14:46 N doubt it; have courage, courage
14:85 cry of the human soul is n unheard
14:85 N does God fail to hear the cry, but
15:31 N count success by money gained
15:43 ground, n once soaring
16:1 N limit that promise
16:32 My overcoming was n, you know, for
16:43 satisfaction they have n found in
16:46 N think that those who have shut
16:83 solution may n be shown you until
17:5 reviling crowds could n know
17:11 give according to need, n according
17:12 relationship to you must n count
18:1 N let yourselves fear anybody or
18:1 N fear poverty or loneliness or of
18:1 N fear their misunderstanding
18:8 sake of my tender, n failing
18:17 must n be a pace that is a truce
18:17 n have harmony if that means your
18:27 N keep anything you are not using
18:28 treasures? You must n do it
18:33 N lose sight of the glorious work to

Nothing

1:24 Keep n for yourself
1:24 Hoard n
1:28 Be careful that you ask n amiss
1:28 n that is not according to my Spirit
1:36 Individual efforts avail n
2:8 N in the day is too small
2:48 N else matters
2:75 N is by chance
3:6 where n unloving can come
3:10 N else is needed
4:23 n that joy and love cannot do
4:27 n lacking in your lives
4:62 N is wrong
4:77 N is small to God
5:28 n is too big
6:18 You have n then to fear
6:20 Let n hinder your risen life
6:96 have not charity, I am n
7:3 toiled all night and taken n
7:31 Leave me out of n
7:48 n that even remembers injury
8:68 Regret n
9:13 n can harm you
9:52 my spirit power, with n to hinder
9:83 Let n less satisfy you
10:81 n but joy and gratitude
10:87 against which n can prevail
11:25 Allow n to disturb your peace
11:35 Let n that others do to you
11:39 until n has the power to spoil
11:88 keep so close to me that n
11:89 n can prevent you
11:89 n can cause you to stray
12:2 Fear n
12:11 Stop short at n less
13:11 needs n so much as a refuge
13:11 where none and n can touch him
13:12 n can make you afraid
13:34 Desire n less than that his
13:52 N fitful
13:72 n is needed but that weak appeal
14:27 n in me to appeal to them
14:28 there is n more to be desired
14:38 n I cannot do
14:46 Fear n
15:14 good for n but to be cast out
15:22 My love can bear n less
15:60 hand of a weak child, n
15:65 n to block the way
15:77 N must daunt you
15:78 N is too small to be faced
16:50 so beautiful as to lack n
16:81 n as compared with my
17:1 hearts see n contemptible in the
17:34 times when I reveal n, command n

Nullifies

5:44 n all the evils against you

Obedience

1:4 Faith and o will remove mountains of evil
6:24 O is one of the keys unlocking the door
6:25 steps of o lead up to the mosaic of joy
6:58 Love for God insures o to his every
6:77 loving o of my disciples brings to my
6:86 Divine control and unquestioning o
7:25 perfect o, all power, all conquest
7:26 that result from o, honesty, order, and
8:3 listening to and o to my bidding
8:35 Remember o, o, o—the straight and
8:75 acceptance of my will, o to it, have not
8:94 go along the arid way of o
9:41 O is your great sign of faith
9:45 walls and roof, by the acts of o
9:47 divinely inspired, the house of o
9:72 Follow the path of o; it leads to the
14:79 steadfast devotion, of o in
15:72 me not only worship and honor, o

Obey

2:6 O my will day in and day out, in the

5:33 Just o me as you would expect a faithful
6:24 the door into my kingdom, so love and o
6:24 No man can o me implicitly without
6:48 O my commands; they are steps in the
9:41 hear my voice and instantly o
9:42 did not obey to the man who built his
9:75 hear my will and then o; o at all costs
12:75 My angels always obey

Obeyed
9:43 I likened the man who o me implicitly
9:53 O, they will bring the answer
11:51 those who o, not seeing but believing
12:19 You have not o in this
12:47 an injunction to be o literally, but

Obeying
1:9 But as you go on o me, walking with me
6:64 Persevere in o my will
9:44 I mean more than o that to those who
9:44 o in all, in the inner guiding that I give

One
1:41 shall guide you o day at a time
1:6 Never let o day pass when you have
1:42 carrying two days' burden on o day
1:55 Drop o here and there
2:13 Does o worrying thought enter your
2:13 o impatient thought?
2:25 O with me
2:25 I and my Father are o
2:25 O with the Lord of the whole universe!
2:25 O with me
2:34 gray day is not o of thankfulness
2:39 Go just o step at a time
2:39 o step at a time is the best way to
2:48 let o ruffled feeling stay for o
2:48 blessing may be checked in o moment
2:65 not o want of the soul that I do
3:22 o or two who followed just to be
3:49 o walking on the waters, like unto the
3:62 making o spot of earth a holy place
3:77 There is only o thing to do
3:84 Not o of your cries goes unheard
4:1 Just o step at a time with me
4:4 alert for o such unguarded spot through
4:38 o poor tool, working all the time
4:43 tender intimacy of o much loved
4:77 o kindly word of more importance than
5:7 o of my disciples is foolish who seeks
5:7 only o place for them—my cross
5:17 lead a soul to me is o thing; to
5:34 no o agency when I am your supply
5:36 there is not o inch too much
5:39 o is no more difficult than the
5:41 into a cheer for o you love
5:42 only if the need is a spiritual o
5:58 o millionth part of all that you can
5:58 think for o moment all that means
5:70 o desire to show you love, more loved
5:77 from my Father's sight for o short
5:81 o garment of spirit for a better o
5:81 aside for a yet finer o, and so on
5:82 among you as o that serves, meek
5:91 I will not lay o test too much on you
6:24 Obedience is o of the keys unlocking
6:25 As o on earth may say of o he loves
6:29 Never yield o point that you have
6:47 when two are o in desire to be with
6:49 when it is lost for even o moment
6:49 help no o when you are agitated
6:54 I and the Father are o
6:68 Send no o away without a word of
6:76 cross on which o hangs alone, untended
6:76 I hang there afresh beside each o
6:77 feel at the loving trust of a dear o
6:94 union with me is the o great
7:4 Any o of these troubles might have
7:9 To love o another is to use God in your
7:38 smiles of the soul at o it loves
7:45 o of my commands that as you seek my
7:48 only o injured, the self, is dead
7:49 o way of feeding a self-life
7:63 only o cure for all its ills—union
7:69 quietly from o duty to the next
7:79 trust, can keep o calm
7:86 Never tolerate them for o second
7:94 How can o judge of another?
8:6 though my Father and I are o
8:14 When o day man sees how marvelously
8:20 O look suffices
8:24 o pull nearer shore and safety
8:26 o hand on the rope and o making
8:50 that there is o who knows
8:50 O who notes every crisis
8:51 I tell you of is o for you to help
8:66 presence of the loved o is sufficient
8:91 of the previous o had been received
9:47 I come to dwell with my loved o
9:73 From o promise or command of mine to

10:22 and my Father and I are o
10:26 on God currents from o to the other
10:34 Does the way seem a stony o?
10:34 Not o stone can impede your progress
10:42 o day be the food of my people
10:60 both o day see the reason for it
10:67 not sin for o who knows me only as
10:68 o who knows me as you do, as friend
10:68 for that o to doubt my purpose
10:69 Expect not o but many miracles
11:26 disturb it for o moment
11:38 help for that little o?
11:42 overcoming of the o who troubled
11:42 own nature aroused by such a o
11:62 o who thinks that money, to be
11:66 Life is o glorious whole
11:69 Make me the o abiding presence of
12:3 My Father and I are o
12:4 He and I are o, and you are mine
12:7 o room, and yet you may become o of
12:9 glorious life, the life of o who
12:44 not to dwell for o moment on your
12:45 as o who runs a race, stumbles and
12:55 offer them up for o troubled soul
12:58 See the o purpose and plan to
12:85 there is o who can never tire
12:93 Do not for o moment lose the
12:95 deal with each o in the best way
13:21 success of o who answered never a
13:30 Our lives are o—yours and mine
13:30 contact is so close we are o
13:33 If your o desire is my kingdom
13:39 from o of discord to o of love
13:58 o and only thing to do is to creep
13:63 My Father and I are o
13:63 O in desire to do good
13:75 Learn of no o but me
14:4 o desire is to do all for me
14:12 for every task I give o of my
14:43 at the thought of o very near and
14:52 called from o task to do o liked less
14:59 o note of joy thrilled through the
14:70 feeling is o of full satisfaction
15:4 o of my disciples in the upper
15:4 o of the two at Emmaus, or o of the
15:28 not bow as o who is resigned to
15:29 for it by o who loves it
15:33 joy of the o who can be calm and
15:52 pressure of a loved o's hand that
16:2 united by o bond in my Spirit, I am
16:16 way must truly be o of delight
16:25 my Father and I, are one and he
16:27 applause given to the o who speaks
16:30 because ye have love o toward another
16:50 as o whom the world would despise
16:51 o who had no form or comeliness
16:64 o with you, voicing the same
16:85 o thing to be sure of is that it is
17:1 in the o despised by the world
17:6 Be o of that throng, and you will
17:15 mighty onslaught from the evil o
17:17 food pass from o to the other
17:40 fear is o of evil's most potent
17:42 love and the Father and I are o
17:68 o corner of it could grow and become
18:4 fear may have been only a small o
18:7 o disappointment or shock and they snap
18:11 as you would to a human loved o
18:40 o with you in tender, loving friendship

Opportunities
7:16 Never make o
7:16 I do the work and I make the o
17:26 o for works in my name would increase

Opportunity
6:32 Man's need is God's golden o for
7:32 o for God to work out your problems

Order
3:36 wait until I give the o to start
7:25 rule of my kingdom is perfect o
7:26 result from obedience, honesty, o
10:7 of creation, of mighty law and o
12:1 out of disorder to o, out of faults
12:3 peace and o out of your little chaos
12:4 It is my divine task to o my affairs
13:62 He can bring o out of chaos
14:55 my divine o of approach
14:72 from those of disorder to o
14:73 right whatever you see is not in o

Ordered
12:3 he who made the o, beautiful world
12:4 yours will be o by me

Orders
1:49 need only your daily marching o

Original
8:87 self, the o man, shrivels up and dies

Others
1:3 disappointment in o and in yourselves
1:6 to help to save o
1:30 Do not worry about o's lives
1:46 stores for your needs and those of o
1:55 Help o
1:57 channel of helpfulness for o
1:57 Feel more tenderness toward o

6:89 Rest, love, joy, p, and work; and the
7:51 Claim joy and p and freedom from care
7:70 Venture there often and you will find p
7:76 your task to maintain your own heart p
7:87 treasures can you have than p, rest, and
7:89 Joy, p, and love; my great gifts
8:13 does man learn strength and gain peace
8:21 Look and into you flows a p beyond
8:38 Be always at p in the busy ways
8:67 p just to know I am beside you, just
9:38 That is the p that only I can give
9:38 To know that p is to have received
9:39 learned that p you are fit to judge
9:40 That p is loving faith at rest
10:48 speaking p to restlessness and fear
10:59 Help and p and joy are here
10:89 'P be still,' to quiet both wind and
11:23 that peace truly does pass all
11:23 that p no man can take from you
11:23 power to disturb that p
11:24 who breaks in and destroys your p
11:26 spoil your p of heart and mind
11:26 training to enable you to acquire this p
11:29 secret of all power, all p, all purity
11:39 power to spoil your inward p
11:42 To attain p quickly in your
11:48 joy and p of conquest shall be yours
11:90 I have promised p but not leisure
12:3 can he not bring p and order out of your
12:24 Look to me for cure, for rest, for p
13:16 Relief brings p
13:16 P brings joy; it is the 'p that passeth'
13:31 I am love and joy and p and strength
13:49 The strength of p and the p of
13:49 the p of strength
13:50 It is my p which gives quietness
13:50 My p flows as a calm river through the
13:51 Success is the result of work done in p
13:52 Love, not rush; P, not unrest
13:62 good out of evil, p out of turmoil
13:73 confidence and p into life
13:74 brings harmony, beauty, p and love
14:23 P is the work of righteousness
14:25 Be calm, quiet, assured, at p
16:47 of each man's happiness, p and rest
16:47 until a soul finds rest and p in me
17:35 with me will bring comfort and p
17:37 I give that p and joy that brings to
18:16 Walk with me in the way of p
18:16 Shed p, not discord, wherever you go
18:16 But it must be my p
18:17 never be a p that is a truce with
18:19 I, the Prince of P, said that I came
18:19 not to bring p but a sword
18:46 only source of happiness and heart p

Peculiar
6:14 p people to make known my name
6:27 my followers are to be a p people
11:4 children of my kingdom are a p people

People
3:8 songs of praise of the p and my
3:67 always pay my p well
4:63 he does not impute evil to his p
4:63 He always sees the good in p
6:14 I called a peculiar p to make
6:27 peculiar p, separated from others
6:45 P waste so much time seeking to work
10:42 I would one day be the food of my p
11:4 my kingdom are a peculiar p
12:6 its statespersons, its law, its p?
18:47 save his p from their sins
18:49 'He shall save his p from their sins'
18:50 'He shall save his p from their sins'

Perfect
1:28 p yourselves at all costs
1:30 p yourselves first in my strength
1:35 'Be ye therefore p' not 'do' p things
1:40 let patience have her p work
2:41 God in whose service is p freedom
2:76 my plans, already p, no detail
3:75 Do not expect a p church, but find
4:38 sharp, keen, p intrument used only
4:38 which turns out p work
4:55 my strength is made p in weakness
4:64 Fear is evil and 'p love casts out'
6:42 To be a p gymnast you must learn
6:42 p balance and poise
6:55 p love which performed those
6:56 P love means p forgiveness
6:82 disturbs your p calm and harmony
6:82 live in that p consciousness of my
6:82 p calm and harmony will be yours
7:25 p order, p harmony, p supply
7:25 p love, p honesty, p obedience
7:36 'Be ye therefore p even as your Father'
7:36 your Father who is in heaven is p
7:79 trust, p trust, can keep one calm
7:92 p silence, p self-control, you can

8:41 in God's service is p freedom
9:61 Rest in me when you need p
10:47 Being p is being like the great
10:47 p as your Father in heaven is p
10:49 what would be the p friend
11:9 why divine guidance is p
11:43 Be ye therefore p even as your Father
11:43 your Father in heaven is p
12:10 resentment to p forgiveness
12:11 'Be ye p even as your Father in'
12:11 Father in heaven is p
13:20 It will be p success, but my
14:41 My strength is made p in weaknes
14:67 it may regard itself as p
14:86 work in p harmony
15:81 mosaic fits into the p pattern
17:41 p trusting love is immediately the
17:42 obtain this p love that dispels fear
17:65 Be ye therefore p even as your Father
17:65 your Father in heaven is p
18:2 fear is the result of a p love
18:2 a p love of me and my Father
18:5 for that p love of me that casts out

Perfection
6:34 long for p and see your bitter
6:34 p because of her sweet love
6:34 faithlessness and crown it with p
10:47 p I enjoined all to have, being
12:1 faults and failure to p
14:34 It leads to p of character
14:67 is cutting and shaping into p
14:76 limitations, my p

Permanent
8:65 their work ceases to be p for me

Persevere
2:15 P! Oh, p! Never lose heart
5:3 P in all I tell you to do
5:62 No discipline can exhaust you; P
5:72 P, p; love and laugh; rejoice!
6:64 P in obeying my will
10:56 P in saying that

Persistent
5:3 p carrying out of my commands
5:26 p prayer, the treasure of my kingdom
5:50 daily p doing of what I have said
6:62 p recognition of my work in daily
8:13 p pleading as a duty upon my

Peter
4:49 P to feel suddenly that his Lord's
4:61 P, urged me to escape the cross
5:87 P was not changed in a flash
5:88 P could never have been the power
5:89 P who was a mighty force for me
5:89 P who said, 'Thou art the Christ'
5:89 rather the P who denied me
9:65 in my name P bade the lame man walk
12:40 P could never have done my work
12:41 protect P from the anger of my Father
12:41 from the hatred of P himself

Petitioned
2:21 p with sighs and tears and much

Picture
9:27 p your soul as a third, being trued by
10:71 p a bodyguard of my servants in

Pity
1:48 p, I withhold too glaring a light
8:73 p him if you saw him bearing the
9:17 righteous need my p for sinners
10:81 no p for yourselves, nothing
16:72 evil or the need, p is worthless
17:37 p of an agonized heart for my

Place
1:34 drop into the secret p of another
2:44 p, the mansion I went to prepare for
2:71 retreat into the quiet p with me
2:71 p you shall find restoration and power
3:49 immediately you will be at the p where
3:62 one spot of earth a holy p
3:67 inspiration the p of aspiration
4:35 Health, joy and peace take its p
5:3 to the p where you would be
5:7 one p for them—my cross
5:12 in the secret p of your being
5:12 which is my secret p too
5:12 inner p of the being to commune with
7:40 in its p put love for me, knowledge
8:76 led out into a large p
10:52 trust me and p your affairs in my
10:74 p him in other deep dangerous waters
10:84 in the secret p of the Most High
12:86 Seek safety in my secret p
11:27 in the secret p of the Father
11:75 secret p of your being, away alone
12:59 difficult p as you ascend, seeing
13:11 He needs a p to hide
13:11 A p where none and nothing can touch
13:13 joy ripples through in its p
13:55 hidden in a sure p, known only to
13:56 Your dwelling p
14:63 from the p of your larger vision
14:70 Live in my secret p

2:37 desire of me: strength, p, joy
2:42 your vision and p, boundless as far
2:49 Any block means my p is diverted
2:50 Its p must flow on
2:71 p and joy and healing
3:7 no limit to my p
3:9 no p on earth that does not fall
3:10 Your faith and my p are the only two
3:15 then my p can become operative
3:16 crutch, and my p shall so invigorate
3:16 Never limit my p for it is limitless
3:27 then my p shall be seen and known
3:29 p to help human weakness
3:31 depend on divine p only
3:32 know and realize my p
3:42 soul to God, faith and p
3:66 let divine p work through them
3:86 rest for your souls and p and joy
4:5 No evil force can hinder my p
4:5 only you have p to do that
4:49 gave them p over unclean spirits and
4:49 that his Lord's p was his
4:87 p, in health, in clothing, to be as
5:29 I am a God of p as well as a man of
5:38 friend, all p is given
5:43 All p is mine
5:44 safety and p it means to you
5:45 battle cry, 'All p is given unto my'
5:45 All p is given unto my Friend
5:45 All p is given unto my Savior
5:49 Never doubt my love and p
5:57 quiet in my love and strong in my p
5:57 possess a p greater than any
5:58 achieve by the p of my Spirit
5:80 miracle-working p
5:86 divine p is being brought to bear
5:88 never have been the p he was had he
6:33 all God needs to manifest his p
6:42 give you p in dealing with the
6:42 That p is already being
6:44 sight is the p that clears away
6:44 have mighty p to do this
6:47 p when two are one in desire to be
6:57 God is love...all p
6:75 Claim p
7:25 all p, all conquest
7:26 often my servants lack p
7:71 Claim the p to work miracles
7:77 doubt your p or wisdom to put things
7:84 the p of two together
7:92 see that as divine p
7:92 p of perfect silence
8:20 To look is surely within the p
8:21 a p new and vital, a wonderful
8:57 because it seems beyond your p
8:58 task beyond its p that must seem!
8:61 readily demonstrating my p
8:61 this p is given to my disciples
8:75 p to vanquish evil that praise has
8:88 love is the p which transforms the
9:11 more restfulness than p
9:12 let all your p be my p
9:12 Man's little p is as clay beside the
9:12 granite rock of my p
9:19 grow in grace and p and beauty
9:23 my p alone which kept them brave and
9:35 thinks the man has magic p
9:49 p to help others will be truly
9:52 act with all my spirit p, with
9:87 Rest and gain p and strength and
10:32 The spoken word has p
10:68 saving p and tender love is wrong
10:85 Know my divine p
11:7 p; once spiritual p is acquired
11:12 strengthened by divine p
11:13 true rest and p
11:20 P goes out to bless through the
11:22 future of unlimited p to bless
11:23 No man has the p to disturb that
11:29 near to me is the secret of all p
11:38 in your p to comfort and bring joy
11:39 until nothing has the p to spoil
11:52 p to see causes for thankfulness
11:68 same miracle working p
11:70 p of my Spirit, my life, is passing
11:76 come forth in p to bless and heal
11:77 My keeping p is never at fault
11:91 Learn of overcoming p from me
12:10 through weakness to p
12:36 to her the possession of divine p
12:37 realize the majesty, the p
12:52 Your p to help other lives will
12:76 a life of p and joy
12:79 p, of sympathy, of all these and
12:80 become a great p to help others
12:88 all within my p to provide
13:1 rise to life and beauty, knowledge and p
13:19 gain your conquering p from me
13:31 p and healing and humility
13:37 My name is the p that turns evil
13:42 soul realizes me and my p, and
13:44 p to see where trust is lacking
13:46 life-power flows through you
13:55 no p on earth can even find it
13:86 My p to save increases as your p
13:86 strength, from p to p
13:87 My miracle-working p is
13:88 No limit to my p to save

13:91 guidance and miracle working p
14:7 p to climb and strive
14:9 my touch still has its ancient p
14:9 that p is promised to you
14:24 in my p to save and keep
14:74 release the imprisoned God p
14:74 That p, once operative, will
14:78 p of your divine brother and
14:82 I gave my p to heal, to raise to
15:12 'Kept hy the p of God' is a promise
15:15 Is my keeping p realized
15:15 p which maintains the salt at
15:18 Temporal p, as money, needs to be
15:24 doubt my p to do all that I have
15:47 no limit to my p
15:54 channel for divine love and p
15:57 P is not such an overwhelming force
15:57 P is just God in action
15:78 all your p, into action
15:92 p was only in action once in time
15:93 p is as manifest there
15:94 nor by p, but by my Spirit
16:3 Think what this means in p
16:3 p that follows two united to serve
16:28 a God-p, simple though it may seem
16:36 untouched by evil and its p
16:39 p you walk unharmed today
16:41 p of vicarious sacrifice is redemptive
16:41 beyond man's p of understanding
17:20 Strength and p will come to you from
17:25 have all my p in the unseen
17:26 not show a greater p nor live a
17:44 my p will so possess you that no
17:40 a soul being kept by my p
17:55 each day must be lived in my p
18:12 p to hurt only those who do not place
18:14 be sure of my conquering p in not
18:17 truce with the p of evil
18:45 live without my sustaining p
18:51 Claim the p it brings

Powerful
5:86 I am all p and all knowing
6:89 most p of these are love and joy
10:22 I am p enough to do everything
12:7 p forces for good in your country
12:15 joyous life, and a p life
14:6 p touch into your very beings
15:58 then all he does is p
15:60 p axe in a master hand
17:40 Evil is p and fear is one of evil's

Praise
2:30 son of p to me is a very crowded day
3:8 it was the songs of p of the people
8:17 pray until prayer merges into p
8:17 your attitude in prayer as p toward God
8:75 P is the devil's death knell
8:75 power to vanquish evil that p has
8:75 Oh, pray and p!
8:90 a sense of failure out with p
8:91 P is the acknowledgment of what I have
8:92 P, which acknowledges my gifts
9:33 To p and thank and steadily fulfill
9:35 paying in thanks and p and promises
11:15 remove mountains is the way of p
11:16 thankful for; P, p, p
11:17 your thankful hearts of p
11:30 Thank and p all the time
13:69 Sing and p my holy name
13:70 P is man's joy-tribute to me
13:70 as you p, thrills of joy surge
13:77 Wing up your prayers on p to heaven
14:54 see that the first step is p
14:62 cries come along the road of p
14:72 Yes, p! And in that moment, in the
14:72 turned to joy, your irrigation to p
17:4 Do not seek the p and notice of men

Pray
1:25 You must p; the way will open
1:27 p and read your Bible and train and
2:16 P daily for faith
2:16 you have to p, but upon your faith
2:31 P more; do not get worried
2:38 You are told to p for faith and you
4:28 P for more faith, as a thirsty
4:30 P daily and most diligently that your
6:28 P for love; p for my Spirit of love
6:51 P about all, but concentrate on a few
6:58 P for much love
6:95 P always that the need may be
7:69 taking time to rest and p between
8:15 p, literally without ceasing
8:16 P until you almost cease to p
8:16 p on because it has become so much
8:17 p until prayer merges into praise
8:25 P it; affirm it; hold on to the rope
8:67 p for more love
8:75 Oh, p and praise!
10:67 Trust and p; it is not sin for one
11:3 Realize fully, and p to realize more
11:22 unto those for whom you p
12:5 p for those wrongs to be righted
12:82 P and deny yourself, and you will
16:47 p to copy the divine unrest until a
16:51 P for the seeing eye, to see the
16:51 p to have the faith to see the
16:52 P until you, with the eyes of faith
16:55 p—not to be able to accept my will

6:44 seems my p ahead, that very sight
6:45 in seeing my p all is done
9:26 Reject it and my p is frustrated
10:64 my eye is my set p—my will
10:68 doubt my p, saving power and
12:58 one p and plan to which all are
13:2 progress gives meaning, a p to life
13:28 I came for that p: to give life for
14:34 your suffering has its p
14:66 so long as it has served its p?
14:80 misunderstanding of his mind and p
16:58 I have my p, my loving p, in cutting

Purposeless
16:53 p now ('having no form nor comeliness')

Puzzles
7:94 me the unraveling of the p of life
16:83 not trouble your souls with p you

Quality
4:78 q of the life that determines the
5:83 service is the finest q of greatness
15:16 by its existing, by its q
16:27 lacks that God q—love

Quiet
2:71 time of retreat into the q place with
4:79 you have to q your heart and still
5:57 q in my love and strong in my power
5:65 Be q
5:66 not to q resignation I give my
10:89 q both wind and waves
10:90 on the q mountain slopes
11:74 times of q communion with my
13:47 Be q, be still
13:48 known that strength lies in q
14:6 you are quiet before me, I lay my
14:25 Be calm, q, assured, at peace
15:7 furnishing the q places of your souls
16:5 They are for the q followers who serve
16:5 Thank me for the q lives
16:6 q service; but I see it, and my reward
16:66 others into the q of your own being
17:5 jeering, a q little throng
17:33 into the q places of prayer
17:34 q time with me will enable you to do
17:57 dearest there are q days
17:58 q gray days are the days for duty

Race
3:54 In a r it is not the start that hurts
3:55 that your r is nearly run?
9:30 discipleship is an obstacle r
12:45 be as one who runs a r, stumbles
15:77 It is as a r

Rapture
2:22 anticipates the r of her child
2:65 r to the jaded, and love to the lonely
4:32 let it fill you with r
6:10 r of her ,'Rabboni' was her
7:50 Try to live in the r of the kingdom
14:34 dwell upon the r of this
14:43 to think of me means joy and r
15:5 r you may know as you hear the

Ready
1:27 instruments must be sharp and r
1:35 Do not be too r to do, just be
5:64 Are you r to live a life apart?
5:82 I am here, your waiting Lord, r at
5:82 r to be used and commanded
5:88 r to lead the other disciples, Peter
6:15 Be r to stand aside and let the
6:16 Be r to confess me before men
6:31 I am always more r to hear than you to
6:95 Do not to too ready to speak to others
7:67 fish r on the shore in their nets
9:37 r for the day of your big demand
10:21 be r for me to do what is best
10:38 joy in life, its r laughter
10:48 A friend is r to help, anticipating
12:33 You are r for the guidance but you
12:61 Be r and willing for my will to
13:25 You must be r to stand apart from
13:82 Be r to prove your sonship by service
13:83 Be ever r to do all you can for
15:9 You must be r to go on trusting to the
15:9 You must be r, like my servant
16:70 companion of the weak, r to supply

Reconcile
7:33 r all your desires and longings

Recurs
7:49 As long as it r to your mind, you

Redemptive
2:75 all sacrifice and all suffenng is r
16:41 sacrifice is r beyond man's power of

Refuge
2:56 nearness of r and safety would have
6:98 he took r in words and more words
13:11 needs nothing so much as a r
13:12 Say to yourself, 'He is our r'
13:13 R; everlasting arms, so untiring, so
15:88 If hopeless, seek from me a r
16:67 Flee to the eternal God, your r
16:68 joy of appreciation of your r

Regret
6:65 Do not r the first; the second is
8:14 r that he prayed so little
8:68 R nothing; not even the sins and

Regrets
7:58 You will have no r

Rejection
1:53 ache of r of my love that I suffered
14:80 Father to save, his r by men
17:2 contempt and r the Son of God

Rejoice
1:54 R; a father loves to see his
2:31 R exceedingly; joy in me
3:35 souls in patience and r
3:45 R! Joy is the spirit reaching out
3:45 So never cease to joy; R!
5:10 Love me; joy in me; R!
5:61 R and be glad; I am your God
5:72 persevere; love and laugh; R!
5:91 Oh, joy! oh, r! I love you
6:12 R in my glad acceptance as you
6:29 discipline; love it and r
6:35 Love and r on the gray days
7:27 R in the springtime of the year
7:53 See me in everything; R in me
8:76 R evermore; Happy indeed if each
9:27 r in sharing, in the discipline and
9:28 R at progress
9:91 R in the sense of security that
10:78 R indeed that you see my hand in
10:88 R, r; I have much to teach you
11:30 Live in my presence; R in my love
12:33 do not r as you should
12:38 r at the wonders to which you are called
13:17 R in it; walk in my love
14:17 R; these are your wilderness days
14:41 R at your weakness, my children
14:46 R even in the darkest places
15:26 it is victory, and the angels r
15:26 your dear ones r, as much as at any
16:20 Not only must you r, but your joy
17:63 R in the fact that you are mine

Reluctantly
2:21 r relinquish the desired treasures

Rely
3:12 R on me
3:31 You must r on me
6:99 R less on words
7:14 r on me to find strength
7:14 r on my supplying the strength
7:77 R on me
8:24 R on it
10:80 R on this and go forward
11:80 R on me alone
12:94 R on me for all
14:12 R on me to keep my promise about this
15:1 does not r upon any merit of yours
15:11 You must r on me alone
18:28 R on me

Remember
1:4 R that you must not see as the world
1:6 R, this must not be
1:47 r that I have spoken to you
2:57 R this—my disciples thought
2:57 R how mistaken they were
3:2 R, as I said to Mary of old
3:30 R, trembling heart, that with God
3:44 R that you are in the hands of a
3:56 R that I am by your side spurring
3:60 R that you must never fail to keep
3:81 R! R, it is the last few yards that
3:83 R my words: 'He that endureth to the'
4:5 R that all you have to do is keep
4:8 R always, doubts delay
4:34 R, I touched her hand and the
4:53 R, it is only struggle that hurts
4:55 R, my strength is made perfect in
4:57 R that truth is many sided
4:63 R that I beheld the city and wept
4:69 R this; if the ground is hard, seed
4:88 R that no thought of sin and
5:6 R, you are only an instrument
5:41 I said, 'Take up your cross daily'
5:28 R, nothing is too big
5:35 R my words to my disciples, 'This kind'
5:48 R this evening time is not to learn
5:80 R this, not what you do, but what you
5:83 R that service is the finest quality
6:18 R that death was the last enemy I
6:27 R that my followers are to be a
6:69 R this; there would be no dark
6:83 R, only the pupil giving great
6:97 R that rarely do I speak to the human
6:99 r that speech is of the senses
7:19 R this to cheer my disciples who have
7:21 r that the varied path does not always
7:35 R that your maker is also your
7:52 R too that I am the same yesterday
7:63 R that; claim the unclaimable
7:64 R, my children, sublime audacity
7:69 R that I can work through you better
7:92 R, by that power of perfect silence
8:4 r I also yield to yours
8:6 R that God is in each of you

8:7 R this in your relation to others
8:9 R, 'He bindeth up the broken hearts'
8:31 R, where I am is victory
8:35 R obedience, obedience, obedience
8:63 R the lesson of the seed
8:88 R that love is the power which transforms the world
9:8 R that I am beside you as your
9:33 confidence and certainty; R that
9:77 R, I long to work miracles as I did
10:16 R now abideth these three: faith
10:20 beyond my love and care; R that
10:23 R, you cannot see the future; I can
10:31 R how I faced the devil in the wilderness
10:64 r that I said, 'I will guide thee'
10:71 R that you are daughters of a King
11:2 R that to me a miracle is only a
11:3 R too that the natural man is at
11:9 R the commands I have given you have
11:65 R that the path of initiation is not
11:70 R that eternal life is the only
12:1 R that always—that out of darkness
12:5 R, no prayer goes unanswered
12:5 R that the moment a thing seems wrong
12:24 R, I am your physician, healer of
12:26 r, sunshine helps to make glad the
12:37 R, there are no limits to my giving
12:46 R no more their sins and failures
12:72 R, I am the supreme being who knows
12:91 R that you are living really in the
13:6 r your friends in the unseen
13:24 R, your great field of labor is
13:59 R that the truths I teach you
13:82 R to serve all
13:85 R, when you serve others, you are
14:16 R that I fed the children of Israel
14:59 R, just as you thank God for me, so
15:40 r, my children, my word is even more
15:61 R, no day is lost on which some
15:68 Forget the past; R only its glad days
15:76 R that life's difficulties and
15:77 R this; it is as a race
15:94 R and often say to yourselves, not by
16:18 R, I was the answer in time to all
16:46 R me, the heavenly beggar, and
16:70 R, I was the companion of the weak
16:73 R that in thinking of your own needs
16:83 R this and strive to be the friend
16:84 R that I have told you so often
17:11 R, as I have told you before, give
17:26 R, I came to found a kingdom
17:56 R that if sometimes there seems a
17:62 R, you may not yet be joyous, but
17:65 r my injunction which followed—Be ye
17:68 R this beautiful earth on which
18:9 R, your master is the Lord of the
18:20 r the first hail must be that of
18:28 R, all I give you will be mine

Remorse
5:89 in his moment of abject r, could best
12:42 shame, r and contempt of themselves
12:43 shame and r must come

Rescuer
2:55 to the drowning man the r comes
2:55 like that of a man toward his r
8:26 hinder the r who has to act with
8:29 leaves all future plans to me, its r
10:74 human r does not save a man from
10:75 learn what I, your r, would do and
11:83 r does a drowning man who is
11:83 r must render him more helpless
11:83 at the will and mercy of the r
14:47 rescued for the r
18:50 friend, joy-bringer and r, leader

Resignation
5:66 not to quiet r I give my blessings
6:59 R to my will keeps me barred out
6:60 only r acceptable to me is when self
8:75 R, acceptance of my will, obedience to
10:30 laughter, not a sorrowful r, mark
16:22 hard dull way of r is not my way

Resist
8:16 a habit that you cannot r
14:18 r the pressure of my hand

Rest
1:4 Leave the r with me
1:13 Everything must r on me
1:13 Force is born of r
1:20 R in my presence brings peace
1:22 R your nerves
1:40 R in me
2:31 R in me
2:31 R in them, as a tired child rests
2:50 no stagnation, not even r
2:63 awards bring heart-r and happiness?
2:64 I will give you r
2:64 turn to me indeed find that r
3:7 can and leave the r to me
3:12 R in this certainty
3:81 R in my love
3:86 have r for your souls and power and
4:5 God does the r

5:19 R; R in that calm and peace
5:20 r in me, than its real life begins
5:57 R in me
5:65 R in my love
5:68 R in my love
6:1 R in me
6:1 r together in my presence
6:39 speaking to me you find soul-r
6:81 R in me
6:89 R, love, joy, peace, and work;
7:10 r before me until you are joyful
7:12 r always precede fresh miracle working
7:13 renewal of spirit force, r of body
7:15 R in me
7:59 I will give you r
7:61 find that r you found in me
7:69 better when you are at r
7:69 taking time to r and pray between
7:70 The r of God is in a realm beyond all
7:87 treasures can you have than peace, r
8:11 Try to r on these words, Seek ye
8:23 R knowing all is so safe in my hands
8:23 R is trust
8:23 you do not r
8:37 r and wait patiently for me
8:38 R
8:83 R in me
9:40 peace is loving faith at r
9:60 R in that truth
9:60 R, that is, cease all struggle
9:61 Do not only r in me when the world's
9:61 R in me when you need perfect
9:86 R
9:87 R and gain power and strength
9:88 R until every care and worry has
10:3 r from the worry and irritation of
10:3 seek some r and shade
10:57 doubts of the day immediately to r
10:90 You shall r with me and learn
11:13 Simplicity brings r—true r
11:74 R more with me
11:87 effort and r, a union of the two
12:1 Out of unrest to r
12:23 R
12:23 R until life, eternal life
12:24 R
12:24 Look to me for cure, for r, for
12:54 I will give you r
12:75 service in every action, even in r
12:79 of r, of fame, of healing, of power
12:92 R in me
12:93 mother's arms, sheltered and at r
13:46 R in me
13:46 rebels, it is her call for r
13:46 R then until my life-power flows
13:49 R in me
13:52 Be calm, assured, at r
13:57 shadow r to make it doubly safe
13:58 So r
13:78 Yes, come for r
13:78 But stay for r, too
13:79 wait until my r fills your soul
13:80 R knows no fear
13:80 R knows no want
13:80 R is strong and sure
13:80 r of soft glades and peacefully
13:81 R
13:81 to gain this r is to come to me
14:25 R in me
14:76 behold my calm, my r
14:34 r upon you for even such a short
16:43 a r, a satisfaction they have
16:43 I will give you r
16:47 man's happiness, peace and r
16:47 until a soul finds r and peace in
16:54 your happiness and spirit r
17:36 silence while I r with you
17:68 for talk and r with me

Resting

7:71 work that results from r with God is
12:65 r, giving up of works, a necessity

Result

1:38 Joy is the r of faithful trusting
1:61 the r is mighty
6:62 discipline r in the constant
6:94 Union with me may be the r of just
7:26 manifestations that r from obedience
8:3 r of frequent conversation with me
8:48 no feeling of responsibility as to the r
8:59 soon you will see the r
9:26 a wonderful molding is the r
11:8 commands and leave the r to me
11:8 according to command, the r will
11:9 circumstances, the required r
11:10 of you and the required r
13:51 Success is the r of work done in
14:20 possession is the r of a yielded will
14:57 r of looking to me, you will be
14:88 r in both holiness and
15:50 joy as the r of effort
15:50 r of trying to force yourself to
16:85 that is not the r of the suffering
16:85 r of the close intimacy with me to
18:2 fear is the r of a perfect love

Results

1:32 heart of man except by seeing r
7:26 as light r from a lighted candle

7:71 work that r from resting with God is
8:13 trust that r, does man learn
11:46 appreciation r from contrary
11:57 heart and mind a oneness r that

Retire
5:12 few r into that inner place of the

Reveal
3:18 I will r my will to you in many
3:76 not what I r to you so much
6:31 r to each the mysteries of the
10:24 by little can I r it to you
10:88 when I do not r more of my truth
16:11 you r to the world something of
17:34 r nothing, command nothing, and

Revealing
1:55 I am r so much to you; pass it on
3:57 r how near they were to victory
5:14 r them, not repeating oft-told

Revelation
1:49 ecstasy of God's r to his own
5:48 not to receive r of the unseen
10:43 wonder of r still to be seen by
13:23 Bend your knees in wonder before my r
14:88 key to divine r is simple acceptance

Reversal
2:62 r from the ways of the world
2:62 r that leads to boundless happiness

Reward
2:38 I am your God, your great r
2:45 given the r and the joy of the next
3:18 r of coming regularly to meet me
4:47 r for not seeking spirit
5:61 I r your seeking with my presence
6:39 persisted in, bring their own r
8:34 persists in bringing its r of me
9:90 faith will receive its r as
11:4 motives and senses of r
13:20 Your r will be sure
13:26 work for me, you have your r
13:26 and expect that r too
13:27 I will give you all necessary r
16:6 my r is not earth's fame, earth's
16:7 My r is joy, whether in the earth
16:7 no r, that can give man that joy
16:8 as the r for patient suffering
16:8 r for activity in my service
17:59 Joy is the r
17:61 Joy is the r of patiently seeing me

Riches
2:37 strength, power, joy and r
10:56 surrounded by r will possess you
18:34 Let no r, no ease, entice you

Rid
6:50 R yourself of self and all is well

Right
1:30 That will be all r
3:67 get the r thought attitude
5:38 friends a r to have it?
7:62 sit on my r hand and on my left
7:77 power or wisdom to put things r
7:77 Ask me to r all as you leave it to me
7:92 alone prove your r to govern
7:94 I can set r all that is wrong
8:39 convinced that the course is r and
8:40 has is his by r
8:41 implies the r to appropriate
8:42 r to use and claim as I have
8:42 Use your r
8:62 That is r, but others have to wait
10:5 I have given the r to enter my
10:20 must be the r ones for you
11:8 the result will be r
13:26 This is not r
13:89 I respect the r of each individual
13:90 call of the soul gives me my r to
14:23 living the r life, living with me
14:58 First get r with me
14:73 seek to r whatever you see is
17:68 I have a r to bring my friends, my

Righteous
3:2 for the r only, and those who had not
9:17 The r need my pity for sinners

Rise
6:17 to r from death to life
6:22 R from your fears and go out into
8:31 R to greater heights than you have
9:29 R above your fears and fancies
10:11 r above the earth life and seek
12:38 R in my strength
13:1 r to life and beauty, knowledge and
15:79 R to conquer
17:63 sun to r on the evil and on the good

Risen
1:3 forward to a new and r life
6:9 r life glad and free can be yours
6:17 all that hinders the r life; to arise
6:20 Let nothing hinder your r life
6:20 'R with Christ,' said my servant Paul
6:20 more and more of that r life
6:20 r life it was truly said, 'I live'
6:22 to meet me, your r Lord
11:21 glory of the Lord is r upon thee

15:96 know that your help and s are sure

Satisfaction
10:40 That is satisfaction
13:25 want the full and complete s you
13:25 the s of the world too?
14:70 feeling is one of full s
16:43 s they have never found in the

Save
1:6 You are to help to s others
1:51 Only scarred lives can really s
2:35 not only to s a world, but also to
4:11 I died to s you from sin and doubt
5:64 times of communion to rescue and s
5:88 No man can s unless he understands
6:32 I love to help and s
6:23 We are out to s
8:24 not shortened that it cannot s
8:26 attempts to s yourself with one hand
10:73 I am meaning to s you even more
10:74 rescuer does not s a man from
10:75 cannot perform and cannot s?
11:82 s you from the sea of poverty and
11:83 man who is struggling to s himself
12:7 Live to serve and to s
12:55 longed to s my world, I let you
12:55 training that shall fit you to s
12:81 prayer if you are to s others
12:82 used marvelously to s and help others
13:86 hand shortened that it cannot s?
13:86 My power to s increases as your
13:88 no limit to my power to s
13:88 my desire and longing to s
13:88 allowed to bless and help and s
14:3 'to share' means 'to s'
14:3 Himself he cannot s
14:4 called to s and share in a very special
14:14 your turn shall s many from poverty
14:24 in my power to s and keep
14:42 beside you, strong, yes, strong to s
14:80 longing of the Father to s
16:40 helping me to s my world
18:47 he shall s his people from their sins
18:49 'He shall s his people from their'
18:50 'He shall s his people from their'

Saved
3:83 end, the same shall be s
3:83 If so, you shall be s
4:25 whereby men can be s
8:19 Look unto me and be ye s, all the ends
8:21 Look and you are s from despair
8:21 Look and you are s from care
8:21 Look and you are s from worry
8:29 s soul trusts me so entirely it no
10:73 my hand that has s you
13:40 under heaven whereby you can be s
14:3 'He s others; himself he cannot save'
14:13 Look unto me, and you shall be s
18:51 'whereby you can be s,' Jesus

Saves
1:7 Joy s
4:24 'Jesus s'—in the face of every
4:25 'Jesus s from poverty'
4:25 'Jesus s from fear'
12:9 the life of one who s
12:57 my life of the suffering that s
15:65 through you, that s and blesses

Savior
3:39 I am your s, your s from slavery to sin
3:39 troubles of life, your s from disease
4:43 Treat me as S and King, but also with
4:72 my tears, the tears of a S, but
5:45 All power is given unto my
5:89 could best speak of me as the s
9:18 God friend, the God-leader, the God-s
10:48 think of all that means; friend and s
10:68 knows me as you do, as friend and s
11:65 sorrow-cry of the world that needs a s
11:65 tender pleas of a s who needs
12:90 I am your s, not only from the
12:90 I am your s
13:21 success of a risen S as he walked
13:42 knows me as helper and S, that soul
14:47 the love of the sinner for the s
15:86 creator or a debt owed to a s
16:11 been with me, your Lord and S
18:50 Jesus is s and friend, joy-bringer

Scales
15:51 s from your eyes, and you see me

Scarred
1:51 Only s lives can really save

Scars
9:12 heal your s and make you strong
15:23 These left their s

Scheme
2:8 too small to be part of my s

Science
7:44 I teach a higher s law than even

Scorn
4:88 approaching s and crucifixion
11:7 worries and s patiently endured
11:39 between you and all s and indignity
12:39 Shield from the s and cover

12:39 from their own s and chiding
12:41 nor from the s of my enemies
13:21 face of the s and torture
14:67 look with s upon the marble
15:23 Do you think the spitting, s
16:22 knowing well that s, reviling

Sculptor
14:67 s who finds a faulty piece of marble
14:67 s is cutting and shaping into

Sea
1:8 soul out of the s of sin or disease
9:84 not think about the Red S that lies
10:79 protected as they crossed the Red S
11:82 save you from the s of poverty
14:16 I made a way through the Red S for

Secret
1:34 s place of another heart
3:84 unlock for you the s treasures
5:12 s place of your being
5:12 which is my s place too
5:64 s times of communion to rescue
6:53 Tender love is the s
10:84 hidden in the s place of the Most High
10:86 Seek safety in my s place
11:27 with me in the s place of the Father
11:29 near to me is the s of all power
11:75 s place of your being
13:19 s of success then is life with me
13:55 so s that no power on earth can
13:57 make it doubly safe, doubly s
14:4 path kept sacred and s for my nearest
14:14 s of prosperity for you
14:70 Live in my s place
16:36 into the s place of the Father

Secrets
1:45 s of my kingdom, the hidden pearls
8:10 share my plans and s with you

Secured
2:7 friendship is s in the drudgery of
8:80 necessary, they are s
10:84 then surely I have s your ladder

Security
1:61 Walking with me is s
3:13 yet had no human s
5:27 peace, assurance, s, health
8:28 truth—safety, s and guidance
8:28 S, 'He set my feet upon a rock'
8:77 feeling of s, a thrill of joy at
9:91 Rejoice in the sense of s that is
11:71 eternal life means s and safety
11:71 consciousness of that s and safety
11:77 failure to be sure of the s of
12:10 through danger to s
15:13 my keeping means s and safety

See
1:4 you must not s as the world sees
1:15 You shall s
1:15 you shall s unfold each day
1:29 S how I have made the purity and
1:41 s I am a master instrument-maker?
1:44 s how vast, how stupendous, is the
1:54 loves to s his children happy
1:65 Then you will s how glorious, how
2:22 s a mother preparing birthday or
2:23 s this as plans unfold of my preparing
2:33 Do you not s it is a lesson?
2:39 Do not want to s the road ahead
2:51 S how many you can bless each day
2:67 I can s the future
2:74 s that your inner lives are all
3:55 s by the nerve and heart rack of the
3:61 All who s you or are in contact with
3:67 s more and more as you get the right
3:77 my work to s your lives and your
3:77 as to s that tomorrow's sun rises
4:1 You do not need to s far ahead
4:10 Could you s, you would understand
4:18 You may not s the work
4:20 You s it all in the bud stage now
4:48 You will s this as you go on
4:51 You may never s it
4:51 s your unlikeness to me
4:57 patience for all who do not s as you
4:71 s my love and tender joy in them
4:72 Those who s not only my tears,
4:81 S the good in everybody
4:81 S your unworthiness compared
4:95 When and how I s best, I will tell you
5:4 s that my leading has been very gradual
5:40 Do you not s this?
5:68 You may not sit, but I do
5:69 I judge the heart and I s in
5:70 I s it only as love's offering
5:73 Do you not s, my children, that you
5:74 Did you not s it with my disciples?
6:34 perfection and s your bitter failures
6:34 I s faithfulness
6:37 Try to s the heart I s, to know
6:41 You will s
6:45 time seeking to work out what they s
6:49 I, your Lord, s not as man sees
6:54 S in them love in operation
6:97 s me in my works done through you and

7:2 S that you walk it with me
7:23 not always s the soul we seek
7:39 S him as the first cause of every
7:46 not s is that you, the self in you
7:53 S me in everything
7:60 s that on it are inscribed the words
7:92 s yourselves absolutely unmoved?
7:92 Try to s that as divine power
8:6 I s God in you, as no man can s
8:7 given to man to s in his fellow man
8:33 To s me you must bring me your cares
8:34 No man can see my face through a
8:43 s my children sitting before my
8:48 responsibility was to s the duty
8:57 unless you s it is not my w for you
8:59 soon you will s the result
8:61 You s others manifesting easily
8:62 others have to wait to s the outward
8:86 no man can s my face and live
9:3 s more and more clearly all that yet
9:7 As you s the slow progress upward made
9:15 each, so does each man s me
9:16 that you s me as others—the world
9:16 s me, but it is necessary that you s
9:18 of mine to man you must s God
9:35 world does not s that the man has been
9:76 S this; to s this with the eyes of
9:83 S others as I see them
10:23 you cannot s the future
10:24 could not bear to s the future
10:28 S me in the dull, the uninteresting
10:28 S me in the laughter of children
10:34 Do not seek to s it
10:49 s a little of what would be the
10:60 one day s the reason for it
10:60 s it was not cruel testing, but
10:63 you will s this had to be
10:78 s my hand in all that happens
10:80 You must s this
10:92 S yourselves as those around you s
11:5 You s a marvelous happening
11:33 s how wonderful life with me can be?
11:33 s that no evil can befall you?
11:52 s causes for thankfulness in his
11:64 S me in all and then it will be an
11:91 s my work had not been affected by
12:6 s lives altered you never touched
12:8 s the mighty work you do, but I s
12:9 S this more and more
12:13 S where I, in the same relation or
12:58 Do not s the small trials and
12:58 S the one purpose and plan to
12:69 s that you cannot be destroyed?
12:86 you will s how rich you are
12:91 each day s more of heaven
13:4 cannot s their many diverse
13:4 s the angels who ministered to me in
13:14 s what you can give away
13:31 s in me, your Lord
13:44 power to s where trust is lacking
13:67 s that, and know him and me as we
13:68 S the Father through seeing me
13:68 To s the Father through me is love
14:13 S no other supply
14:29 S me as I really am
14:54 s that the first step is praise
14:63 s the faith of the day before as
14:70 s this in your mind
14:71 S yourselves as daughters of a king
14:73 you s is not in order there
14:75 s all you could and do desire in me
14:76 s my unfailing patience
14:90 s the same fulfillment of divine
15:10 known even when you cannot s
15:10 before you s my deliverance
15:11 unseen, not in those you s
15:19 though you may not s it, conquest
15:25 I s the loving and striving, not the
15:25 I s the conquest of your
15:30 raise your head and s the glory, joy
15:32 around you s worked out in your lives
15:48 Do you not s how you wrong me?
15:51 scales from your eyes, and you s me
15:59 try to s it is not you, but the
15:60 s that it is not the instrument
15:81 will s that every step was planned
15:83 s stone by stone and trust the
15:94 will s, and in seeing, will give me
16:6 world may s the humble, patient
16:6 I s it, and my reward is not earth's
16:10 dazzling for mortals to s in full
16:14 Train it to s more and more
16:17 When you s me face to face in that
16:21 Men must s and know your joy
16:26 S that only love matters
16:34 followers, would s a lost cause
16:36 Man could not s my Spirit untouched
16:37 man could s my risen body and learn
16:39 man could s that proved beyond
16:41 may not s it, but the power of
16:48 hath eyes to s let him s
16:50 Yet when we shall s him, there is
16:51 s the beauty of my character, of my
16:51 faith to s the beauty of my love
16:52 s all that you could desire in what
16:77 s the majestic figure of the Son of
16:80 ideal man I s in him—the man he
16:82 friend I s in my vision of you

17:1 hearts s nothing contemptible in the
17:13 temptation is to s it as temptation
17:24 s my spiritual kingdom though
17:51 Try to s your lives as that
17:52 S your lives not only as calm and
17:61 of trusting when you cannot s
17:67 S there the abundance of delights
17:67 S wonders, ask wonders, bear wonders

Seek

1:46 S my wonderful truths and you shall
1:50 if men s the battle of the world
1:55 S to find a heart-home for each
2:10 S to know and then to do my will
2:18 As you s to do, you feel your
2:46 S to carry out all I say
2:62 When you s to follow me
3:23 you s me just to dwell in my presence
3:72 Do not s the spiritual through
3:73 S this time as a time of communion
4:33 S sometimes not even to hear me
4:33 S a silence of spirit understanding
5:17 to s to say with it as interpreter mars
5:46 S not to know the future
5:62 S me; love me; joy in me
6:1 S this evening time just to be with me
6:20 S to know more and more of that risen
7:16 Do not s to work for me
7:23 not always see the soul we s
7:24 S and ye shall fmd
7:45 as you s my forgiveness, so you
8:11 'Seek ye first the kingdom of God'
9:54 s my help and guidance as to what
9:64 S me early
9:72 only to those who diligently s me
10:3 when you s some rest and shade
10:7 When men s to worship me they think
10:11 s to soar higher, to the kingdom
10:27 Always s to understand others
10:34 Do not s to see it
10:37 S in every way to become childlike
10:37 S, s, s until you find, until the
10:51 In all things s simplicity
10:86 S safety in my secret place
11:55 S diligently for something to be
11:68 s by constant contact to know me
11:69 S to do less and to accomplish
12:31 You s my presence and they who s
13:34 told to s first the kingdom of God
13:34 S to advance his kingdom in all
13:35 S in all things his kingdom first
13:36 s material gain when that gain will
13:45 s to go up this path to me
14:73 s to right whatever you see is
15:18 S to conquer in all things
15:19 s daily to obtain this self conquest
15:50 Do not s to realize this fullness
15:56 s to live, knowing no other desire
15:88 If hopeless, s from me a refuge
17:3 always s to judge only according
17:4 Do not s the praise and notice of
17:28 All men s for me, but all men do not
17:30 to s communion with my Father
18:45 lives that s to live without my

Seeking

2:61 let that be your daily s
3:70 s silence must help in the rush
4:47 reward for not s spirit communication
5:61 I reward your s with my presence
6:45 waste so much time s to work out
7:22 We are s lost sheep
12:64 And s you shall find
17:28 s because they are dissatisfied
18:27 s the means to do my will and work

Sees

1:4 not see as the world s
4:63 He always s the good in people
6:44 s my purpose ahead, that very sight
6:49 I, your Lord, see not as man s
7:18 s me with his human sight it does
8:14 s how marvelously his prayers
9:34 s a man who can unexpectedly draw
9:35 s the man of faith make a sudden
10:74 He then s him to his home
12:81 see it and evil s it
13:48 world s strength in action
15:44 eye that s all, the ear that hears
15:44 It s and knows the heart of love it
16:69 s your struggles and conquests

Self

1:18 Uproot s—the channel-blocker
1:62 Kill the s; every blow to s is used
1:62 Did s prompt that?
1:63 I died embodying all the human s
1:63 on the tree, I bore the s human nature
1:64 As you too kill s, you gain the
1:64 you have to conquer, only the s in
2:53 As s, fears and worries depart from
2:73 no thoughts of s, banish these
3:66 turn the s out of their lives
3:2 Only s can cast a shadow on the way
3:5 your poor, puny s impedes their onward
3:58 elimination of s is the key to holiness
4:93 entrance and do not keep it out by s
5:9 to crucify the s which hinders progress

5:9 That s prevents the flow through your
6:9 Die with me to s—to the human life
6:50 Rid yourself of s and all is well
6:60 when s, ousted by my claims, accepts
6:97 atmosphere of love and s-effacement
7:40 S dethroned; that is the lesson, but
7:41 S, not only dethroned, but dead
7:41 A dead s is not an imprisoned s
7:41 an imprisoned s is more potentially
7:41 let s die
7:42 each blow to the life of s you must at
7:43 not a dead s that men have to fear
7:43 thwarted, captive imprisoned s
7:43 That s is infinitely more s-centered
7:43 the s allowed full play
7:44 than even freedom of the s
7:44 I teach death to the s
7:44 Petty s life exchanged for divine life
7:46 the s in you, can never forgive
7:46 thought of them means s in the
7:46 The s cannot forgive; kill self!
7:48 Aim at killing the s now, in your
7:48 only one injured, the s, is dead
7:49 one way of feeding a s-life
7:74 is not the belittling of the s
7:74 It is forgetting the s
7:74 more than forgetting the s
7:91 What joy follows s-conquest!
7:92 perfect s-control, you can alone
8:87 The s, the original man, shrivels
10:49 perfect friend: a tireless, s-less
11:6 unflinching desire to conquer s
12:43 facing of the real s has to be done
15:17 conquest of the physical, the s-life
15:19 seek daily to obtain this s-conquest
15:60 turn s out
15:66 block there can be in your channel is s
15:66 Keep s out and know that my Spirit
15:70 'Who his own s bore our sins in his
16:64 I am present too, a s-invited guest

Senses
4:39 How little man knows and s my need
4:79 quiet your heart and still your s
4:80 five s are your means of communication
6:99 remember that speech is of the s
7:17 Contact with me is not gained by the s
11:2 s only regards it as something
11:4 motives and s of reward

Separated
6:27 a peculiar people, s from others
7:11 I s myself from my disciples and sat

Sermon
9:44 even living my s on the mount

Servant
1:39 Paul, my s, learned this lesson
2:59 You are the s of all
2:59 let him be the s of all
3:41 Did not my s of old say, 'All thy'
4:74 s and messenger as any saint who has
5:2 s Isaiah say, 'They that wait upon'
5:85 have no position—just be a s
5:87 My s Peter was not changed in a flash
6:14 My s Paul said that my followers
6:20 'Risen with Christ,' said my s Paul
6:47 message of my s Paul now plain:
6:99 Make it your s, never your master
7:35 your maker is also your s, quick
9:48 s Paul spoke and which he urged his
13:83 As a s of all think no work beneath
14:4 s Paul did, all things but loss so
14:26 my s Isaiah spoke of the wonderful
14:51 You are my s
14:52 s who avoids extra work, who
14:52 ill served by such a s?
15:10 s Abraham, to climb the very hill
15:58 s of mine, however weak he
16:74 s is not above his master, certainly
18:22 friend and s of sinners

Servants
5:76 my s have gone to their betrayal
6:34 s, you long for perfection and see
7:1 kept my s, in times of peril, in
7:26 often my s lack power, conquest
8:40 no longer s but friends
10:71 bodyguard of my s in the unseen
11:49 Think much about my s of old
12:65 s, which made resting, giving up of
14:89 adjusted to my s shoulders, and

Serve
2:34 for those who ask to s me well
2:61 How best can you s?
2:67 not s your purpose, are being moved
6:53 Love those who s you
7:83 s me that when this time of
9:71 s at my direct command, my Spirit
9:74 material will s only to attain the
10:70 hosts throng to s and protect you
11:63 longing to s me has offered me all
12:7 Live to s and to save
12:20 only my will and only to s me
12:75 'They s him continually,' can be
13:3 live to s and s they truly do
13:3 They s me and those they love
13:3 They s ceaselessly
13:5 earthly friends who can s them in
13:5 can s them so much better
13:25 try to s God and mammon

13:25 s, then claiming the wages of both God
13:33 s that kingdom, then truly your whole
13:82 Remember to s all
13:83 S; S; S
13:85 s others, you are acting for your
14:51 S me as simply, cheerfully and readily
14:51 as you expect others to s you
14:53 not how you so often s me?
16:3 power that follows two united to s me
16:5 s me unobtrusively yet
16:79 you should s your brother man

Served
2:60 I s indeed the humblest and the
2:61 not how best can you be s
6:15 my kingdom are thereby s
12:21 had I been s by many such two souls
14:52 ill s by such a servant?
14:66 so long as it s its purpose?

Serves
5:82 I am among you as one that s, meek
14:48 s to answer the prayer, 'Make me love'

Service
1:7 love, every trifling s—joy
2:41 God in whose s is perfect freedom
2:60 S is the byword of my disciples
2:60 My highest powers were at their s
5:83 s is the finest quality of greatness
6:13 love and s, my children must stand
8:41 in God's s is perfect freedom
9:70 seen s for me as activity
9:70 more than all the s man can offer
12:75 S is the law of heaven
12:75 love there is continuous s in every
12:76 new life consecrated to my s
12:87 I can command your obedient s
13:82 ready to prove your sonship by s
13:84 gladness in s, joy in doing my will
13:85 In s for others, express your love
14:61 bring joy to my heart by faithful s
14:61 By faithful s in the little things
14:79 loving s, as an atonement for the
15:74 Your s becomes so different when you
16:6 s; but I see it, and my reward is not
16:8 reward a for activity in my s
16:9 gateway into it may be s or it may be
16:11 s, purity, or whatever it may be
16:40 Offering your day's s to me in that
18:23 steps: humility, s, worship

Set
2:26 S your affections on things
3:76 Forces are already s in motion
4:24 S your standard very high
4:95 limit is s by your own spiritual
7:94 I can s right all that is wrong
8:27 s my feet upon a rock
4:28 Security, 'He s my feet upon a rock'
9:69 I will s you on high because you have
9:89 path of duty I have s before you
10:64 my eye is my s purpose—my will
10:70 Once I have s on you my stamp
10:93 I will s you on high because you have
11:4 They are s apart
11:25 S yourselves this task
12:3 s the stars in their courses
12:86 s your affections on things above
14:21 accepted it, to s an example
14:12 there is s aside all that is
15:93 to s my apostles free
16:16 More and more s your hopes on me
16:20 A candle must not be s under a
17:3 to s aside the valuation of the
17:51 fountains s in the midst of a mighty
18:34 path upon which your feet are s, of

Shadow
1:1 My s is thrown backward, over the
4:2 Only self can cast a s on the way
13:57 Over that home shall my s rest to
13:57 mother bird wings that s rests
13:58 ventured out of that protecting s
17:56 if sometimes there seems a s on your
17:56 It is my s as I stand between you and

Share
1:19 carry a little day's s
4:19 S your love, your joy, your
4:73 joy if you s in her joy now
4:74 S her joys and travails, and great
7:53 S all life with me
7:53 S all with me as a child shares its
8:10 I s my plans and secrets with you and
8:41 We s the Father's property
8:71 you mock me to expect me to s it
9:91 s your troubles
9:9 you s my patience and my strength
9:27 then you will s, and rejoice in sharing
10:38 its desire to s all with all men
11:59 Together we s and joy in the
13:63 him to s his goodness with them
13:63 God is good, anxious to s his
14:11 would be able to s that human life
14:2 s, in the sufferings and
14:3 'to s' means 'to save'
14:4 you are called to save and s in a
16:38 you must s my tribulations
18:23 S it with me

Sharing
7:54 Give me the joy of s all with you
9:27 you will share, and rejoice in s
9:82 only by living with me and s my life
16:40 s my life work and helping me to
18:25 myrrh is your s in my sorrows and

Sharp
1:27 instruments must be s and ready
4:38 compared with the s, keen perfect

Shelter
10:11 The eternal arms s you
11:77 not whether I can provide a s
11:77 sure of the security of that s
13:58 do is to creep back into s again

Shield
2:66 I am your s; have no fear
11:39 I am your s; no buffets of the world
11:39 indignity there is a strong s
12:39 S from the scorn and cover
12:39 Often I have to s my disciples from
12:43 protect them with a s of love

Shore
7:4 sat on the s and mended those nets
7:67 fish ready on the s in their nets
8:24 one pull nearer s and safety

Shrivels
8:87 self, the original man, s up

Silence
1:33 Cultivate s
1:33 a s, a soft wind, can be a
1:47 times when you sit in s, when it
3:58 listened to me in the s as the two
3:70 Simply seeking s must help in the rush
3:86 Wait in s a while
4:33 Seek a s of spirit understanding
6:49 Go back into the s to recover this
7:92 by that power of perfect s
13:39 in the s of your hearts, it will
14:6 Wait in s before me to feel that
17:36 asking you to wait in s while I

Simple
4:92 Choose s things always
4:92 reverence the humble and the s
4:92 Have only s things here
5:26 s trust and persistent prayer
5:70 s offering of a child, brought with
5:87 s fisherman to a great leader and
6:39 S tasks, faithfully done and
10:13 rigidly doing your s duties
10:38 s trust, but for its joy in life
10:44 s and the loving heart that
10:50 s rules I gave to my followers are
14:60 s doers of my word, not hearers only
14:61 Do your s tasks for me
14:79 s acts of steadfast devotion, of
14:88 revelation is s acceptance of my will
16:28 s though it may seem, while the mighty
17:38 s tasks done in my strength and love
18:24 heaven is for the lowly, the s

Simplicity
4:92 S is the keynote of my kingdom
10:51 In all things seek s
11:13 Have I not taught you to love s?
11:13 S brings rest—true rest and power
11:37 joy and cheer and comfort in its s

Simply
3:70 S seeking silence must help in
6:50 s needs an unblocked channel
6:98 commune with his God s and naturally
7:15 s and naturally use the body as need
11:5 happening so easily, so s, so free
11:6 This has not happened easily and s
13:38 Use my name in that same way—s
13:70 feel you can s claim help, and so
14:51 Serve me as s, cheerfully and
15:16 s by its existing, by its quality
17:59 Think s of the march
18:27 s seeking the means to do my will

Sin
1:8 soul out of the sea of s or disease
3:39 Savior from slavery to s
4:11 I died to save you from s
4:24 every s, every evil or every fear
4:88 no thought of s and suffering, of the
5:77 bore the weight of your s
6:17 from s, sloth, depression, distrust
6:18 S is also conquered and forgiven, as you live
6:52 Yours is the fault, the s, if that
7:12 except as far as s is concerned, to
8:89 It is the only weapon with which s
8:89 Drive s out with love
10:14 wrecked his physical being with s
10:15 go and s no more
10:15 burden of the consciousness of her s
10:30 for s, for all you may encounter in
10:67 not s for one who knows me only as
12:10 through s to salvation
12:13 such a s, mistake or omission be avoided

12:90 not only from the weight of s
14:88 at its foot the burdens of s

Sing
2:30 'S unto the Lord'
2:40 S with joy

Singing
10:83 struggled on, s as they went
12:94 on your way rejoicing, s and free
18:18 Not when it means s the song of

Sinner
5:77 I was shut out with man, the s, from
5:88 unless he understands the s
14:47 love of the s for the Savior
18:22 earth's s, you stand by me as I am

Sinners
8:88 the publicans, the s, the harlots
9:17 righteous need my pity for s
18:22 friend and servant of s

Sins
1:63 I bore your s in my own body on the
8:68 Not even the s and failures
10:45 down with the s and sorrows of the
12:19 not being punished for past s
12:44 not to dwell for one moment on your s
12:46 Remember no more their s and
14:68 Lay upon me your s, your
15:70 bear the burdens of his s himself
15:70 our s in his own body on the tree
15:71 If you do not forget the s of
16:65 weakness, your s and shortcomings?
18:4 doubt of me, and so many other s
18:47 save his people from their s
18:48 's,' read not only vice and
18:49 save his people from their s
18:50 save his people from their s

Slopes
10:90 s (not during the storm) that I
10:90 time of the mountain s will come

Soar
10:11 earth life and seek to s higher
12:50 earthbound spirit that cannot s

Solvents
2:13 Love and trust are the s for the

Son
3:48 waters, like unto the S of Man
4:1 know—the S of Righteousness
5:23 my Father and me, the S sent by
5:77 I, the S of God, bore man's weight of
5:89 Thou art the Christ, the S of the
7:60 the words, 'The Son of Man'
7:60 I must feel, I—the S of man
8:42 s or daughter appropriates
11:74 If I, the S of God, needed those
16:77 majestic figure of the S of God
17:2 contempt and rejection the S of God
17:31 persuade men I was the S of God?
18:36 so shall the S of Man be three days

Song
2:30 take the most crowded day with a s
2:30 s of praise to me is a very crowded
4:84 joy from the s of the birds
4:90 s as a message from my Father
18:18 means singing the s of the world

Songs
3:8 s of praise of the people
8:76 Go with s of rejoicing
10:83 there must be s on the way

Sorrow
1:1 hiding trouble and s and
1:60 depression and s in the Garden
4:60 there was no cup of s to dnnk
7:1 of peril, in adversity, in s
8:18 S may endure for a night, but joy
8:18 night of s that underlying joy that
8:84 the wine of s and disappointment
9:4 no sense of s now cause you trouble
10:29 Whatever s or difficulty the day
10:30 middle or old age, for s, for sin
11:65 s-cry of the world that needs a
13:37 Spoken in fear, in weakness, in s
14:39 every s over failure, every weakness
14:48 experience in your life of joy or s
14:65 rung was made, whether of joy or s
14:72 your s is turned to joy
14:88 way to the cross may be a way of s

Sorrows
10:45 sins and s of the world
14:4 way of s, if walked with me, the
14:4 man of s, is a path kept sacred and
14:44 thought of me is the balm for all s
15:71 bear them, then you add to my s
17:1 the need for the man of s
17:7 keep very close to the man of s
18:25 myrrh is your sharing in my s and

Soul
1:8 lift another s out of the sea of sin
1:44 work of any s that has eternal life
2:2 s-balance and poise, in a vacillating
2:36 power from the s that dwells near me
2:36 s who lives in my presence
2:65 want of the s that I do not supply

2:74 battlefield of the s are these things
3:35 joy than that s knows
3:42 line from the s to God, faith and
3:42 no s can be overwhelmed who is
3:60 If every day each s, or group of
3:74 food for the s I have provided
4:2 s-disturbance, or of a ruffling of the
4:4 surround the city of man's s and are
4:41 speaking to the s matters so much to
4:88 tree is impressed upon your s
4:89 beauty becomes part of your very s
4:90 Let is sink into your s
5:1 s, renewer of your youth
5:11 life, the very breath of your s
5:13 Wherever the s is, I am
5:17 lead a s to me is one thing; to seek
5:18 when it involves the s and me
5:20 s finds its home of rest in me, then
6:4 Each s is so different
6:39 speaking to me you find s-rest
6:74 me, the s's lover, the s's friend
7:18 that s I have to span the physical and
7:23 not always see the s we seek
7:38 smiles of the s at one it loves
7:56 window of your s open toward me
7:81 in the individual s of the worker
7:89 Any s can feel this in a harbor
8:29 saved s trusts me so entirely it no
8:51 s I tell you of is one for you to help
8:79 prayer links up the s and mind and
8:81 s, being linked to God in prayer
8:81 s, when in human form, also needs the
8:82 s's transformation is the way of divine
8:87 my image becomes stamped upon the s
9:19 s live, it shall grow in grace and
9:25 It is for the s
9:25 what best suits the s
9:25 I permit only what best suits the s
9:27 picture your s as a third, being
9:28 Stand apart from your s with me and
9:44 I speak to each individual s, the
10:30 Leave every s the braver and
11:56 union between a s that loves me and
12:27 Faith is the s's breathing in the
12:28 Mind, s and body need helping
12:30 distances between a s and me
12:55 offer them up for one troubled s
12:63 ladder which a s can climb from the
13:12 until its truth sinks into your s
13:33 eye of the s is the will
13:41 It expresses the s's progress
13:42 As a s realizes me and my power, and
13:42 s believes in me more and more
13:43 s's progress—an increased belief
13:79 until my rest fills your s
13:89 the right of each individual s
13:90 call of the s gives me my right to
14:22 s attains this calm can there be
14:22 s and body be strong to conquer and
14:85 cry of the human s is never unheard
15:12 joy and beauty for the believing s
16:47 until a s finds rest and peace in me
16:60 s finds me, I have to begin our
17:17 union of a s with God in which
17:19 S-starvation comes from failing to do
17:50 s being kept by my power
18:49 name lifts the s away from petty

Source
14:13 Look to no other s for salvation
18:46 only s of happiness and heart peace

Sovereign
4:23 Joy is the s balm for all the ills

Space
2:53 world, there is no empty s
5:77 from my Father's sight for one short s

Sparrow
4:77 s is of greater value than a palace

Speak
1:43 words you s, the influence you have
1:47 'bid he not s to us by the way?'
3:17 Listen to me; I will s
3:20 I s to the listening ear
3:20 Sometimes I may not s
3:40 I s as all to you both
3:68 Even if I were never to s to you
4:41 few wait to hear me s to them
4:42 To hear me s is to find life and
4:46 words that I s unto you, they are
5:89 could best s of me as the Savior
6:38 s to anyone, ask me to act as
6:79 I that s unto you am he, your master
6:95 Do not be too ready to s to others
6:96 'Though I s with the tongues of men
6:97 rarely do I s to the human heart in
6:97 Do not feel that you have to s
8:46 before you allow yourself to s to, or
9:10 I s very quietly
9:44 injunctions I s to each individual
9:83 S much of me
12:53 I s to you today, my loved ones
12:91 S to me
14:45 Then think of me and s to me
15:14 I s of as the salt of the earth
16:6 s only of passing into that fuller
16:80 s of your fellow man as
17:35 I may s no word that you could write
18:2 S to me about everything

Speed
7:80 world has to learn s to attain its
15:76 progress, but to increase your s

Spirit
1:14 My s shall flow through you and
1:28 not according to my S
1:36 work of the universal S—my S—
1:55 poor s-impoverished friend
1:61 coming of my S into a life
2:5 Bathe your s in it
2:48 Keep your s life calm and unruffled
2:50 My S brooks no stagnation
2:53 S, that you crave so, rush in
3:43 s life sap flows silently, secretly
3:45 Joy is the s reaching out to say
3:53 be led by the S of God and trust me
3:64 lead man back to s-conversation with
3:73 s-wings down with earth's mud
4:2 Be more afraid of s-unrest, of
4:2 or of a ruffling of the s than of
4:15 healing of body, mind and s comes from
4:15 contact of your s with my S
4:16 Silently the work of the S is done
4:23 s cure for every ailment
4:32 hearing of s sounds is more than
4:33 s understanding with me
4:46 they are s and they are life
4:47 for not seeking s communication
4:47 of s communication as you
4:68 work must be done in my S
4:68 How silently my S works
4:74 embodied spirit of my thoughts of
4:80 links between your real s life and
4:80 you wish to hold s communication
4:93 gently breathing in my S
4:93 If you give that S free entrance
4:94 a medium for any s, other than mine
4:95 know of my s kingdom
5:5 quickened responsive s nerves
5:9 my invigorating life and S
5:11 Draw near in s to me
5:18 only real S that understands it
5:58 achieve by the power of my S
5:81 You are changed by my S
5:81 shedding one garment of s for a
6:22 s of the tomb or in the s of
6:23 choose the s of resurrection
6:23 reject the s of the tomb
6:28 Pray for my S of love to be
6:39 Live in a s of prayer
6:50 accomplished by my S
6:95 My S has been driven out by the
7:2 Once you are born of the S, that is
7:5 not mean my S is not supplying wisdom
7:13 renewal of s force, rest of body
7:15 nervous body has driven a s
7:15 The s should be the master always
7:17 S consciousness replaces sight
7:56 Breathe in my very S in pure air
7:56 Keep the eye of your s ever upon me
8:30 The conquering s is never crushed
8:30 difficulties in the s of conquest
9:51 but the movement of my S
9:52 I can act with all my s power
9:71 my S could operate more and
9:85 revives your fainting s
10:31 sword of the s which is the word of
10:38 child-s only for its simple trust
11:9 worked out by me in the s world to
11:20 man actuated by the Holy S
11:46 Even in the s world, appreciation
11:67 flow of life eternal through s
11:70 done in the power of my S
11:70 All done in that S-life is undying
11:75 Refilling with the S is a need
11:80 s of trust that more will come to
12:27 Trust is the s sun, with your being
12:27 being wrapped in the divine S
12:28 soul's breathing in the divine S
12:30 In the s kingdom we measure
12:37 kneeling in a s of humility, turn
12:50 only the earthbound s that
12:64 breath of desire and my S is
12:65 s but of the guiding of the S
12:89 only the watering of a grateful s
13:15 lets the S of my supply flow clear
14:6 divine S flows through that healing
14:26 to those who were S guided
14:32 led by the S is a proof of sonship
14:32 led by the S of God, they are the
14:8 Home build in the S now
14:11 Trust in the s forces of the unseen
15:59 not you, but the divine S in you
15:63 My S cannot fail to pass through
15:63 know that my S is flowing through
14:67 S flowing through you as a channel
14:94 but by my S, saith the Lord
15:2 united by one bond in my S
16:6 passing into that fuller s life
16:7 earth world or in the s world
16:33 who could read my undaunted S
16:35 S was free, unbroken and unharmed
16:36 Man could not see my S untouched
16:40 s, a blessing will attend all you
16:50 to the seeing eye, the S that dwelt
16:51 beauty of my character, of my S
16:54 lies your happiness and s rest

16:61 This is the way of the S
17:8 s world contains the first law of
17:25 my power in the unseen—the Holy S
17:66 done in love and in the s of true

Spoil
11:26 s your peace of heart and mind
11:39 power to s your inward peace

Spoken
1:47 remember I have s to you, as I spoke
8:93 awe, will accompany the s word
10:32 The s word has power
13:37 S in fear, in weakness, in sorrow

Spring
1:43 s from the life within you, my life
3:43 sun of s comes new life, leaves
4:13 Take your fill of joy in the s
4:73 joy of the s shall be yours
8:94 come to the glad s of water
11:55 joy and gratitude will s to greet
13:18 joy, a s, a gladness in the walk
13:50 flowers of life to s forth and yield
17:37 second s—the youth they sacrificed

Stage
4:20 bud s now—the glory of the open
8:29 Guidance is the final s when the
10:80 entered upon the s of success
12:44 That is a s in development
12:44 but only a s
13:45 this path to me, each s nearer to me
16:84 s by s, can you proceed in your

Stagnation
2:50 My Spirit brooks no s, not even rest
13:15 There is always a s, a blockage, when
14:65 kingdom, and there can be no s

Stamp
9:38 received the s of the kingdom

Stamped
8:87 my image becomes s upon the soul

Stand
1:11 s between the years
1:31 No man can s upon the threshold
3:11 I choose to let it s between you and
4:25 No evil can s against that, for
6:13 My children must make a s
6:13 my children must s out
6:15 Be ready to s aside and let the
6:21 despair and tears come as you s by
9:28 S apart from your soul with me and
10:52 No man or woman can s against my will
13:25 ready to s apart from the world
15:37 friend with whom you s by the grave
16:45 I s a beggar, knocking, knocking
17:56 I s between you and your foes
18:22 earth's sinner, you s by me as I am baptized

Start
3:1 S a new life tomorrow
3:1 old mistakes away and s anew
3:1 I give you a fresh s
3:36 wait until I give the order to s
3:54 it is not the s that hurts, nor the
5:79 s anew from today
12:46 a fresh s from today

Starvation
17:19 Soul-s comes from failing to do

Stay
1:58 Gold does not s in the crucible
2:48 ruffled feeling s for one moment
5:17 s with it as interpreter mars the
9:80 s for a while in my presence
10:83 s on alone and friendless in the
11:89 no alternative but to s at my side
13:78 But s for rest, too
18:9 S or go as that pressure—love's

Step
1:18 the way will unfold s by s
2:35 Every s was necessary to their
2:39 Go just one s at a time
2:39 one s at a time is the best way to
3:13 Just go s by s
4:1 Just one s at a time with me
7:2 must walk s by s the way to freedom
10:12 less stony with every s you take
10:21 first s is always to lay your will
10:22 second s is to be sure, to to tell me
10:84 if I have asked you to s on and up
12:60 think of each s as leading to the
13:34 first s is to make sure your will
14:50 s with a firm s of confidence in me
14:54 see that the first s is praise
14:58 That is always the second s
14:66 S up the ladder, then cast
15:81 see that every s was planned
15:84 s by s, and stage by stage, can
17:13 first s toward conquering temptation
17:47 Wait for guidance in every s
18:23 S out beside me

Stop
1:21 devil will try to s them by any means
2:49 s everything until absolute calm

15:32 Your s is measured by the amount
18:41 forces that will ensure your s

Suffering
1:3 of s, of loss
2:75 all s is redemptive, to teach
4:88 no thought of sin and s, of the
5:77 God, had this not been my s, then I
11:44 s is the only path into my kingdom
11:92 s, friends and angels even now are
12:57 my life of the s that saves others
13:90 hardest of all my s for humanity
14:34 So your s has its purpose
16:7 midst of pain and poverty and s
16:8 may come as the reward for patient s
16:9 S must in time bring joy, if borne
16:9 into it may be service or it may be s
16:85 not the result of the s, but the
16:85 with me to which s drove you

Summit
12:60 s of achievement from which

Summon
10:4 s at will the God of the world?
10:5 s me to their bedside, to their worship
15:51 Calling my name does not really s me

Sun
1:1 radiance of the s of righteousness
3:43 s of spring comes new life
3:77 as to see that tomorrow's s rises
4:14 S and air are my great healing forces
4:26 vanish as night when the s arises
6:5 lives with the warm s of my presence
12:27 medicines are s and air, trust and
12:27 Trust is the spirit s, with your
17:10 makes his s to shine on the evil and
17:63 'He maketh his s to rise on the evil

Supernatural
3:66 s men, men who will persistently turn

Supplicates
8:42 A beggar s

Supply
2:43 broke with an overabundance of s
2:65 want of the soul that I do not s
3:31 I am your Lord, your s
3:33 on me, your strength, your help, your s
3:34 Am I your s or not?
3:37 if you know that I am your s
3:87 before him means immediate s
3:88 I long to s
5:34 when I am your s
5:39 have a need I cannot s
5:40 spiritual s is fashioned from love
5:42 a constant s, but only if the need
6:57 God is love...all s
6:75 Claim s; claim what you will
6:86 only conditions of s being ample for
6:87 have no connection with s
6:87 commands are mine and the s is mine
6:92 branch continually ask the vine to s it
7:25 perfect s, perfect love
7:26 s, harmony, and think I fail in my
8:40 he has—when your s is exhausted
8:54 There was a s left over
8:56 God's s is abundant
8:80 whatever s and other things are
10:55 Say, 'the s for it is not here yet'
10:56 feeling is your faith claiming my s
11:80 more will come to meet your s
11:80 quickly to ensure a divine s
11:81 It is a law of divine s
11:84 ask to understand divine s
11:84 so dependent on material s
13:14 When s seems to have failed, you must
13:15 blockage, when s seems short
13:15 lets the Spirit of my s flow clear
14:13 See no other s
14:14 Regard me as your only s
15:47 My law is that of an unlimited s
15:47 unlimited s, but poor blocked
16:70 ready to s their hunger
16:75 know that I will s your need
17:12 As you receive, you must s the

Supports
10:84 Its s may be out of your sight
14:8 helping hand s you when you faint

Sure
3:18 You shall have more s knowledge
4:29 s that I can never fail you?
4:29 As s as you are that you still

Surprise
4:17 s you, all that I have planned for
4:70 by the lakeside—a little glad s
9:35 to its s that demand is met
15:29 s being prepared for it by one who
15:30 glory, joy and wonder of your s
18:3 seeks to s you in some fear

Surrender
2:44 Complete s of every moment to God
12:31 s to my will in the small as in

Swift
4:28 My help comes s and strong
9:2 Molding means s recognition of

Sympathy
1:57 Have more s
12:79 of s, of all these and many more
14:40 My tender s is yours
16:71 no s for the fainting, exhausted
16:72 divine s includes responsibility
16:73 s goes, you must go too, if

Task
2:4 replenish after each t, no work can
2:48 your great t, to remain calm in my
2:49 yours is the t to stop everything
3:62 presently your appointed t
6:50 Never feel inadequate for any t
7:8 occupy themselves with the t I give them
7:76 your t to maintain your own heart
8:47 delivered or that the t is done
8:47 Never relinquish any t or give up
8:57 the thought of any t because it
8:58 What a t beyond its power that must
8:58 it carries out that t
9:12 your t to let all your power be my
10:76 I complete every t committed to me
11:25 Set yourselves this t
11:64 then it will be an easy t
11:91 the agony, but the t was finished
12:4 It is my divine t to order my affairs
13:24 your first t, the weeding, the planting
14:12 for every t I give one of my
14:52 from one t to do one like less?
14:82 deserters I gave the t of bringing
14:90 interruption, in each t, however small
14:91 Accept each t or interruption; say
17:34 Your daily t is to grow more and more
18:30 Perform every t, however humble, as
18:43 With men your t may be impossible, but

Tasted
5:89 He who had t my forgiveness, in his

Teach
2:75 redemptive, to t the individual or to
3:15 I cannot t a man to walk who is
3:17 Walk with me; I will t you
5:48 t you all things and be the very
7:13 I had to t renewal of spirit force
7:13 t them that ceaseless activity
7:44 I t a higher science law than even
7:44 I t death to the self
7:63 T it that there is only one cure for
7:73 reliance on mine will t you humility
8:25 illustration t you a great truth
10:88 I have much to t you both
11:40 needed to t you a lesson
13:59 truths I t you have all been given
17:27 t the truths of my kingdom to them

Teachers
3:19 school for which there are many t
13:75 T are to point the way to me

Teaching
1:16 Accept t; be as a child
3:23 to be near me, not for t, or material
5:4 definite t and guidance
6:42 I am t you balance and poise
6:83 unwearied discsipline, t and
7:94 Leave to me the t of understanding
10:17 t time has not been in vain
11:15 t both of you my way of removing
12:25 Live in my presence and my t

Teachings
1:65 marvelous my revelations and t are
11:6 self, to do mywill and to live my t
13:61 t out in their daily lives, they

Temporal
2:42 t affairs submit to limitations too
5:3 spiritual, mental and t things are
10:62 Success in the t world would not
10:62 Great success, in both t and
12:86 (the lower, t things), and you will
13:76 even controlling your t life
15:17 over the material and the t
15:18 T power, as money, needs to be
15:19 conquest over t forces and powers
16:15 t needs look to me, owner of all this
17:63 it was of t and material blessings
17:66 bestow t blessings, as does my

Temptation
10:33 t to be attacked and overthrown
11:46 t, also find a way of escape that ye
11:88 no t, and no other thing can come
16:32 I overcame each t and each difficulty
17:13 conquering t is to see it as t
17:14 not think of t as something resulting

Temptations
11:10 t must be lacking to some extent
17:16 t come, you will recognize them
17:43 Treat all the t of fear in a like

Tempted
9:17 The t and fallen need my salvation
11:46 not suffer you to be t above that

Test
3:34 This is the great t
3:35 After the waiting t, when I crown it
4:70 only t and train and bend to my will

5:91 not lay one t too much on you
8:66 T your love for me by this
15:11 This final t has to come to all
16:28 The t of all true work and words is

Thank
1:54 say 't you' for everything, even
1:54 attitude of 't you' to me
2:33 Never forget your 'T you'
2:33 say 'T you' on the grayest days
8:93 'T you,' as a courtesy, with
9:13 T me if you knew the darts of worry
9:14 T me for dangers unknown, unseen, but
9:33 t and steadily fulfill your promises
11:17 Say, 'T you' all the time
11:30 T and praise all the time
14:55 Than bless and t
14:59 t God for me, so I t God for his
16:5 T me for the quiet lives

Thankful
3:4 only bless glad, t hearts
3:13 t for this time when you felt peaceful
5:66 glad, very happy, very t
8:50 be t, both of you, that there is
8:92 shower yet more on the t heart
8:93 thrill of joy, of t awe, will
11:16 all you have to be t for
11:17 remover of mountains—your t hearts
11:52 gift of a brave and t heart
11:55 t about in every happening

Thanks
3:45 reaching out to say its t to me
9:35 man has been paying in t and praise
14:91 interruption; say your t for it

Thanksgiving
9:36 sacrifice of t and pay your vows to
11:54 t, is indeed a sweet incense going

Thought
1:2 Encourage yourselves by the t
1:3 Bury all t of unkindness and
1:15 all that my love has ever t, you shall
1:20 Take no t for tomorrow
1:28 soon every fleeting t will be
1:34 t of yours can be like a pearl that
1:36 Dwell in t on this more and more
2:13 worrying t enter your mind, one
2:13 one impatient t?
2:20 Dwell on this t
2:21 t of a grudging God who has to be
2:26 your t is called into being
2:27 To dwell in t on the material, when
2:57 disciples t that in sleep I had
3:8 my t carried out in action
3:11 a t from me, and it is gone
3:63 every t, every activity, every
3:82 t it was too late and that they
4:25 every t of want or lack, 'Jesus saves'
4:85 beautiful t, I made a lovely flower
4:87 flower is my expression of t
4:87 in spiritual beauty, in t-power
4:88 no t of sin and suffering, of the
4:89 a kind t or a prayer
5:15 say what they t about my truth
5:41 I t of you and a bud opened
6:6 Put aside all t of the future and of
6:29 Mountains can be removed by t, by
6:54 Dwell on the t, God is love
6:77 t of the joy that the patient
7:14 not indifference as they t
7:30 expression of eternal t in time
7:30 Grasp the eternal t
7:46 t of them means self is in the
7:52 t about the world called it into
7:52 t for you, I can call into being all
8:5 words and actions and by tender t
8:57 give up the t of any task because it
9:54 put from you t of trouble
10:4 t what it means to be able to summon
11:1 Joy in that t
11:61 wishes every action, t, word and
11:92 Let this t comfort you
12:44 weighed down with the t of its
12:78 no mean t in your heart
12:78 Of love, of t, of all you have, give
13:39 raise the standard of talk and t
14:43 t of one very near and dear
14:44 t of me is the balm for all sorrows
14:59 t of the souls who had kept my word
14:66 cast away all t of the manner of
15:59 t with you through the days in
15:75 t of you as my friends and of the
15:78 Bring all your t, all your power
15:95 t upon all I accomplished on earth
17:8 time, your love, your t, yourselves
17:11 t of supplying a real need, you must
17:22 beautiful they had t it to be
17:24 t material forces had proved too
17:47 t of this loving leading should
17:62 t for others are as sure signs of
17:66 interchange of t would be impossible
17:68 once only a t of divine mind
17:68 from your t one corner of it could
18:2 at once some t of me for the fear

Throne
6:60 inevitable and resigns the t for me
9:72 It leads to the t of God

7:84 the power of two t
7:85 t will know that I am the divine third
11:59 T we share and joy in the harvest
12:9 You are fellow workers t with me
14:33 you may also be glorified t
16:2 t in my name, united by one bond in
16:63 be 'gathered t in my name, bound by
17:40 Love and fear cannot dwell t

Tool
4:38 one poor t, working all the time

Touch
3:9 at my miracle-working t
4:35 My t is still a potent healer
4:35 Just feel that t
5:5 Man's ecstasy is God's t on quickened
9:60 No evil can t you
11:29 How dare any foe t you when you
13:11 none and nothing can t him
14:6 powerful t into your very beings
14:7 arm with a gentle t to point the
14:7 my t brings strength and healing
14:8 My t of the strong and helping
14:9 my t still has its ancient power
16:37 powerless to t me
17:8 or whose lives t yours

Touched
4:34 I t her hand and the fever left
10:86 cannot be t or harmed there
12:6 lives altered you never t, laws

Tower
10:87 you were in a really strong t

Tragedy
17:37 t of living and the pity of an agonized

Train
1:27 t and discipline yourself
2:35 world, but also to t my disciples
4:70 only test and t and bend to my will
7:5 help of t or car has not learned a
11:27 T yourself to make sure that no
16:14 T your sight by constantly getting
16:14 T it to see more and more, further

Training
1:29 Welcome the t
2:34 requires a great and careful t
2:35 all a part of their t
3:83 is my t too hard?
5:90 My apostles needed a many sided t
6:53 Love those you are t
6:83 Life is a t school
6:83 discipline, teaching and t
6:84 consider this t not as harsh, but
7:7 to me the necessary correcting or t
7:21 mean that you need the varied t
7:41 In all t (in mine of you, and in
8:37 t is different for different spirits
9:27 sharing, in the discipline and t
9:28 from your soul with me and welcome t
10:17 This t and teaching time has not
11:27 t to enable you to acquire this peace
12:30 your t must be severe
12:55 t that shall fit you to save

Transmitters
10:27 Be t these days; love and laugh

Treasure
1:34 recipient finds the t and realizes its
6:7 earth t that he has no hand to receive
9:72 Your t lies at the end of the path
13:60 Hunt for it as for hidden t

Treasures
2:21 relinquish the desired t
3:3 You would crush my t
3:84 unlock for you the secret t
5:26 prayer, the t of my kingdom
7:53 newly found t, joys and little work
7:86 come in to take your t
7:87 What greater t can you have than
9:21 reaching after the t of my kingdom
18:28 Could you think of me hoarding my t?

Trees
1:2 use the past as the t use my sunlight
3:43 t, stripped of their beauty, pruned
13:50 causes the t and flowers of life
17:51 butterflies and t and playing fountains

Trouble
1:1 hiding t and sorrow, and
7:86 Turn out all thoughts of doubt and t
9:4 now cause you t and dismay
9:7 others whose imperfections t you
9:26 progress is delayed, t and grief are
9:36 call upon me in the day of t and I
9:38 world surrounded by t and difficulty
9:42 In times of storm and t he is overthrown
9:54 put from you thought of t
11:16 When t comes, think of all you have
11:26 Do not let anyone without, any t
12:56 live on after the t and distress
12:68 Trials and t may seem to overwhelm
13:11 Man, in his t and difficulty, needs

13:58 fears assail you, and cares t you
15:77 Whatever difficulty and t, it must
17:83 Do not t your souls with puzzles you

Troubles
3:39 Savior from all the cares and t of
5:61 Courage and joy will conquer all t
7:4 t might have made them feel my help was
8:49 unknowing of your heartaches and t
9:9 I share your t, failures, difficulties
9:64 before I get crowded out by life's t
11:53 t crowd in, then definitely look
12:91 Lift up your heads from earth's t
13:7 Earth's t and difficulties will
14:54 bless the Lord even when t seem to
15:76 t are not intended to arrest
15:78 aside is to be preparing big t

Truce
18:17 a t with the power of evil

True
3:14 learning of t trust in me
3:41 For of him it was t, 'He came from'
3:46 certainty of your t discipleship
3:74 me, the t bread of life
5:65 Be calm; be t; be quiet
6:12 expresses the t love of the giver
6:43 That gives you t balance
6:61 t discipleship, and in the t spiritual
6:92 'I am the t vine and you are the
7:47 as all t love is of God, and is God
7:47 all t forgiveness is of God
8:17 note on which t prayer should end
8:40 t friend—has is his by right
8:41 t friendship—implies the right to
8:86 as t today as it was in the days of
9:19 t beauty, the beauty of holiness
9:23 kept them brave and strong and t
9:39 fit to judge t values, the values of
10:45 Look for the loving, the t, the
10:80 It is t; it is t
11:13 Simplicity brings rest—t rest

Trust
1:4 year in my hands—in t for you
1:9 T on, love on, joy on
1:53 t me always; never rebel
1:53 The t given to me today takes away
2:13 Love and t are the solvents for the
2:32 from all evil; t me; fear not
2:67 T me absolutely
2:69 T me for all
3:7 Peace and t will come; fear not
3:14 time of learning of true t in me
3:26 T and be not afraid
3:31 T to the uttermost limit
3:31 T and do not be afraid
3:33 You must wait, t, hope, and joy in me
3:40 T me for help
3:42 T, t, t; never be afraid
3:50 Wait and t; wait and do not be afraid
3:53 be led by the Spirit of God and t me
3:53 Give me gladness as well as t
3:78 worries in the divine hands; so t
4:6 You must t me wholly
4:9 T my tender love; it will never fail
4:29 Do you t me as much as you would a
4:42 T me in all things
5:24 You need to t me for everything
5:25 Just t me in everything
5:26 Seize from me, by firm and simple t
5:29 Can you really t me? I am a God of
5:30 Just t; I cannot and I will not fail
5:56 My message to you is to t and wait
6:30 just t me wholly
6:77 joy I feel at the loving t of a dear
6:86 T in me; do as I say each moment and
7:35 Oh, children, t me
7:53 Joy in me; t in me
7:79 Calm is t in action
7:79 Only t, perfect t, can keep one calm
8:13 calm t that results, does man learn
8:16 because t has become so rocklike
8:23 Rest is t
8:34 cares and show me your heart of t
8:39 There is a t that waits patiently
8:39 also a t that tolerates no delay
9:29 T me; love me; call upon me
9:52 Love and t; let no unkind thought
9:60 Walk in my way and t me
10:21 if you t me, what I do for you will be
10:29 Learn daily the sublime lesson of t
10:38 child-spirit only for its simple t
10:52 if you t me and place your affairs in
10:54 T me, the captain of your salvation
10:67 T and pray
10:76 So t and do not be afraid
10:77 child's joyful trust, for the next
10:85 Know my divine power, t in me
10:85 T in me; dwell in my love
10:91 others will say is a lack of t in me
11:37 simplicity, its love and its t?
11:79 Children, t
11:80 Pay all out in the spirit of t that
11:81 fear of the future, a lack of t in me
11:82 you must t wholly in me
11:83 T wholly; t completely
12:2 T me wholly; fear nothing; hope ever
12:27 medicines are sun and air, t and faith

12:27 T is the spirit sun, with your being
12:61 T me absolutely; know that I will do the
12:70 T and go forward unafraid
12:71 T me; am I not leading you safely
12:74 Tell me you t me in this
13:42 falling short of absolute t in me
13:43 conquer all unbelief, all lack of t
13:44 more power to see where t is lacking
13:52 Sow in prayer, water by t, bear flower
13:62 He is good; t in him; know that all
13:64 T and be not afraid
14:16 milk and honey; so t; be led
14:42 T me, my children; I know all
14:49 T and know that I am leading you
15:9 You must t to the end
15:11 T in the spirit forces of the unseen, not
15:11 T and fear not
15:83 t the pattern to the designer
15:94 T in me; have a boundless faith in me
16:21 springs from t in me, from living with
16:23 So t, so conquer, so joy
18:35 Love and laugh; t and pray; ride on

Trusting
1:38 Joy is the result of faithful t
3:15 teach a man to walk who is t in a crutch
3:26 Open childlike t eyes to all I am doing
3:29 a t cry, ever reaches the dear divine
4:8 Are you t all to me or not?
7:65 drift with the tide, t to the current
8:30 Keep a brave and t heart; face all your
10:37 your nature that of the t child
11:62 the t understanding love
14:35 means to feel a little t hand in yours
15:9 ready to go on t to the last hour
17:41 perfect t love is immediately the
17:61 dark days, of t when you cannot see

Trusts
7:65 The oarsman who t in me does not lean
8:29 when the saved soul t e so entirely
15:93 Wherever man t wholly in me and

Truth
1:55 Each t is a jewel
1:55 find a heart-home for each t I have
3:74 Grasp the t and find me
4:57 t is many sided; have much tender love
5:15 what they thought about my t
8:24 t is as a rope flung to a drowning
8:25 illustration teach you a great t
8:25 Lay hold of the t
8:28 three steps of that wonderful t
8:62 before they realize this spiritual t
9:60 Rest in that t
10:88 do not reveal more of my t to you
12:62 Cling joyfully to that t
12:63 This t, accepted and firmly
13:12 say it until its t sinks into your
15:61 some spiritual t becomes clearer
16:48 prophet realized the t which I said
16:62 I am the t; every word of mine
18:24 Accept the t that the kingdom of

Truths
1:45 ponder on these t I give you
1:46 Seek my wonderful t and you shall
1:55 More t will flow in
5:14 I am telling you t, revealing them
9:22 Dwell on these t
10:90 I taught my disciples the t of my
13:23 seeing spiritual t is a great joy
13:59 the t I teach you have all been given
17:27 to teach the t of my kingdom to them
17:27 In those t they were to live and work

Twenty-four
1:70 weight of t hours and no more
8:72 coming t hours, you must face as you

Two
1:42 carry t days' burden on one day
3:10 my power are the only t essentials
3:22 one or t who followed just to be
3:58 silence as the t of you meet with me
4:48 I sent my disciples out t by t
6:47 intensified immeasurably in power when t
6:63 Joy is of t kinds
6:63 t joys lie discipline
7:84 the power of t together
7:85 those who visit the t of you together
8:53 you are t of my disciples present
8:64 The t growths are necessary
11:87 effort and rest, a union of the t
12:20 I rarely find t souls in union who
12:21 served by many such t souls
12:22 It was always t and t
12:47 When I sent my disciples out, t by t
12:47 without t coats, without money
14:81 Learn t lessons from these words
15:4 one of the t at Emmaus, or one of the
16:1 when t who love me meet, I am the
16:2 Whenever you t are together in my name
16:3 power that follows t united to serve
16:65 For t to agree about the wisdom of
16:65 not the same as t agreeing to pray

18:41 t forces that will ensure your success

Unafraid
2:52 Go forward u; health and strength
5:51 Go forward boldly and u
7:68 Go forward u; I am beside you
10:82 conquer; go forward u
12:70 Trust and go forward u
14:9 forward into the future bravely and u
18:43 Go forward gladly and u

Unbelief
6:59 barred out from more hearts than does u
9:77 many mighty works because of u
13:43 Help thou mine u
13:43 plea to conquer all u, all lack of
14:63 I will indeed help your u
14:63 faith of the day before as almost u
15:24 it is not the u of my enemies that

Unbelievers
6:47 unequally yoked together with u

Unbroken
7:75 others are in u accord with you
16:35 my Spirit was free, u and unharmed?

Undernourished
17:19 talks of bodies that are u!
17:19 What of the souls that are u?

Understand
1:65 You could not u them
1:65 listening to me, you will u
1:76 beyond your finite mind to u
4:10 Could you see, you would u
4:71 surprises for those who u and joy
5:75 You u this, my children, I know you
6:41 alone u perfectly the language
10:27 seek to u others and you cannot
11:83 So u my leading
11:84 You both ask to u divine supply
11:84 fail to u because they have
13:5 They u better, protect better, plan
13:86 your power to u my salvation increases
15:1 u that my knocking does not rely
15:67 U this, and you will think it natural
17:35 Only friends who u and love each
17:65 My followers do not always u this
17:65 u if they remember my injunction

Unemployed
15:20 u, let him make himself a conquering

Unemployment
3:67 All u would cease
4:65 afraid of u, afraid of sickness
15:20 U would cease if man realized that

Unequally
16:47 Be ye not u yoked together with

Unhelped
14:87 response and unsaved and u by it

Union
6:92 from the very u with the vine
6:94 u with me is the one great overwhelming
6:94 U with me may be the result ofjust
7:63 all its ills—u with me
11:56 no bond or u on earth to compare with
11:56 u between a soul that loves me and me
11:87 effort and rest, a u of the two
12:20 rarely find two souls in u who want
12:20 The u is miracle working
13:86 We go in u, from strength to
14:34 u with me and God, the Father
17:17 majestic u of a soul with God in

United
8:81 linked to God in prayer, u to him
16:2 u by one bond in my Spirit, I am 'there
16:3 follows two u to serve me
17:53 cannot be u in your great friendship

Unlock
3:84 I will u for you the secret treasures

Unrest
4:2 Be more afraid of spirit-u, of
6:82 u disturbs your perfect calm
12:1 Out of u to rest, out of disorder
13:52 Peace, not u
14:76 In your u behold my calm, my rest
16:47 pray to copy the divine u until

Unseen
1:58 marching of the u host, rejoicing
5:48 not to receive revelation of the u
5:54 U forces are controlling your
9:14 dangers unknown, u, but averted
10:71 bodyguard of my servants in the u
12:91 you are living really in the u
13:6 remember your friends in the u
13:6 as you live more in the u world
13:51 in the u that your life's future
15:11 spirit forces of the u, not in
17:25 power in the u—the Holy Spirit

Untroubled
13:78 feverish haste and be calm and u

Uproot
1:18 U self—the channel-blocker

Upward
1:10 Refuse to be checked in your u climb
5:68 steady progress u
5:61 grandeur, or even of his u progress
6:73 u way is a glorious way with its
8:68 failures that marked his u path
9:7 slow progress u made by you, in spite
9:49 Steep steps lead u, but your power to
9:50 You will not go u alone
9:50 thoughts will be helped u by you
16:84 can you proceed in your journey u

Valuation
17:3 set aside the v of the world

Value
1:34 treasure and realizes its v for
4:38 small v compared with the sharp, keen
4:77 sparrow is of greater v than a
4:78 life in all that has v
4:78 life that determines the v
15:64 are of little v to my world
16:47 v to me, his God, of each man's

Values
4:38 Heaven's v are so different from the
4:38 from the v of earth
9:39 peace you are fit to judge true v
9:39 v of the kingdom
9:39 v of all the world has to offer
13:35 Know no v but spiritual v
13:36 Get away from money v altogether
17:2 v of heaven and those of the world
17:3 according to the v of heaven

Venture
7:70 V there often and you will find
7:73 Be afraid to v on your own as a child

Vicarious
16:41 v sacrifice is redemptive beyond

Victor
3:35 when I crown it v, heaven itself
3:36 No disciple of mine can be v who

Victory
1:58 host, rejoicing at your v
1:59 rejoicing when he's won the v
3:16 shall indeed walk on to v
3:56 your side spurring you on to v
3:57 revealing how near they were to v
5:45 then you pass on to v
6:18 with death my v was complete
7:89 v come to those alone who sense these
8:31 Remember, where I am is v
11:39 have won a marvelous v
15:25 I count it v, a glad v
15:36 For you it is v, and the angels
15:79 path of v I would have you tread
18:35 Ride on now in loving humility to v

Violence
2:56 storm is at its full v
5:26 kingdom of heaven suffereth v

Violent
5:26 v who take it by force

Vista
2:39 grant the long v to my disciples

Vital
3:88 your contact with me is v
8:21 a power new and v, a wonderful joy

Voices
9:10 Never heed the v of the world
12:52 Broken v can regain a strength and

Wait
1:25 Just love and w
1:31 W; wonders are unfolding
2:19 I w with a hungry longing to be
2:56 my method to w until the storm is at
3:31 w to give you all that is lovely
3:20 w in my presence
3:33 You must w, trust, hope, and joy
3:35 You must w until I show the way
3:36 w until I give the order to start
2:46 waiting, and yet I say w
2:46 W until I show you my will
2:47 Again, I say w
2:48 W; I will not overly tax your
2:50 W and trust; w and do not be afraid
2:69 W before me; learn patience
3:86 W in silence a while
4:41 few w to hear me speak to them
4:93 W before me, gently breathing in
5:2 They that w upon the Lord shall renew
5:12 Though I w in many hearts, so few
5:56 My message to you is to trust and w
6:5 W in love and longing to feel their
6:5 as you w, courage and hope will flow
8:37 busy man is asked to rest and w
8:62 w to see the outward manifestation
9:75 W to hear my will and then obey
10:77 w, with a child's joyful trust
13:79 w until my rest fills your soul
14:6 W in silence before me to feel that

9:81 w for so many in my poor world to keep
10:2 common w, the weary w, the steep w
10:2 may seem a w to heaven if the
10:12 the w will lighten
10:34 Does the w seem a stony one?
10:37 Seek in every w to become childlike
10:42 w in which I would one day be the
10:61 w that seems painful to you
10:61 just not that is the only w
10:73 keep you in the w you should go
10:83 there must be songs on the w
11:12 meant to walk with me in this w
11:15 my w of removing mountains
11:15 w to remove mountains is the w of
11:28 you shall know the w
11:28 I am the w
11:41 no obstacles in his w, but to him
11:44 joy-w into the kingdom can be taken
11:45 choice of ways, the guidance in the w
11:46 traveler who has forced his w
11:46 w of escape that ye may be able
11:86 my w is a sure w, that my paths are
11:89 I am the very w itself
11:89 prevent you from being in the w
12:19 I have been showing you the w
12:20 plan that can only be revealed in this w
12:29 Let her have her way with you both
12:66 my w may seem a narrow w
12:94 you can go on your w rejoicing
12:95 deal with each one in the best w
13:5 serve them in such a limited w
13:38 Use my name in that same w
13:51 in this w can work yield its
13:53 This is the w
13:53 The w of uncertain future
13:53 It is my w
13:75 Teachers are to point the w to me
14:4 share in a very special w
14:4 The w of sorrows, if walked
14:7 gentle touch to point the w
14:8 supports you when you faint by the w
14:16 I made a w through the Red Sea
14:18 endeavor to go your own w
14:88 w to the cross may be a w of sorrow
15:17 know the w of conquest over the
15:24 cannot walk all the w with me
15:30 Bow in such a w, just waiting to
15:35 quickest w possible to work out
15:65 nothing to block the w so that
16:16 w must truly be one of delight
16:22 w of resignation is not my w
16:24 Love colors the w
16:28 word of love goes winged on its w
16:40 day's service to me in that w, you
16:56 in the best and quickest w
16:59 with me is really the wrong w
16:61 This is to be your w of life
16:61 This is the w of the Spirit
17:9 first practice giving in this w
17:42 w to obtain this perfect love
17:47 Wait to be shown my w
18:1 or of not knowing the w
18:3 In the same w evil lurks around you
18:11 'Have your w then'
18:11 make that w as easy for your feet as
18:16 Walk with me in the w of peace
18:30 Live, love and work in this w

Weak
2:38 have w knees and hearts that faint
9:17 The w need my strength
12:42 of their w selves
13:71 or a turning of w appeal
13:72 nothing is needed by that w appeal
14:36 fail that child, as faulty and w
14:41 When you are w, then I am strong
15:58 w he humanly may be, allows God to
15:60 same in the hand of a w child
16:70 I was the companion of the w
17:41 w vacillating love can soon be routed
18:3 find some w spot, attack that
18:4 affords evil a w spot to attack and

Weakness
3:29 divine power to help human w
4:54 conscious not of strength but of w
4:55 my strength is made perfect in w
5:71 conscious of the w of his stumbling
5:88 power he was had he not learned his w
10:33 fear, not as a w on your part due to
12:10 through w to power, through sin to
13:37 in w, in sorrow, in pain, it
14:7 spiritual w, my touch brings strength
14:39 sorrow over failure, every w
14:41 Rejoice at your w, my children
14:41 My strength is made perfect in w
16:13 w, lift your eyes to the hills of
16:66 your w, your sins, and shortcomings?
18:51 from w, 'There is none other name'

Weary
1:64 power I released for a w world
2:63 honor, and wealth are w and
2:64 unto me all ye that are w and heavy
2:64 w and disappointed who listen and turn
2:65 I am joy to the w
4:73 nature is w too of her long months of
5:2 they shall run and not be w
5:8 like a w man bearing a heavy load

6:71 Many a w troubled heart needs you
7:11 I was w too, when on earth, and I
7:59 The way is long and w
7:59 It is a w world
7:59 So many today are w
7:61 The w and heavy laden must come to you
8:14 Never w in prayer
8:58 forced its w way up that sunlight and
8:74 my poor world is heartsick and w
9:86 When w, do as I did on earth
10:2 w way, the steep way, may seem a way
10:41 faint and w be satisfied and healed
12:29 nurse for tired souls and w bodies
12:53 tired, and pain-w as you may seem
12:53 your tired noise-w ears, I speak
12:59 how w and profitless your climb

Welcome
1:29 W the training
2:73 W love, joy and peace
4:17 give them a royal w
4:17 W all who come with the love of
6:40 W all who come here
6:60 to w my will gladly, rapturously
6:66 love them, w them, shower little
8:24 W the knowledge
9:28 soul with me and w training
11:46 fireside of home be more w than
12:28 W my treatment for you both
14:90 w my will in the great decisions

Welcomed
6:59 My will should be w with a glad

Wide
12:66 w enough so that I can walk beside

Wilderness
1:60 conquered Satan in the w
2:6 in the w plains as well as the

Will
1:20 Love me and do my w
1:38 acceptance of my w when it seems not
2:6 Obey my w day in and day out
2:6 do my w in all things
2:66 other than my w for you
3:13 My w shall be revealed as you go
3:18 reveal my w to you in many
3:46 Wait until I show you my w
3:76 Only my w is coming to pass
4:70 test and train and bend to my w
5:33 choice but mine, no w but mine
5:69 single desire to do my w
5:77 bore it of my own free w
6:59 Hearts eager to do my w send out a
6:59 Resignation to my w keeps me barred
6:59 My w should be welcomed with a glad
6:60 w, to welcome my w gladly
6:64 Persevere in obeying my w
8:57 see it is not my w for you
8:75 acceptance of my w, obedience to it
9:45 the loving doing of my w
9:75 Wait to hear my w and then obey
10:21 lay your w before me as an
10:24 Accept my w, and it will bring you
10:30 mark real acceptance of my w
10:52 can stand against my w for you
10:64 my eye is my set purpose—my w
10:65 To guide you with my w is to bring
10:65 oneness with my w and my desires
10:66 My w guides you
10:66 when my w is your only w
11:6 to do my w and to live my teachings
11:40 sought to do my w in the matter
12:20 union who want only my w and only
12:31 w in the small as in the big things
12:61 willing for my w to be done
12:68 cannot do more than work my w
12:68 said that w is your w
13:33 eye of the soul is the w
13:34 make sure your w is for that kingdom
13:84 joy in doing my w for others
14:19 do my w, there must be gladness
14:19 Delight to do my w
14:20 is the result of a yielded w
14:88 simple acceptance of my w
14:89 acceptance of my Father's w in all
14:90 my w in the great decisions of
15:31 measure of my w and mind that you
15:32 measured by the amount of my w that
15:63 only to know my w and to do my work
16:54 desire and love my w because therein
16:55 accept my w, but to know and love
16:63 desirous only of doing my w
17:18 To do the w of God is the very
17:19 and to delight in doing, my w
17:20 your meat to do my w
18:27 means to do my w and work

Wings
3:72 weighing beautiful spirit-w down with
5:2 They shall mount up with w as eagles
12:44 w of a butterfly if it remains
12:52 Clipped w can grow again
13:57 Like brooding mother bird w that

Wisdom
1:5 each day I shall supply the w and

7:5 Spirit is not supplying w and
7:73 Doubt your own w; reliance on mine
7:77 Always doubt your power or w to
7:77 I am w
7:77 Only my w can rightly decide
14:11 assurance that the w and strength
16:65 For two to agree about the w

Wisest
11:10 by earth's w might lead to disaster
18:25 truly the gifts of earth's w

Withdraw
1:50 battle of the world, then I w
2:3 Use it; if not, I w it
5:19 W into the calm of communion with me

Within
1:43 life w you, my life, eternal life
2:41 w the narrow limits of a baby
4:15 body, mind and spirit comes from w
7:1 w you is the life of life; the life
8:20 look is surely w the power of everyone
8:31 Forces of evil, w and without you
8:58 life w the seed compelling it, it
12:88 sufficiency of all w my power to
14:74 all reform is from w out, you will
14:74 release the imprisoned God power w
16:60 working this time from w out

Word
1:33 heart without voice or w
1:34 Each w or thought of yours can
2:29 When my w has gone forth, all are
3:11 If not, a w, a thought from me, and
4:77 one kindly w of more importance than
4:89 loving w or a kind thought
6:68 Send no one away without a w of cheer
6:92 spat upon, and answering never a w
6:92 never a w
8:80 a look or w of love or confidence
8:93 will accompany the spoken w
9:41 things that I say, was my w when
9:66 w before which all the hosts of evil
10:31 spirit which is the w of God
10:32 aloud; the spoken w has power
11:46 Take this w of cheer to heart
11:61 thought, w and moment to be mine
12:30 A false w, a fear inspired failure
12:83 that w is unfailingly true
13:21 answer never a w in the face
14:20 my meaning of the w meek
14:59 souls who had kept my w
14:60 simple doers of my w, not hearers
14:60 daily tasks and ways they kept my w
15:30 loving w to raise your head
15:39 My w is the Scriptures
15:40 my w is even more than that
15:41 w was made flesh and dwelt among us
16:18 I was the W of God
16:28 a smile or a w of love goes winged
16:62 Every w of mine is true
17:35 I may speak no w that you could write
18:48 In that w, 'sins,' read not only

Words
1:43 w you speak, the influence you have
1:44 Its w and influence go on down
2:11 w, and deeds toward others
3:38 not always expressed in w
3:83 Remember my w
4:34 Not many w, just a momentary contact
4:42 My w are life
4:46 The w that I speak unto you, they
4:46 w I spoke to my disciples of old
5:4 look back over my w to you, you will
5:16 My w need none of man's explanations
5:35 Remember my w to my disciples, 'This'
5:79 Study my w and carry them out
6:95 Spirit has been driven out by the w
6:95 W, w, w; many have called me Lord
6:96 W perish
6:97 do I speak to the human heart in w
6:98 he took refuge in w and more w
6:99 Rely less on w
7:60 w, 'The Son of Man'
7:82 there will be other w for you
8:5 love by countless w and actions
8:11 w, 'Seek ye first the kingdom of'
9:2 actions, w and thoughts, and
9:37 w of faithfulness in my great storehouse
10:14 I had no w of reproach for any I
12:11 let my w ring out, 'Be ye perfect'
12:19 Take my w, revealed to you each
12:81 Take my w as a command to you
13:17 Beyond all w is my love and care for
13:17 These w mean much
13:76 The w of eternal life are all the w
14:81 two lessons from these w
16:4 These w are whispered in the ears
16:4 These w are not said often to the great
16:6 These w do not speak only of passing
16:28 while the mighty w of an orator
16:28 w is—are they inspired by love?

16:42 Ponder again these w and learn from
16:65 all that lies behind the w
17:1 That these w strike a note of beauty
17:17 Those were my w to my disciples in
17:29 lives, sufferings, w and love

Work
1:27 That is your w—mine is to use
1:36 only the w of the universal Spirit
1:40 let patience have her perfect w
1:44 w of any soul that has eternal life
1:45 W at them in your minds and hearts
1:48 you should miss your daily path and w
2:4 after each task, no w can be too much
2:16 Certainly you have to w, you have
2:18 all you need for my power to w
2:34 great w requires a great and careful
2:72 carry on the w I have given to you
2:74 Then the w is accomplished
3:34 Every great w for me has had to
3:46 There is no w in life so hard as
3:47 marred their w and hindered the
3:62 Though you must w and spend yourselves
3:62 doing the greatest w either of you
3:65 sufficient for all the w in the world
3:66 let divine power w through them
3:67 always have plenty of w to be done
3:67 attitude about the w being mine only
3:70 silence must help in the rush and w
3:77 it is as much my w to see your lives
4:11 All your doubts arrest my w
4:16 Silently the w of the Spirit is done
4:18 You may not see the w
4:35 Sense my presence and the fever of the w
4:36 to your friendship and your w
4:37 hours of w may be profitless
4:38 all the time but doing bad w
4:38 but which turns out perfect w
4:67 No w that employs this enemy of mine is w
4:68 W for me, with me, through me
4:68 To last, all w must be done in my
5:6 Make yourself very fit to do my w
5:17 let me do my own w
5:24 Is this w mine or not?
5:40 spiritual need to carry on my w
5:41 Increased health means w for me
5:63 process precedes all real w and success
5:70 feel that your w has been spoiled
5:87 miracle w is not the w of a moment as
6:13 in life and w, in love and service
6:17 w inspired by love and joy, to rise
6:18 as you live and move and w with me
6:34 imperfect w of her child and invests
6:45 seeking to w out what they see
6:50 All w here is accomplished by my
6:53 Love those who w with you
6:59 if I am to do my w in the heart and
6:62 recognition of my w in daily happenings
6:67 leave him to do his w
6:83 future good w would be singled out
6:89 Rest, love, joy, peace, and w;
6:93 w of the branch is to provide a channel
7:8 would leave my w to me and occupy
7:10 stop all w, everything, and rest
7:15 My w in the world has been hindered
7:15 by w, w, w
7:16 Do not seek to w for me
7:16 I do the w and I make the opportunities
7:34 for God to w out your problems
7:53 joys and little w with its mother
7:69 I can w through you better when you are
7:71 All w that results from resting
7:71 with God is miracle w
7:71 Claim the power to w miracles
7:81 All great w for me is done first in
8:36 disciples must w out their own salvation
8:65 their w ceases to be permanent for me
8:78 smooth the day's w, then fear will
9:1 It is not only my w but yours
9:3 a w that requires cooperation, mine and
9:3 w that brings much sense of failure
9:3 w proceeds, you see more and more
9:34 earned by faithful w in many ways
9:48 I am giving you w and hope
9:48 W for the gray days
9:62 further the w of my kingdom
9:74 All your w for the moment is in the
9:77 I long to w miracles as I did when
9:87 w will come to you as it came to me
10:60 wonderful life w you are both to do
11:25 Stop all w; stop all
11:27 make sure that no w, no interruption
11:62 to be used in this good w or that
11:65 accomplish his great w of salvation
11:91 crucified I could see my w had
12:8 never see the mighty w you do
12:12 acquaintances, your country and your w
12:23 It is wrong to force w

12:23 Then w, glad w, will follow
12:24 Tired w never tells; rest
12:30 w for me to be unhindered
12:40 Peter could never had done my w
12:68 cannot do more than w my will
13:26 If you w for me, you have your
13:51 result of w done in peace
13:51 way can w yield its increase
13:83 servant of all think no w beneath
14:22 calm can there be true w done
14:23 Peace is the w of righteousness
14:52 blame the servant who avoids extra w
14:53 view your day's w in this light
14:83 for the great w of my kingdom
14:86 w in perfect harmony, so is
15:16 What a work! My keeping is not
15:35 possible to w out your salvation
15:58 allows God to w through him
15:62 The fruit is not the w of the
15:62 It is the w of the vine, that sends
15:63 know my will and to do my w
15:93 w miracles of wonder and healing
16:26 only the w of God remains
16:28 test of all true w and words is
16:29 much w done in my name is not
16:40 happenings as w you can do for me
16:40 you are sharing in my life w
16:58 cutting you away from other w
16:59 to w from large interests and a desire
17:15 fulfill your mission to w for me
17:15 frustrate you and prevent your good w
17:25 which had hindered my w on earth
17:26 kingdom were to do the work
17:27 My w on earth was to gather around
17:27 truths they were to live and w
17:30 I left my work—seemingly the
17:30 greatest w, that of saving souls
17:53 friendship and bond to do my w
17:58 W in the calm certain that I am with
18:26 sufficient for your needs and for my w
18:27 means to do my will and w
18:30 Live, love and w in this way
18:33 Never lose sight of the glorious w
18:41 W and prayer represent the two
18:41 Your w and my w

Works
2:16 answer to your prayers—your w
2:18 yet, 'Faith without w is dead'
2:18 you need w, too, to feed your faith
4:68 How silently my Spirit w
4:93 enable you to do the same w I did
4:93 enable me to do the same w, and even
4:93 even greater w than I did when on
4:97 Man will see me in my w done through
9:77 I cannot do many mighty w because of
9:78 belief can I do miracle w now
10:69 under my control, are miracle w
11:2 the man who w and understands through
11:18 'The w that I do shall ye do also'
11:18 greater w than these shall ye do
11:19 'Greater works!' The blind
11:19 'And greater works than these'
12:65 resting, giving up of w, a necessity
14:77 'greater works than these shall ye'
17:26 greater w than I was able to do
17:26 opportunities for w in my name would

World
1:2 me, the light of the w
1:4 you must not see as the w sees
1:42 serving another master—the w, fame
1:48 w, but sometimes in tender pity, I
1:50 babble of the w, then I withdraw
1:63 I bore the self human nature of the w
1:64 power I released for a weary w
2:2 vacillating, changing w
2:35 not only to save a w, but also to
2:53 spiritual (as in the material) w
2:62 reversal from the ways of the w
2:63 w's awards bring heart-rest and
2:63 w has most rewarded with name
2:64 jangle of the w's discordant cries
3:60 poor sick w would be cured
3:65 sufficient for all the work in the w
3:65 To know that would remake the w
3:66 The w does not need supermen, but
3:82 w's prayers have gone unanswered
4:23 balm for all the ills of the w
4:24 Aim a conquering a w, the w all around
4:41 many in the w cry to me
4:65 Fear is the curse of the w
4:74 thoughts of beauty for this w
4:80 communication with the material w
4:82 laugh, w (your little w) happy
4:89 Look for beauty and joy in the w
4:89 given back to the w again by you
4:90 back to the w in ways I have said
4:92 standard must never be the w's
5:7 burdens of the w are laid on my cross
5:11 Shut out the distractions of the w
5:64 In the w and yet apart with me?
6:15 customs of the w go by when my glory
6:35 w happier for your being in it

5:24 w about how rent and rates should be
5:55 w because ahead lay a river and he
7:48 forgive those who w or wronged you

Worries
1:54 even seeming trials and w
2:53 fears and w depart from your lives
3:78 placing difficulties and w in
6:6 on earth, its cares, its w, even
8:45 w and cares and burdens to accumulate
11:7 w and scorn patiently endured develop
11:23 world and its w and distractions in

Worry
1:30 Do not w about others' lives
2:13 solvents for the w, cares, and
2:14 w corrode, and in time they would
3:3 Why do you chafe and w so?
3:3 lives are soiled with w and irritation
8:70 help in the rush and work and w
4:11 save you from sin and doubt and w
7:2 You must never doubt, never w
7:3 This means no w, no anxiety, but it
7:23 ways that will w and tire, just to w
8:21 Look and you are saved from w
9:13 darts of w and evil they turn from
9:88 w has gone, and then let the tide of
10:30 rest from the w and irritations of
10:33 w, but as a very real temptation

Worrying
2:13 Does one w thought enter your

Worship
4:59 W me
7:55 Then w would be instinctive
9:47 of a disciple's adoration and w
10:5 to their w—and I am there
10:7 When men seek to w me they think of
10:7 they feel the awe that precedes w
10:7 feel the desire to w me in wondering
12:34 W is not supplication though
12:34 Bow low in w, conscious not only
15:72 as man gives me not only w and honor
18:21 first hail must be the w of humility
18:22 Then comes the w of repentance
18:23 steps: humility, service, w

Worthless
16:27 w if it lacks that God quality—love
16:72 for the evil or the need, pity is w

Wounded
15:22 often 'w in the house of my friends'

Wounds
6:78 w in the hands and feet hurt little
6:78 compared with the w in the heart
6:78 w, not of my enemies, but of my
8:9 hands as I bind up your w
9:29 heal all your sores and w
14:66 of w or healing balm, so long as it

Wrong
1:29 can become witchery in w hands
4:62 he was ill; nothing is w
4:94 Spiritualism is w
7:79 rushes to action; it is w
7:94 I can set right all that is w
10:68 power and tender love is w indeed
11:42 w in your own nature aroused by
12:5 the moment a things seems w to you
12:6 What's w in your country, with its
12:23 It is w to force work
15:48 Do you not see how you w me?
16:59 life with me is really the w way
17:9 w to give money and material things
17:62 lives are all w if you do not feel it

Wronged
7:48 forgive those who worried or w you

Year
1:1 presence is flung across the y to come
1:1 thrown backward, over the past y
1:4 I hold the y in my hands
1:11 burdens can you lighten this y?
6:7 Easter is the wonder time of all the y
7:27 Rejoice in the springtime of the y

Years
1:11 stand between the y
2:48 Y of blessing may be checked in one
2:6 1900 y my message, 'Come unto'
5:21 my kingdom we do not measure in y, as
5:75 mine in manhood's y on earth
8:70 weighted down with the past of y
8:73 uniforms of past marches and y?
10:25 months and y that lie ahead
10:37 y have added to your nature that of
10:43 hundreds of y and much of what I
12:53 across the y yet close and near to
14:1 founded my three y' mission on earth

Yielded
14:20 possession is the result of a y will

Yoked
6:47 Be ye not unequally y together